Women's Diaries as Narrative in the Nineteenth-Century Novel

CATHERINE DELAFIELD
University of Leicester, UK

ASHGATE

Published by
Ashgate Publishing Limited
Wey Court East
Union Road
Farnham
Surrey, GU9 7PT
England

Ashgate Publishing Company
Suite 420
101 Cherry Street
Burlington
VT 05401-4405
USA

www.ashgate.com

British Library Cataloguing in Publication Data
Delafield, Catherine
Women's diaries as narrative in the nineteenth-century novel
   1. English fiction – 19th century – History and criticism 2. Diaries – Authorship
   3. Diaries in literature 4. Women – Diaries 5. Women and literature – England –
   History – 19th century
   I. Title
   823.8'099287

Library of Congress Cataloging-in-Publication Data
Delafield, Catherine.
   Women's diaries as narrative in the nineteenth-century novel / by Catherine Delafield.
      p. cm. — (The nineteenth century series)
   Includes bibliographical references and index.
   ISBN 978-0-7546-6517-5 (alk. paper)
   1. English fiction—Women authors—History and criticism. 2. English fiction—19th
century—History and criticism. 3. English diaries—Women authors—History and criticism.
4. Diaries in literature. I. Title.

PR115.D46 2009
823'.8099287—dc22

               2008050243

ISBN: 978-0-7546-6517-5

d bound in Great Britain by
ks Ltd, Bodmin, Cornwall.

Contents

The Nineteenth Century Series
General Editors' Preface

The aim of the series is to reflect, develop and extend the great burgeoning of interest in the nineteenth century that has been an inevitable feature of recent years, as that former epoch has come more sharply into focus as a locus for our understanding not only of the past but of the contours of our modernity. It centres primarily upon major authors and subjects within Romantic and Victorian literature. It also includes studies of other British writers and issues, where these are matters of current debate: for example, biography and autobiography, journalism, periodical literature, travel writing, book production, gender, non-canonical writing. We are dedicated principally to publishing original monographs and symposia; our policy is to embrace a broad scope in chronology, approach and range of concern, and both to recognize and cut innovatively across such parameters as those suggested by the designations 'Romantic' and 'Victorian'. We welcome new ideas and theories, while valuing traditional scholarship. It is hoped that the world which predates yet so forcibly predicts and engages our own will emerge in parts, in the wider sweep, and in the lively streams of disputation and change that are so manifest an aspect of its intellectual, artistic and social landscape.

Vincent Newey
Joanne Shattock
University of Leicester

A Note on Texts

The diaries of Frances Burney exist in a complex variety of forms and any discussion of her writings must address this issue. Overall, however, reference to Burney's diary in *Women's Diaries as Narrative* has been simplified to allow readers to follow the discussion within standard editions to the fullest extent possible. Chapters 2 and 3 differentiate between the recovered text of Burney's journals and letters and its published form in the 1840s. Chapter 2 considers her diary as a representative text written at the time, reflecting the composition of a personal record by a woman of the period. Chapter 3 addresses the text presented to the market and refers specifically to entries and passages retained by Burney, her editor and publisher which then circulated in the nineteenth century. This circulation was re-emphasized in January 1843 by Macaulay's famous review of the first five volumes of her *Diary and Letters* which was almost immediately reprinted in his *Critical and Historical Essays* in April 1843.[1]

The rationale adopted here is as follows. All references to diaries or letters are supplied with a date. If reference can be made to the Oxford University Press Clarendon editions edited by Joyce Hemlow and Lars Troide then this is done. In the present instance there are two notable exceptions to this. Any reference to Charlotte Barrett's 'Editor's Introduction' or to the Court Journal sequence which is still forthcoming from Clarendon uses the original edition: *Diary and Letters of Madame D'Arblay: author of 'Evelina', 'Cecilia', &c.* (7 vols, London: Colburn, 1842–46).

In the case of Dinah Mulock Craik's novels where there is no standard edition, the rationale followed is that applied in Sally Mitchell's *Dinah Mulock Craik* (Boston: Twayne, 1983) where reference is made to the chapter by number. A page reference is also supplied from the edition listed in the bibliography.[2] For all the novels discussed, subsequent references within the text are to the editions first cited within each chapter.

---

[1]   *The Edinburgh Review* (January 1843): 523–70. The Burney review was further prioritized because it was the first chapter in Volume III of *Critical and Historical Essays* which Macaulay boasted was in its seventh edition by 1849. It was reprinted many more times after Macaulay's death in 1859.

[2]   *A Life for a Life* can also be found online at http://www3.shropshire-cc.gov.uk/etexts/E000329.htm and *John Halifax Gentleman* at http://www.gutenberg.org/etext/2351. In addition, *The Spectator* can be found at http://meta.montclair.edu/SPECTATOR/ and Wilkie Collins's collected short stories *After Dark* (1856) in their original diary-framed format at http://www.gutenberg.org/etext/1626.

Introduction:
Performing to Strangers

In the opening lines of 'Book the Fourth' of Wilkie Collins's novel *Armadale*, the fictional female diarist Lydia Gwilt returns to the diary she closed on her marriage and asks herself: 'Why have I gone back to this secret friend of my wretchedest and wickedest hours?' She answers her own question immediately: 'My misery is a woman's misery and it *will* speak – here rather than nowhere; to my second self, in this book, if I have no one else to hear me.'[1] Gwilt is a consummate actress who has convinced a young man called Ozias Midwinter to marry her in his real name of Allan Armadale, the name he shares with his best friend whose father was murdered by Midwinter's father. The two men have 'second selves' in each other; the woman's 'second self' is in her diary.

The concept of a second self is frequently explored in Collins's fiction.[2] He also uses documents as narrative in many of his novels and one of those documents is a woman's diary which he uses in *Armadale* to give direct access to Lydia's thoughts. The fictional diary operates as a second self, acting as both internal personal narrative and a separate, secretly performed life. Lydia Gwilt and other female fictional diarists are in their turn operating within the ideological climate of the nineteenth century which created for middle class women a life dependant on household management and codes of domesticity. The existence of these diaries creates a fear that the diary may be the life and the domesticity a performance.

This book examines the appearance of the fictional diaries of women in the nineteenth-century novel considering the effect of the diary as a literary device and the impact of the gender of the diarist. These are areas which have received some critical attention but a number of new developments are proposed. Firstly, this study takes its departure from the date of the first woman's diary to be published, that of Frances Burney, between 1842 and 1846. The influence of this publication on the fictional diary is specifically explored. A model of women's diary writing is derived from Burney's *Diary* and other non-fictional examples and applied to a range of novels of the mid to late nineteenth century. Secondly, the life-writing 'second self' is assessed in conjunction with the diary's specific role as a document which is on show or performing a life. This conflicts with nineteenth-century concerns with self-representation by women. In terms of narrative, a theory of

---

[1]   Wilkie Collins, *Armadale*, ed. Catherine Peters (Oxford: Oxford University Press, 1989), p. 532.

[2]   This is the opening discussion of Catherine Peters's biography of Collins, *The King of Inventors: A Life of Wilkie Collins* (London: Minerva Press, 1991), pp. 1–4.

diary narrativity is presented in Chapter 9 and finally, at the level of the assembly of the overall novel, a new derivation, a narrative of inclusion is proposed.

The book thus constructs a model of nineteenth-century diary-writing by women and uses it to examine a group of novels which employ the device as narrative. It considers the interaction of the fictional diary with its non-fictional counterpart and the acts of editing which put women's private writing into the marketplace. By considering the emergence of the non-fictional diary in print and the other forms of literary production which become narrative, it posits a fictional diary chronology for the later nineteenth century.

The method of the book is dependent on a number of overarching concepts both in the terms used – 'diary', 'journal' and 'performance' – and in the choice of structure. The word 'journal' is of Middle English origin from Old French 'jurnal' and late Latin 'diurnalis'. 'Diary' is a more recent coinage of the sixteenth century from the Latin 'diarium' originating in 'dies'. Both terms clearly arise from a concept of daily recording or 'dailiness'. A journal originally signified a more public financial or administrative record or else an allusion to a travel itinerary. The two terms appear to become applicable to a personal record around the beginning of the seventeenth century at the recommendation of Bacon's *Advancement of Learning* (1605) which nonetheless suggests that the diary should concern itself with great events. The term is, however, used in the sense of a more trivial record in Ben Jonson's *Volpone* in the same year. William Cowper makes a distinction between the overall text and the entries in his long poem *Conversation* (1781) when he suggests the need for cultivation in the art of communication and not 'An extract of his diary - no more, / A tasteless journal of the day before'. Nineteenth-century usage, however, aligns the two terms and the analysis which follows uses them interchangeably.[3]

The concept of performance is also a theme throughout the book. The discussion addresses the discrepancy between the nineteenth-century woman in the private sphere and the public narrative of the self which the published diary, fictional or non-fictional, represents. In Chapter 31 of *Pride and Prejudice*, Elizabeth Bennet teases Mr Darcy about his being 'ill qualified to recommend himself to strangers' drawing a parallel between her lack of practice on the piano and his disinclination to make conversation. He replies, 'We neither of us perform to strangers.'[4]

There is a sense within Judith Butler's definition of gender as 'a stylized repetition of acts' that the diary functions as a reinforcing record, 'a set of repeated acts within a highly regulatory frame'.[5] In a later essay, Butler adds that a 'performative

---

[3]   *The Oxford English Dictionary* (12 vols, Oxford: Clarendon Press, 1989), 'Diary', vol. 4, p. 612 and 'Journal', vol. 7, pp. 279–80.

[4]   Jane Austen, *Pride and Prejudice*, ed. Tony Tanner (Harmondsworth: Penguin, 1972; reprinted 1980), p. 209.

[5]   Judith Butler, *Gender Trouble: Feminism and the Subversion of Identity* (London: Routledge, 1990), p. 139.

act' is the 'coincidence of signifying and enacting'.[6] The diary is performative for the nineteenth century because it is an element in gender signification within the 'regulatory frame' of femininity. The diary is stylized in its repetition and the non-fictional model discussed identifies codes which allow women to access life-writing through their daily record. The diary is also performative in the sense of being a physical text which is shown within the narrative. Whilst acting as diagetic narrative it is also mimetic, a showing as well as a telling.[7] This is reinforced in the novels under discussion by the internal dramatization of the acts of writing and of reading which introduce the diary into the marketplace through a level of fictional strategy to be termed the narrative of inclusion.

There is a wider discussion of the fictional diary in narrative terms in Part 3. This is informed in part by Shlomoth Rimmon-Kenan's distinctions between classical and postclassical structuralist narratology which form the coda to her discussion of theory in *Narrative Fiction*. She suggests that structuralism should turn to interpretation in a context wider than linguistic analysis.[8] *Women's Diaries as Narrative* is in turn prompted to consider the cultural and historical context of diary narrative using an interpretative paradigm derived from women's non-fictional diaries. Rather than proposing a comprehensive narratology, it takes a view of the narrativity of the fictional diary.

When he discusses the use of diary narrative in *The Tenant of Wildfell Hall* and *The Woman in White*, Bernard Duyfhuizen uses the idea of a competitive narrative matrix.[9] This is a concept which can be usefully opened up to accommodate the non-fictional diary, women's fictional writing and a wider range of nineteenth-century texts and approaches which flourished in the cultural context of the period under examination. In Part 2, the model of nineteenth-century diaries is examined as a fictional vehicle for narrative within the novel.

In terms of the book's structure, Part 2 comprises a series of essays which analyse the fictional diary against other competing narratives. This approach, as opposed to a series of chronological chapters organized by text or author, presents material in a form suitable for readers interested in specific genres as well as those researching the novels themselves. This thematic approach also allows the diary to be explored in the broader context of nineteenth-century culture and reading practices. This, in turn, opens up the number of possible readings of the chosen

---

[6]   Judith Butler, 'Burning Acts: Injurious Speech', in Andrew Parker and Eve Kosofsky Sedgwick (eds), *Performativity and Performance* (New York: Routledge, 1995), pp. 197–227.

[7]   Andrew Parker concludes that 'performativity concerns the set of conditions in which saying is itself a kind of doing' (Andrew Parker, 'Praxis and Performativity', *Women & Performance: A Journal of Feminist Theory*, 8/2 (1996): 268).

[8]   See Shlomoth Rimmon-Kenan, *Narrative Fiction: Contemporary Poetics* (first published 1983; 2nd edition, London: Routledge, 2002; reprinted, 2003), p. 142.

[9]   Bernard Duyfhuizen, *Narratives of Transmission* (London: Associated University Presses, 1992), p. 123.

texts and allows the meaning of the diary as a narrative device to interact with a range of literary productions.

Part 1, therefore, traces the tradition of diary-writing in the nineteenth century with specific reference to women's life writing and the publication of diaries. Chapter 1 discusses the traditions of diary-writing in the nineteenth century by analysing the non-fictional diary and assessing the role of real women in producing diaries as household and personal narrative. It then reviews the diary as life writing for women and defines the concept of diary fiction by reviewing the work of recent critics.

In Chapter 2 these non-fictional diaries are represented by Frances Burney's *Diary and Letters of Madame D'Arblay* (1842–1846; written 1768–1839), *The Journal of Emily Shore* (1891; written 1831–1839), Elizabeth Gaskell's *Diary* (1923; written 1835–1838) and the diary of Anne Lister (partially serialized 1887–1892; written 1806–1840). These examples illustrate the specifically nineteenth-century deployment of the diary model at the moment when women's diaries became vehicles for fiction. The diaries of Burney, Shore, Gaskell and Lister demonstrate that there was an approved and evolving form for the diary written in private which was part of female culture.

Chapter 3 acts as a springboard for the concepts which are further explored in the essays of Part 2. It investigates the terms on which a woman's diary, that of Burney, becomes part of the print culture of the period. This leads into an introductory consideration of the fictional female diarist who is the subject for Part 2. The nineteenth-century woman's diary interpreted as a feminine form, as a type of life writing and as a public document is contextualized within a core group of six nineteenth-century novels: Anne Brontë's *The Tenant of Wildfell Hall* (1848), Dinah Mulock Craik's *A Life for a Life* (1859), Wilkie Collins's *The Woman in White* (1859–1860), *Armadale* (1864–6) and *The Legacy of Cain* (1888) and Bram Stoker's *Dracula* (1897).[10] These novels variously maintain, challenge and resolve an ideology of nineteenth-century womanhood through their exploitation of the real diary in a published form. They demonstrate elements of the diary fiction model devised by later critics and they all use a hybrid narrative form which creates competition within the text for control of both the narrative and the evidence presented within it. They bear the imprint of the real diary and recreate the way in which a daily record is constructed through the need for a narrative occasion. They exploit the lack of a language which the choice of a woman's viewpoint offers. In this way the events of the plot are endowed with the power of elliptical suggestion authorized by the act of writing (or failing to write) which is itself recorded by the

---

[10]   *The Tenant of Wildfell Hall* and *A Life for a Life* were both quickly reprinted with additional material by their authors. All three of the novels by Collins were serialized and *The Woman in White* was revised for its second edition because of chronological errors identified by the critic E.S. Dallas. (See 'Appendix C' to Wilkie Collins, *The Woman in White*, ed. John Sutherland (Oxford: Oxford University Press, 1996; reissued 1998), pp. 662–8.)

diarist. Against Linda Anderson's definition of 'interiority',[11] these novels also dramatize the 'exteriority' and machinery of diary publication demonstrated by the editing process which puts them onto the printed page. The fictional diary's progress to publication is contextualized by the story-telling process and as David Seed observes of *Dracula*, the physical text narrates its own assembly.[12]

Part 2 uses the 'competitive matrix' and narratives of inclusion to explore the use of the diary as a narrative device. Chapter 4 asks how women writers utilized their own heritage in adapting the diary for narrative and considers the response of critics to the diary as a device. This introduces the two earliest of the six core texts and considers the reaction of contemporary critics to diary fiction within the matrix of approved writing for women.

Chapters 5 to 8 explore the competitive interaction of diary narrative with other forms of literary production. These essays refract the fictional diary against a range of published material which circulated in the marketplace of the later nineteenth century namely: the epistolary narrative, the periodical, the factual document and the fiction of sensation. In these discussions a range of other representative texts are also introduced including Samuel Richardson's *Pamela* (1740), Burney's *Evelina* (1778), Mary Shelley's *Frankenstein* (1818), Emily Brontë's *Wuthering Heights* (1847) and other works by Craik and Collins.

Chapter 5 traces the development of the epistolary format of daily correspondence with an addressee which became part of print culture in the mid eighteenth century and considers how the diary evolved as a similar story-telling medium by the nineteenth century.

Chapter 6 attempts to reconstruct a reading experience of the diary in print as part of the miscellany consumption of the serialized novel within a periodical. The woman reader and the reception of the printed word in periodical form gives a further nuance to the diary as a serial record interacting with the narrative as a serial story.

Chapter 7 considers the role of the printed word circulating more widely in the bureaucracy of nineteenth-century life. The novel format questions the documents which can tell the truth. This in turn links with a particular development in the documentary role of personal record where the diary and letter forms can be considered as categories of documents given in evidence. As a result, the evidence of texts like diaries, letters and even death certificates can be exploited within fiction.

---

[11]   See Chapter 1, p. 17. Anderson discusses the diary as a text which 'allows the woman to remain hidden while providing her with a place to actualise her interiority' (Linda Anderson, 'At the Threshold of Self: Women and Autobiography', in Moira Monteith (ed.), *Women's Writing: A Challenge to Theory* (Brighton: Harvester Press, 1986), p. 60).

[12]   David Seed, 'The Narrative Method of *Dracula*', *Nineteenth Century Literature*, 40/1 (June 1985): 73.

Chapter 8 explores the context for sensation which the diary helps to create and demonstrates how the particular impact of sensation fiction reflects the use of the diary as evidence, document and woman's autobiography.

Part 3 (Chapter 9) draws together the evidence from the core texts. It considers the literary and cultural significance of the female diarist within the novel; the role of the text as a physical artefact in competition with other documents and the fictional diary within the narrative structure of the novels as a whole. Across a fifty-year time span, there is an identifiable continuity in the treatment of the diarist and her text.

This book assesses the treatment of women's diaries as commodities in fiction; it examines their role in telling a story and in telling women's stories. The diary is an ideological tool which can be seen to operate in conflict with its received place in the home. Its authority as a life-writing opportunity for the nineteenth-century woman comes into conflict with its concept as a site for domestic and spiritual record. The act of a diary being read or transmitted within an edited and shaped framework allows a story to be both validated by dailiness and shown in public. It is in this sense that the diary is 'performing to strangers'.

PART 1
The Diary Model

Chapter 1
The Diary in the Nineteenth Century

The fictional diary in the nineteenth-century novel is based on the model of the non-fictional diary. This chapter considers the diary-writing traditions that existed in the nineteenth century and the ways in which women's diaries accommodated these traditions. It assesses the diary as life writing for women and concludes by briefly examining the published diary in the nineteenth-century and the fictional diary discussed by twentieth-century critics.

Four identifiable traditions for diary writing have emerged by the early nineteenth century. These are the accounts of a household or business; the spiritual improvement or book of reflections; the family record or chronicle; and the travel diary.[1] In the nineteenth century, diaries were being kept or composed as economic records and domestic memoirs, and as both spiritual and secular autobiography.

In the financial accounting sense of the daily journal, records of economic dealings took place within literate households. These practical records might be seen as the most basic form of daily recording on a factual basis. They were public in the sense that they were available for consultation and review but rarely publish-worthy. Over time these records acquired personal commentary and fuller descriptions of events and personalities and from these initially pragmatic and circumscribed processes of entering information emerged a second tradition, the family history or domestic memoir. This was more consciously a record of achievement and an account of stewardship and position. A family history or shared journal of this kind represented an assessment of worth in terms not merely monetary. Such a history would have value in public as an acknowledgement of a life and of a circulating heredity; the original document on which it was based would usually remain private.

In parallel, the growth of Non-Conformism stimulated the development of the spiritual diary as a vehicle for the assessment of one's life against a pattern of moral management, accounting for one's soul to God. The daily record of actions measuring progress against a moral standard would be reread and shared to offer guidance to others. The idea of setting up a model approach was also a stimulus to publication so that the most worthy or most improved members of the community

---

[1]   For surveys of this evolutionary process see Robert A. Fothergill, *Private Chronicles: A Study of English Diaries* (London: Oxford University Press, 1974), pp. 14–28; Cheryl Cline, *Women's Diaries, Journals and Letters: An Annotated Bibliography* (New York: Garland Press, 1989), pp. xiv–xxi; Stuart Sherman, *Telling Time: Clocks, Diaries and English Diurnal Form 1660–1785* (Chicago: University of Chicago Press, 1996), pp. 50–59 and Christina Sjöblad, 'From Family Notes to Diary: the Development of a Genre', *Eighteenth Century Studies*, 31/4 (1998): 517–21.

could share that model with a wider range of beneficiaries. One of many popular examples was that of *The Memoirs of Miss Hannah Ball ... Extracted from her diary of thirty years experience: in which the devices of Satan are laid open, the gracious dealings of God with her soul, and all his sufficient grace, are exemplified in her useful life and happy death.*[2] Robert Fothergill outlines the self-improvement model of diary keeping which emerges, 'intensifying the writer's surveillance over the conduct of his life and the condition of his soul'.[3] Miss Matty's diary in *Cranford* appears to be a form of spiritual accounting. The novel was published in 1853, but Miss Matty is looking back from the 1830s to her own childhood in the 1790s. She tells Mary Smith about the two-column format proposed by her authoritarian father: 'we were to put down in the morning what we thought would be the course and events of the coming day, and at night we were to put down on the other side what really happened. It would be to some people rather a sad way of telling their lives.'[4]

A fourth strand, the travel diary, operated in a composite tradition reflecting a number of the other functions of diary-writing. Travel, exploration and migration stimulated a need to record. By keeping basic records but also recording events with both public and private aims, the resultant diary of a journey could act both as a reminder for later memoirs and as the basis for more immediate letters and family news.[5]

The diary in its received nineteenth-century guise is discussed in a well-known and much reprinted text, Isaac D'Israeli's *Curiosities of Literature*. In his discursive essay, 'Diaries Moral, Historical and Critical', D'Israeli draws an important distinction regarding the intended audience of a diary: 'We converse with the absent by letters, and with ourselves by diaries'.[6] He distinguishes the diary from the letter as 'the honester pages of a volume reserved only for solitary contemplation; or to be a future relic of ourselves, when we shall no more hear of ourselves'.[7] This is an equivocal statement which suggests that although it is possible to be more honest in private, these pages will nonetheless be 'contemplated' and reread to contribute to the shaping of entries made at later dates. The idea of a 'future relic' also suggests collection and collation for more public view and D'Israeli proposes

---

[2]   *The Memoirs of Miss Hannah Ball By Joseph Cole* (York: Wilson, Spence & Mawman, 1796; reprinted London: John Mason, 1839). Fothergill cites John Beadle's *The Journal or Diary of a Thoughtful Christian* (1656) as the first published work on this model (Fothergill, pp. 15–17).

[3]   Fothergill, p. 66.

[4]   Elizabeth Gaskell, *Cranford* in *The Works of Elizabeth Gaskell*, ed. Joanne Shattock (10 vols, London: Pickering and Chatto, 2005), vol. 3, ed. Alan Shelston, p. 257.

[5]   See Andrew Hassam, '"As I Write": Narrative Occasions and the Quest for Self-Presence in the Travel Diary', *Ariel*, 21/4 (October 1990): 33–47.

[6]   Isaac D'Israeli, 'Diaries Moral, Historical and Critical', *Curiosities of Literature*, vol. 2 (New edition London: Warne, 1881), p.206. The essay was originally published in 1793.

[7]   Ibid.

that, at the very least, a reread diary might act as consolation for the family of a public man out of favour.

D'Israeli describes diaries within a spiritual-economic tradition as 'books of account' which 'render to a man an account of himself to himself'. He regards them as better than history, 'a substitute to every thinking man for our newspapers, magazines, and annual register' although never a substitute for action.[8] Writing at a time of burgeoning interest in the past and in the publication of memoirs, he observes: '[W]e their posterity are still reaping the benefit of their lonely hours and diurnal records'.[9] He accepts the concept of the diarist as an isolated figure at the time of writing even though his examples all appear to have been men of action, and the 'reaping' of benefit again assumes an audience although clearly in the spiritual improvement tradition.

In deriving these diary-writing criteria, D'Israeli pictures the isolated, private writer engaged in a 'diurnal task'. He describes the practice of using portable daily books or tablets but he cautions against the exhaustiveness of presenting the daily record – 'to write down everything, may end in something like nothing' – which suggests the need to edit or shape material. He presents the diary formed from a literary man's studies as 'the practice [of] ... *journalizing the mind*'. He also suggests that there is a hierarchy of diary texts, doubting, for instance, the need for a daily record of dreams: 'Works of this nature are not designed for the public eye; they are domestic annals, to be guarded in the little archives of a family'.[10]

Two other factors are also vital to an understanding of the context of diary-writing and publication in the early nineteenth century. Firstly, the value of private experience became a relevant concept within the Romantic tradition. The urge towards self-expression and definition was fired by a new sensibility giving both a voice to the concept of 'I' and a link to the subjectivity and authority of private experience. Secondly, at a practical and commercial level, the publication of diaries was linked inevitably with the growth of literacy, the cheapness of the printing process and the availability of material.[11]

Within this nineteenth-century context, any analysis of the diary model must also take account of the work of twentieth-century diary critics like Robert Fothergill, William Matthews and Andrew Hassam. The diary as a genre in its own right has been described by Fothergill as a 'serial autobiography'. Observing that no one can record exhaustively, he defines the diary as a 'non-linear book of the self', a record which tends to be valued according to the time of discovery rather than the time of writing.[12] He describes the diarist as 'a fugitive and cloistered genius'

---

[8]   Ibid., p. 209.

[9]   Ibid., p. 207.

[10]   Ibid., p. 215.

[11]   See for instance Linda K. Hughes and Michael Lund, *The Victorian Serial* (Charlottesville: University Press of Virginia, 1991), p. 4.

[12]   Fothergill, pp. 2, 62.

and identifies a tendency to shape entries and to employ literary forms.[13] Self-projection, and thus performativity, is seen by Fothergill as the key to the genre: 'the diary ... creates its own reader as a projection of the impulse to write'.[14]

William Matthews, whose *Bibliography of British Diaries* published in 1950 was Fothergill's starting point, revisits the diary in a later article. He specifically identifies the absence of an audience and 'a natural disorder and emphasis', the lack of a value system.[15] Although neither Fothergill nor Matthews specifically refers in any detail to female diarists, their observations draw attention to the concepts of creating an internal reader and valuing the daily which are significant for women keeping diaries within the ideological constraints of the nineteenth century.

Andrew Hassam in turn challenges the sense of an audience for the journal using the French critic Rousset's typology of the diary as '*texte sans destinataire*', without an addressee. Hassam puts together a spectrum of authorial intention based on the status of the addressee in the text relative to publication and this suggests that the diary comes into existence for a range of performative reasons.[16] Additionally, he identifies a dilemma for the reader or editor arising from the diarist's authorization to read, and this is a useful concept for an analysis of the unauthorized and 'licensed violators' who read fictional diaries within the novels and so become accidental narratees. Hassam comments: 'The position of the researcher reading an unpublished diary would be the same as that of an editor, that of licensed violator of the secrecy clause.'[17] In a later article, Hassam also describes the act of writing a travel diary as being based on the availability of the 'narrative occasion' or 'moment of stasis'[18] which provides an opportunity to write within the dailiness or busyness of travelling. Hassam observes that: 'The diary is self-referential in that the diarist employs language to construct both the space and the occasion in which to write.'[19] It is this concept which confers performative agency on the diarist through her text.

The nineteenth-century female diarist was writing and living within a tradition which valued her as a moral touchstone and domestic object. Kathryn Gleadle observes that language was used to make sense of lives and that 'the discourses of

---

[13]   Ibid., pp. 12, 62.

[14]   Ibid., p. 96.

[15]   William Matthews, 'Diary: A Neglected Genre', *Sewanee Review*, 85 (1977): 286, 287.

[16]   Andrew Hassam, 'Reading Other People's Diaries', *University of Toronto Quarterly*, 56/3 (Spring 1987): 435–6.

[17]   Ibid., p. 442, n. 7.

[18]   Hassam, '"As I Write"': 33; the phrase 'narrative occasion' was originally coined by Gerald Prince, 'The Diary Novel: Notes for the Definition of a Sub-Genre', *Neophilogus*, 59 (1975): 478; this definition is further discussed below.

[19]   Hassam, '"As I Write"': 35–6.

separate spheres contributed to the construction of individual subjectivities'.[20] The published discourse of womanhood maintained this ideological position and one of the ways in which domestic space was identified and constructed was through advice manuals which located women's lives in the moral sphere of the home. Elizabeth Langland points out that these books of etiquette for the early nineteenth century were 'aimed specifically at enabling the middle class to consolidate its base of control through strategies of regulation and exclusion'.[21] Women were defined within these regulated texts by their relational status within the ordered garden of the kingdom where, Sarah Stickney Ellis tells the 'Daughters of England': 'Society has good reason for planting this friendly hedge beside the path of a woman.'[22] The dailiness represented by a diary might reflect a woman's duties as defined by writers such as Ellis or Thomas Gisborne. Their manuals codified a woman's life as an alternative to the masculine world of work. The maintenance of the home was a matter of moral and patriotic duty addressed to the 'Wives of England': 'To make [her] husband happy, to raise his character, to give dignity to his house, and to train up his children in the path of wisdom — these are the objects which a true wife will not rest satisfied without endeavouring to attain.'[23]

In terms of the diary, of course, the very act of writing by women is a vexed question for the nineteenth-century adviser on etiquette. Like the diarist valorizing the daily, Ellis seeks authority for her own writing when she explains that she is making public the 'apparently insignificant detail of familiar and ordinary life' for instructional and patriotic purposes: 'a nation's moral wealth is in your keeping'.[24] In his *Enquiry into the Duties of the Female Sex*, Thomas Gisborne advises the female writer of letters by differentiating between types of writing for women. He distinguishes between an authorized and 'good' domestic communication and

---

[20]   Kathryn Gleadle, 'Our Separate Spheres': Middle-class Women and the Feminisms of Early Victorian Radical Politics', in Kathryn Gleadle and Sarah Richardson (eds), *Women in British Politics, 1760–1860, The Power of the Petticoat* (Basingstoke: Macmillan, 2000), p. 134. Simon Morgan discusses the civic identity which women could nonetheless adopt in *A Victorian Woman's Place: Public Culture in the Nineteenth Century* (London: Tauris, 2007).

[21]   Elizabeth Langland, *Nobody's Angels Middle Class Women and Domestic Ideology in Victorian Culture* (New York: Cornell University Press, 1995), p. 9. See also Amanda Vickery's observation that 'we should not presume without evidence that women (or men) mindlessly absorbed a particular didactic lesson like so many pieces of blotting paper' in Amanda Vickery, 'Golden Age to Separate Spheres? A Review of the Categories and Chronology of English Women's History', *Historical Journal*, 36/2 (1993): 408.

[22]   Sarah Stickney Ellis, *The Daughters of England Their Position in Society, Character and Responsibilities* (London: Fisher and Son, 1842), p. 220; see also *The Women of England* (London: Fisher and Son, 1839) and *The Wives of England* (London: Fisher and Son, 1843). Thomas Gisborne, *An Enquiry into the Duties of the Female Sex* (London: Cadell, 1797) was still in print in the 1840s, reaching its 14th edition in 1847.

[23]   Ellis, *Wives of England*, p. 59.

[24]   Ibid., pp. 5, 8.

an overwritten performance: 'Tinsel and glitter, and laboured phrases, dismiss the friend and introduce the authoress.' [25] In Gisborne's judgment, being an 'authoress' produces artificiality and an undesirable loss of simplicity. The diarist writes a naïve plotless text which ostensibly guards against the dangers of such authorship.

A diary could accommodate those forms of information management which linked clearly with the administration of home duties. As such, the model of the diary received into nineteenth-century practice could appear specifically to exclude any personal expression on the part of the diarist. Within the authorized lines of daily record, as Ellis informed the 'Wives of England', 'it is her sacred privilege to forget herself'[26] or at least to conceal herself within the subjects permitted by the domestic code. The diary helps to define women's private, domestic and relational status. It is ostensibly a form of writing without an addressee and creates a type of female writer somewhere between a 'friend' and an 'authoress'.

The woman's development of her authorized occasion for writing as economic record produces specifically feminized elements in diary discourse. In her 'descriptive bibliography' of diaries in manuscript, Cynthia Huff concludes that the diary often took on the role of 'an understanding friend'.[27] She observes that keeping a diary allowed women to 'sift and evaluate the past, whether it was measured by the recurrence of birth and death or by the tallying of accounts'.[28]

The physical appearance of a diary, whether customized or pre-printed, would shape its entries to some extent, offering indications of class and social distinction. The manuscripts Huff has examined for her study also include inked-over pencil entries, the evidence of editing and of sharing as family documents. This process appears to anticipate a reading or listening audience, a narratee or addressee in Andrew Hassam's terms. The diaries are structured by regular anniversaries like birthdays or deaths which might be the occasion for a special address to God.[29] Marriage inevitably provides both a framework and a change of lifestyle, and diary entries also appear to have had some use as a reference document on experiences in childbirth for both the writer and her female friends.[30] The diary functioned equivocally as a private document in such circumstances acting – as Elizabeth Gaskell's did – as an extension to the advice manuals themselves.[31]

D'Israeli's diarists in his essay of 1793 are all men. He mentions women only briefly and then only as biographers of their husbands.[32] One third of the diaries listed in Robert Fothergill's concluding bibliography are by women but the main

---

[25]   Gisborne, p. 112.

[26]   Ellis, *Wives of England*, p. 96.

[27]   Cynthia Huff, *British Women's Diaries: A Descriptive Bibliography of Selected Nineteenth-Century Women's Manuscript Diaries* (New York: AMS Press, 1985), p. xxiv.

[28]   Ibid., p. ix.

[29]   Huff, p. xix.

[30]   Ibid., pp. xxix, xxx.

[31]   See Chapter 2, pp. 31–2.

[32]   D'Israeli, p. 212.

text of his book *Private Chronicles* of 1974 discusses women only briefly with reference to Elizabeth Barrett Browning, Dorothy Wordsworth, Alice James and Anaïs Nin. More recent critics argue that the personal diary is a feminine form of writing which rebels against the ideology of the home which creates it. This process demonstrates the applicability of the diary to women's life writing and its ability to accommodate the daily record which valorizes women's experiences for auto/biographical purposes.

The diary presents the unmediated reflection of a life without interpretation whilst autobiography overwrites a life already lived with knowledge of narrative closure. Sidonie Smith observes that autobiography is a genre, 'assigning meaning to a series of experiences, after they have taken place, by means of emphasis, juxtaposition, commentary, omission'.[33] Fothergill makes a similar distinction which also raises the performative aspect of the diary in the process of composition: 'Unlike the autobiography, which may tell in retrospect the history of self-development and the resolution of internal conflict, the diary receives the actual form and pressure of these processes.'[34] More recently, Aaron Kunin muses on the function of the diary to 'know no more than the day knows'[35] and these elements of the diary which question the right to record and validate the act of recording without retrospect are practices identifiable as part of the negotiation within the female-authored diary.

Women's diaries as sources of autobiography have come under extensive scrutiny particularly within a feminist critical agenda. This originates in part from Estelle Jelinek's observation that the 'anecdotal and disruptive' nature of diaries has fitted them to the task of accommodating women's stories. She suggests that women's lives are themselves reflected by the diary form and devalued by association with it; that 'these discontinuous forms…are analogous to the fragmented, interrupted and formless nature of their lives'.[36] The private sphere and the discontinuity of female occupations are personified in the act of diary-writing itself. The diary and by extension the diarist is thus made safe by dailiness and private status. Smith contends that the non-fictional diary is a form in which the woman is 'culturally silenced' and 'doubly estranged' because she is both marginalized by the choice of text and denied the possibility of self-writing, of saying 'I'.[37]

The narrative viewpoint of autobiography asks the autobiographer or diarist to act as both narrator and protagonist in her own story. This impinges on issues of self-representation in Victorian culture. The act of identifying and valuing herself

---

[33]   Sidonie Smith, *A Poetics of Women's Autobiography: Marginality and the Fictions of Self-Representation* (Bloomington: Indiana University Press, 1987), p. 45.

[34]   Ibid., p. 128.

[35]   Aaron Kunin, 'From the Desk of Anne Clifford', *ELH*, 71 (2004): 601.

[36]   Estelle C. Jelinek, 'Women's Autobiography and the Male Tradition', in Estelle C. Jelinek (ed.), *Women's Autobiography Essays in Criticism* (Bloomington: Indiana University Press, 1980), p. 19.

[37]   Smith, pp. 43–4, 49.

in public, without the moral advantages of the home, would separate the woman from her socially constructed role as exemplar and ideal of femininity.[38] Mary Jean Corbett and Valerie Sanders regard the diary with its apparent emphasis on private life as an opportunity to write within that gendered ideological position but they recognize that the issue of the devalued and trivial dailiness of the genre remains.[39] The diary is coded as a private and domestic document and thus a suitable form for limited self-expression in marginalized writing permitted as a relational duty and linked with the authorized adjacent forms of letters, family history or spiritual autobiography. In a similar context, Linda H. Peterson argues that women needed 'private, culturally sanctioned forms of life writing because they were excluded from others', and the three strands of her analysis – spiritual autobiography, domestic memoir and *chronique scandaleuse* – are in close parallel with diary tradition. She suggests that women could select from the existing traditions and that in this way the diary comes within the bounds of acknowledged life writing forms.[40]

This incorporation of gendering through existing forms reflects the role of the diary traditions already discussed. The life-writing potential of the diary has also been identified as a site for specifically female rebellion, and non-fictional women's diaries have been studied intensely as a means of recovering marginalized lives. Felicity Nussbaum describes diaries as 'sites of resistance' within power relations.[41] These lives are seen to offer challenges to patriarchal structures and modes of expression. In her study of 'centuries of female days', Harriet Blodgett points out that time taken out for diary-writing 'counters the patriarchal attack on female identity and self-worth'.[42] She contends, however, that the woman's diary is still pervaded by unease about the act of writing because her pen is 'clogged' by social role and 'moral-sexual status ... restricted and unauthentic language ... lack of privacy'.[43] Elizabeth Barrett Browning's fear of display is expressed in her diary entry for 4 June 1831: 'How could I write a diary without throwing upon paper my thoughts, all my thoughts — the thoughts of my heart as well as of my head — & then how could I bear to look on them after they were written?'[44]

---

[38]   See Smith, p. 53.

[39]   Mary Jean Corbett, *Representing Femininity: Middle Class Subjectivity in Victorian and Edwardian Women's Autobiographies* (Oxford: Oxford University Press, 1992), pp. 12–15 and Valerie Sanders, *The Private Lives of Victorian Women* (Hemel Hempstead: Harvester Press, 1989), p. 12.

[40]   Linda H. Peterson, *Traditions of Women's Autobiography: The Poetics and Politics of Life Writing* (Charlottesville: University Press of Virginia, 1999), pp. 28, 20, x.

[41]   Felicity A. Nussbaum, *The Autobiographical Self: Gender and Ideology in Eighteenth-Century England* (Baltimore: The Johns Hopkins University Press, 1989), p. xii.

[42]   Harriet Blodgett, *Centuries of Female Days: Englishwomen's Private Diaries* (New Brunswick: Rutgers University Press, 1989), p. 5.

[43]   Ibid., p. 62.

[44]   Quoted by Fothergill, p. 89.

The diary could thus be viewed as a form of unmediated life writing caught between its authorized daily record and its potential to be overwritten for public consumption. For a woman it might be the basis for a more public family history or a biography of a male family member, a production which might also result in her own effacement. It might also be a document which can circulate in its own right as an advice manual as Gaskell's seems to indicate or be read as a record of nature like Emily Shore's as discussed in Chapter 2. The act of writing and the text produced are also performative indicators of the restrictions of role, reticence and language.

A number of critics have tackled the issue of the diary as a specifically 'feminine form'. Linda Anderson regards it as a vehicle for women's private authorship which can challenge the historical prohibition against self-representation allowing 'the woman to remain hidden while providing her with a place to actualise her interiority'. [45] The diary is a 'space where the traditional ordering of narrative and meaning could be undone'.[46] Anderson uses James Boswell as a case study, distinguishing Boswell's approach as masculine and suggesting that he felt the need to draw that distinction clearly. She quotes from his diary of 1791: 'as a lady adjusts her dress in the mirror, a man adjusts his character by looking at his journal'.[47] The issue of a diary's privacy would thus be a point of tension for the (male) public self. Anderson concludes that the diary was viewed as a 'private repository for those errant selves which proved inconsistent with the public character'.[48] Since women were deemed to have no 'public character', the diary for a woman could only be 'errant self-representation'.

The revaluation of detail within the daily is one aspect of the diary's status as a feminine form. Picking up the idea of the alternative record of women's experience, Valerie Raoul describes the diary as a 'memory bank', irregular, non-retrospective and *in medias res*. She claims that 'the original non-public, non-literary nature of the "genuine" diary is the first feature which made it a form of writing considered appropriate for women'.[49] Rebecca Hogan regards the diary as 'engendered autobiography' because it 'valorises the detail in both the realms of ornament and everyday',[50] a statement which challenges Matthews's concept of the lack of a value system in the diary. The lack of a hierarchy is a necessary

---

[45]   Linda Anderson, 'At the Threshold of Self: Women and Autobiography', in Moira Monteith (ed.), *Women's Writing A Challenge to Theory* (Brighton: Harvester Press, 1986), p. 60.

[46]   Linda Anderson, *Autobiography* (London: Routledge, 2001), p. 34.

[47]   Ibid., p. 36. This entry is also contemporary with D'Israeli's essay although Boswell's diaries were not published until 1950–1989.

[48]   Ibid., p. 37.

[49]   Valerie Raoul, 'Women and Diaries: Gender and Genre', *Mosaic*, 22/3 (Summer 1989): 61, 58.

[50]   Rebecca Hogan, 'Engendered Autobiographies: The Diary as a Feminine Form', in Shirley Neuman (ed.), *Autobiography and Questions of Gender* (London: Cass, 1991), p. 96.

female strategy for a woman who has no part in the public male world and yet is seeking, within the codes of Victorian womanhood, to question the morally redemptive framework imposed on her by her domestic role.

Janet Bottoms also pursues the idea of the diary as a feminine form in reviewing the diary-writing of Alice James, invalid sister of Henry. Bottoms writes: 'The diary is very much a woman's form because it is secret — it makes no open claim to notice — and yet to record oneself in this manner is, after all, to make an assertion that one is worthy of record.' She describes the diary as having a 'defining shape ... imposed on contingency'.[51] In the case of Alice James, this was the circumscription imposed both by her subordinate role within the family and by her own knowledge of her impending death.

Considering this gendering of texts, Kathryn Carter sees a more subtle force at work when she discusses 'the fiction of the diary's privacy'.[52] She suggests that the privacy and sincerity of a diary written without an audience was proof against the threats of the mid century marketplace and 'evidence of unexploited creative labour'. She continues: 'it might also (illusively) demarcate authentic writing from that which was commercialised, publicised or circulated and thereby denigrated'.[53] The trivial and undervalued became a symbol of security but Carter adds that the text as a commodity could nonetheless slip into public notice through court cases via the permeable boundary with the private.[54]

The diaries of nineteenth-century women demonstrate the elements of tradition and practice already identified but they also offer nuances specifically geared to the culture and gender of the diarist herself. Discontinuity and fragmentation are part of the daily domestic life of trivial incident which gave women their superior status outside the industrial world of men. The 'hidden interiority' of the ostensibly private diary could allay unease about self-representation and performance; and yet within its pages a woman could challenge patriarchy in an attempt to recover her self-worth. A diary could function to evaluate and 'sift' experience in the mode of the spiritual diary. It could also account for women's gendered experiences recorded and shared retrospectively using the diary. This was particularly significant where there was no agreed language for the expression

---

[51]   Janet Bottoms, 'Sisterhood and Self-Censorship in the Nineteenth Century: Writing Herself: the Diary of Alice James', in Julia Swindells (ed.), *The Uses of Autobiography* (London: Taylor and Francis, 1995), p. 111.

[52]   Kathryn Carter, 'The Cultural Work of Diaries in Mid Century Victorian Britain', *Victorian Review*, 23/2 (Winter 1997): 251.

[53]   Ibid., 255.

[54]   Ibid., 256–62. Carter cites two nineteenth-century plays and a real-life adultery action where diaries are publicly employed as true representations of private events. A number of the novels to be examined using the diary model concern the fictional diary of a woman performed as evidence in public: *The Woman in White*, *The Legacy of Cain* and *Dracula* are the most obvious examples as discussed in Chapter 7. *The Tenant of Wildfell Hall*, *Man and Wife* and *The Law and the Lady* use some elements of the diary as evidence scenario.

of life events like marriage and childbirth. Incapacity, reticence and the lack of a language and audience might also contribute to silences and gaps in recording. Finally, the physical appearance and preservation of the diary are integral issues in the process of its production. Privacy and the ability or opportunity to write were necessary conditions for both the diary entry and the text itself to exist.

D'Israeli focuses on rendering an account and preserving the memory and on the diary as 'a moral instrument'.[55] His essay reflects the interest in diary-writing which emerges from the need to write history. For him, this often revolves around the lives of great men and he looks back at the fruits of the sixteenth and seventeenth centuries developed from manuscript family records. Manuscripts with appropriate provenance were valued for their perceived accuracy and public lives recorded in private could be made public again through modern printing.

The ability to print and to sell such texts in public seems to have emerged at the beginning of the nineteenth century.[56] Diaries and journals of the eighteenth century were often travel-oriented, presented as evidence of tours or expeditions.[57] The publication of hitherto manuscript diaries appears to have begun with that of John Evelyn's in 1818. Samuel Pepys's diaries were decoded and published in 1825.[58]

The cultural positioning of these two texts can be seen from their full titles. John Evelyn's exploits his status as a gentleman and Fellow of the Royal Society and makes illustrious connections:

> *Memoirs Illustrative of the Life and Writings of John Evelyn Esq., F.R.S. comprising his diary, from the year 1641 to 1705-6, and a selection of his familiar letters. To which is subjoined, the private correspondence between King Charles I. and his Secretary of State, Sir Edward Nicholas, whilst His Majesty was in Scotland, 1641, and at other times during the Civil War; also between Sir Edward Hyde, afterwards Earl of Clarendon, and Sir Richard Browne ... The whole now first published, from the original MSS ... Edited by William Bray [or rather, for the most part edited by William Upcott under the supervision of W. Bray].* (London: Henry Colburn, 1818)

---

[55]   D'Israeli, p. 206.

[56]   Martin Hewitt observes that diaries were part of a publishing tradition by the 1830s (Martin Hewitt, 'Diary, Autobiography and the Practice of Life History', in David Amigoni (ed.), *Life Writing and Victorian Culture* (Aldershot: Ashgate, 2006), p. 25).

[57]   For instance James Purefoy, *Diary of a Journey from Manchao...to Canton, in the years 1804 and 1805* (London, 1825); Henry Mathews, *The Diary of an Invalid; being the Journal of a Tour...in Portugal, Italy, Switzerland and France in the years 1817–1819* (London, 1820); Samuel Johnson, *Diary of a Journey into North Wales in 1774* (London, 1816). Perhaps there was also an element of vanity publishing as in John Beard, A *Diary of Fifteen Years' Hunting, viz. from 1796 to 1811.* (Bath: printed for the author, by W. Meyler and Son , 1813).

[58]   Aaron Kunin suggests that this was the effect of a Cambridge diary responding to an Oxford one (Kunin: 598).

The first edition of Samuel Pepys's diary insists on its documentary provenance despite the decoding process:

> *Memoirs of Samuel Pepys. Comprising his diary from 1659 to 1669, deciphered by the Rev. J. Smith, from the original short-hand MS. in the Pepysian Library, and a selection from his private correspondence. Edited by Richard, Lord Braybrooke.* (London: Henry Colburn, 1825)

The sense of originality and verisimilitude is made abundantly clear with dates, derivation and the addition of 'private correspondence'. The shorter titles echo one another in the definition of the works as 'memoirs'. Although the use of this category gives retrospective distance, both works are described as 'comprising his diary' rather than being 'compiled from' which might be a more formal biographical approach.[59] Both are nonetheless 'edited' and require the supporting testimony of the antiquarian Bray and the aristocratic editor Braybrooke.

It has since been established that these earliest examples of the published diary were heavily edited and expurgated for unacceptable matter, a fact which might countermand their claims to verisimilitude. The nineteenth century could not bear too much original material which might offend the reading public although it is only the expurgation which would allow them to be publishable once deemed publish-worthy. It should be noted that both of these men's diaries were published by Thomas Colburn who will later influence the selection and presentation of the diaries of Frances Burney discussed in Chapter 3. There was thus a market in the early nineteenth century for works purporting to be unexpurgated diaries. In addition to the four evolving traditions and the features outlined by D'Israeli, the published diary could be seen as an influence on the private diary from the 1820s. The diary in print also emerged as a feature of fictional narrative in the context of other evolved literary forms within the novel.

The representation of the non-fictional diary within its fictional counterpart can be traced through the epistolary novel into the mid nineteenth century. Defoe and Richardson had already exploited the diary's potential as first-person authenticated narrative in the context of the emerging novel format in the eighteenth century. Richardson's Pamela composes a journal when her letters can no longer be dispatched and Robinson Crusoe writes in journal form when he is isolated on his desert island.[60] In the terminology of H. Porter Abbott, these are literally 'cloistered' or 'moated' writers.[61] Involuntarily without an addressee, the diarist 'journalizes' and turns to the diary for her audience.

---

[59]   An 1828 publication also by Colburn insists on the diary direct: *Diary of Thomas Burton, Esq. member in the Parliaments of Oliver and Richard Cromwell, from 1656 to 1659: now first published from the original autograph manuscript. With an introduction, containing an account of the parliament of 1654; from the journal of Guibon Goddard Esq. M.P. also now first printed.* (London: Henry Colburn, 1828).

[60]   Daniel Defoe, *Robinson Crusoe* (1719); Samuel Richardson *Pamela* (1740). See also Daniel Defoe, *A Journal of the Plague Year* (1722).

[61]   H. Porter Abbott, 'Letters to the Self: The Cloistered Writer in Nonretrospective Fiction', *PMLA*, 95 (1980): 23.

In terms of the novel, the use of diaries as narrative has been the subject of study by twentieth- century scholars beginning with Gerald Prince's 'Notes for the Definition of a Sub-Genre' in 1975. This was followed by a number of book length studies by Valerie Raoul, H. Porter Abbott, Lorna Martens and Andrew Hassam.[62] These critics use the general analysis of the diary form to understand its particular function as a narrative device. Raoul identifies the 'code' of the real or non-fictional diary interacting with the 'code' of the novel. [63] Her focus is on French fiction and Hassam's on modern fiction. Abbott and Martens take a broader view and analyse nineteenth-century literature as a stepping stone to postmodern works. Martens provides a structured argument for the genre and Abbott is specifically concerned with the isolation of the fictional diarist.[64] None of these studies discusses diaries enclosed by other forms of narrative, their aim being to analyse fictional diaries with a single viewpoint. Their models and critical techniques, however, provide a vital part of any analysis of the diary acting as a fictional narrative.

Gerald Prince's 'Notes' present a simple outline of the features of the 'diary novel' which he describes as 'a first-person novel in which the narrator is a protagonist in the events he records'.[65] Prince identifies the features of fragmentation and 'several narrative occasions' as well as loneliness, the quest for the self and a theme of diary writing within the text itself.[66] He indicates a stress on authenticity and origins as well as an overt interest in how the words become text and in the physical shape of the diary volume itself.[67] These features are directly influenced, of course, by the non-fictional diary and describe significant elements of nineteenth-century women's diaries analysed in Chapters 2 and 3.

Lorna Martens points out that the diary novel is a subgenre of the first-person novel, 'a first-person narrative that the narrator writes at periodic intervals and essentially for himself'.[68] She sees the influence of the actual diary in the diary novel's periodic narration in the present, its discussion of the fiction of writing,

---

[62] Valerie Raoul, *The French Fictional Journal: Fictional Narcissism/Narcissistic Fiction* (Toronto: University of Toronto Press, 1980), H. Porter Abbott, *Diary Fiction: Writing as Action* (Ithaca: Cornell University Press, 1984), Lorna Martens, *The Diary Novel* (Cambridge: Cambridge University Press, 1985) and Andrew Hassam, *Writing and Reality: A Study of Modern British Diary Fiction* (Westport: Greenwood, 1993). Raoul and Hassam have produced articles which also supplement their work referring to the non-fictional diary: Valerie Raoul, 'Women and Diaries'; Andrew Hassam, 'Reading Other People's Diaries', and '"As I Write": Narrative Occasions and the Quest for Self-Presence in the Travel Diary'.

[63] Raoul, *The French Fictional Journal*, p. vii.

[64] Two articles become the more extensive study in 1984. Abbott picks up on Richardson's heroines and also on the journal inserted into *Robinson Crusoe* but he concentrates on single-perspective diary as fiction.

[65] Prince, 477.

[66] Ibid., 478; 479.

[67] Ibid., 479–80, 481.

[68] Martens, pp. ix, 4.

its secrecy and the presumed authority of the first person.[69] She touches briefly on the idea of the inserted journal which forms the main occurrence of the diary in the nineteenth-century novel. She contends that this device allows the author to maintain a grip on the narration whilst giving the reader access to thoughts and feelings.[70] Martens's book is an important study which provides a definition of diary fiction in terms of the interest evoked by the single-person viewpoint. It is the dialogic and nested narrative form of the fictional diary in the nineteenth-century novel which demands further attention within the terms she provides.

H. Porter Abbott, writing at about the same time, observes that readers of diary fiction are left with 'non-retrospective perceptions' but that the diary allows the author – equated by him with the overall producer of the text – 'a sharp dissociation between his present wisdom and the wisdom, or lack of it, that records the words on the page'.[71] Like Prince, Abbott observes that the production of the narrative becomes part of the plot – 'the event recorded and the event of recording' – and that fiction produced in the diary format draws attention to the act of writing.[72] The tale is told through an act of writing which ostensibly takes place without full knowledge of the outcome and an added layer of drama derives from the effect of the diarist's being 'cloistered' with her pen as sole resource. [73] Abbott finally adds that the impact of the isolated diarist 'is enabled by a proportional suppressing of other ... writing by narrators or correspondents'.[74] This again highlights his concentration on the single viewpoint since the fictional diary within a framing narrative very specifically provides multiple viewpoints and fragmented narrative.

The treatment of the fictional diary by this group of critics acknowledges the influence of real diaries particularly with reference to the lack of retrospection and the contribution of the physical text to its own narrative. The analyses by Abbott and Martens move firmly into a European and 'pure' diary fiction tradition leaving the nineteenth century largely untouched. Martens describes the use of the diary in nineteenth-century realism as 'a vehicle for convoluted plots'.[75]

The work of Bernard Duyfhuizen explores the use of the diary in the context of the documentary construction of the novel. He discusses the Abbott and Martens approaches in a review article which also helps to position his own full-length work, *Narratives of Transmission*. Duyfhuizen observes that a novel which operates

---

[69]   Ibid., p. x.

[70]   Ibid., p. 36.

[71]   Abbott, 'Letters to the Self': 23.

[72]   H. Porter Abbott, 'Diary Fiction', *Orbis Litterarum*, 37 (1982): 21–2; H. Porter Abbott, *Diary Fiction*, p. 9.

[73]   Abbott, *Diary Fiction*, pp. 39, 11. Martens similarly states that diary fiction uses its form to convey a message 'obliquely' and that the influence of the actual diary highlights the passing of time (Martens, pp. xi, x).

[74]   Abbott, *Diary Fiction*, p. 11.

[75]   Martens, p. 37.

through a 'narrative matrix' of voices whether linear, enclosed or alternated shows a form of competition which he also terms a 'drama of intertextuality'.[76] This reflects the other critics' references to the act of writing being itself part of the plot. For the interacting or intercalated narrative form, the transmission as well as the production of the text is a significant feature of a novel's construction. Duyfhuizen specifically discusses Anne Brontë's *The Tenant of Wildfell Hall* and Wilkie Collins's *The Woman in White* where women's diaries enter this competition, acting out the transmission of the novel through the gendering of the diarist, the physical appearance of the text and the structure of the narrative in relation to other texts. The novels under discussion in Part 2 of this book exemplify the ways in which the diary narrative of the nineteenth-century novel employs this more complex form of intertextuality as part of what Duyfhuizen terms a 'hybrid' narrative.[77]

In its non-fictional form, the diary was a product of accounting and the assessment of worth in economic, spiritual and dynastic contexts. The traditions described vary in their degree of closeness to the originally produced text: a spiritual diary was edited by content to deal with only the spiritual life but appeared in a published diary format; the family chronicle recorded everything but was edited for publication; the travel diary migrated through letters which were rewritten for another audience. Diaries in their public form were thus valued by the audience's differing chronological relationships with their original material and the experiences (re)presented by that material. The relationship between the text and its audience, the traditions and their publish-worthy character together with the role of daily record as evidence are vital concepts in the migration of the diary to a fictional narrative.

The diary or journal is in essence a daily record which owes its veracity to its recording method. It may be loosely formatted or more tightly structured by entries in a pre-printed volume. It may also have the appearance of daily record retrospectively reimposed. Non-fictional diaries refer to real unfolding events but are nonetheless composed, crafted and filtered by their controlling intelligence. Their composition and transmission is negotiated by a self who questions the existence of an audience. The diary model which appears as a narrative device in the novel is a response to the diary of a nineteenth-century woman which is ideologically positioned within existing diary traditions. This overview of the received practices of diary-keeping begins the process of understanding the composition and reception of a woman's record which animates the fictional diaries of women in nineteenth-century novels.

---

[76] Bernard Duyfhuizen, *Narratives of Transmission* (London: Associated University Presses, 1992), p. 123.

[77] Ibid.

Chapter 2
The Female Diarist in the Nineteenth Century

As Bernard Duyfhuizen points out, the diary is a democratic form, accessible to every literate person.[1] Analysis of the diary-writing practices of real women demonstrates how nineteenth-century women were able to converse with themselves and to engage in life writing through the medium of a journal. The application of the model to nineteenth-century female diarists is illustrated in this chapter using the unpublished versions of the diaries of four women: Frances Burney, Emily Shore, Elizabeth Gaskell and Anne Lister. The discussion specifically addresses the diaries produced in their own time rather than the published edited versions which have since emerged. It should be noted that Burney's diary has a complex textual history and the original is in the process of being recovered through the continuing work of the Burney Centre at McGill University.[2] Lister's diary has conversely been given a modern form which makes publication and consumption possible through severe editing and a degree of interpretation.[3] In so far as it is possible, the following is a discussion of the diaries written at the time by the four women within the traditions and criteria established in the late eighteenth and early nineteenth centuries. The reception as a public document of a diary written by a woman is explored in Chapter 3 using the published version of Burney's *Diary and Letters*.

Emily Shore kept a detailed diary for eight years but died in relative obscurity aged only nineteen. Elizabeth Gaskell was a public figure in her own lifetime and kept a sporadic record in a diary for three years in her mid-twenties but channeled her creative energies into writing letters and novels. Anne Lister and Frances Burney, however, kept personal records for most of their lives. Much of what Burney wrote between the ages of 15 and 88 has been retained. She was a consciously public person from the age of 25 following the publication of her first

---

[1]   Bernard Duyfhuizen, 'Diary Narratives in Fact and Fiction', *Novel A Forum on Fiction*, 19/2 (Winter 1986): 171.

[2]   The projects include *The Journals and Letters of Fanny Burney*, ed. Joyce Hemlow (12 vols, Oxford: Clarendon Press, 1972–1984) and *The Early Journals and Letters of Fanny Burney*, ed. Lars E. Troide, (6 vols, Oxford: Clarendon Press, 1988–). Where available, references are to these editions as *Journals and Letters* and *Early Journals* respectively. The six-volume *Court Journals 1786–91* are forthcoming.

[3]   See Anne Lister, *I Know My Own Heart: The Diaries of Anne Lister (1791–1840)*, ed. Helena Whitbread (London: Virago, 1988); unless indicated all references to the text are from this edition. See also Jill Liddington, *Female Fortune: Land, Gender and Authority: The Anne Lister Diaries and Other Writings 1833–36* (London: Rivers Oram, 1998).

novel, *Evelina* in 1778. Her long life passed through a number of phases leading from her father's involvement with the circle of Dr Johnson, to her time at Court and her marriage at the age of 41 to the French émigré Alexander D'Arblay.

Burney's diary as originally composed was initially addressed to 'Nobody': 'To NOBODY, then, will I write my Journal! since To Nobody can I be wholly unreserved – to Nobody can I reveal every thought, every wish of my Heart, with the most unlimited confidence, the most unremitting sincerity, to the end of my Life!' (27 March 1768, *Early Journals*, vol. 1, p. 2). Burney later addresses journal letters to her mentor Samuel 'Daddy' Crisp, to her sisters Susan and Charlotte and to her friend Frederica Locke of Norbury Park. These were variously circulated as semi public documents and sewn into book form by Susan but they ultimately returned to Burney on the deaths of their recipients as was the practice at the time.[4] Burney began writing in the mid eighteenth century and her diary illustrates the emerging private model of diary keeping. Felicity Nussbaum observes that by this period 'a private subject who engaged in constant self-scrutiny throughout her or his life is a commonplace'.[5] Burney spent much of the period between 1817 and 1840 reviewing family material at the time when diary publishing came into vogue and her example illustrates the ideological position which pervades the diaries of nineteenth-century women.

Burney announces her intention to provide unmediated accounts for posterity in a prospectus written at the age of fifteen. This is the first surviving diary entry:

> To have some account of my thoughts, manners, acquaintance & actions when the Hour arrives in which time is more nimble than memory, is the reason which induces me to keep a Journal: a Journal in which I must confess my *every* thought must open my whole Heart! (27 March 1768, *Early Journals*, vol. 1, p. 1)

The final document of some 1200 letters and journals exists as both daily record and retrospective reconstruction from memoranda written at the time. The fragmentation, dailiness and non-retrospection of the diary are nonetheless part of its complex negotiation for existence. On 15 September 1773 she tells her sister, 'I must give you this last Week all in a *lump* – for I have no Time for Daily Datings' (*Early Journals*, vol. 1, p. 309). From Streatham on 26 September 1778 she explains: 'I have, from want of time, neglected my journal so long, that I cannot now pretend to go on methodically, and be particular as to dates' (*Early Journals*, vol. 3, p. 167). In a letter of March 1787, she describes how she intends to reconstruct: 'I find no further memorandums of my winter Windsor expeditions of this year. I will briefly record some circumstances which I want no memorandums to recollect, and then tie my accounts concisely together till I find my minutes

---

    [4]   See Joyce Hemlow, 'Letters and Journals of Fanny Burney: Establishing the Text', in D.I.B. Smith (ed.), *Editing Eighteenth-Century Texts* (Toronto: University of Toronto Press, 1968), p. 27.

    [5]   Felicity A. Nussbaum, *The Autobiographical Self: Gender and Ideology in Eighteenth Century England* (Baltimore: The Johns Hopkins University Press, 1989), p. 201.

resumed.'[6] The language of 'memorandums', 'record', 'accounts' and 'minutes' suggests the discipline of an accounting system and the responsibility for family communications which she clearly felt.

Joyce Hemlow describes how the 'Teignmouth journal' created between 1 August and 17 September 1773 was in private circulation and lent out by Crisp.[7] The Bath journal was also reconstructed later: 'I have kept no regular memorandums, but I shall give you the history of the Bath fortnight of this month as it rises in my memory' (31 August 1791, *Journals and Letters*, vol. 1, p. 37). The Windsor journal of her time at Court was a mock communiqué written when her onerous duties permitted and probably as an antidote to them. The 1786 journal was a 200-page introduction to court life and she writes to her father and sister in November 1785: 'As you don't quite hate one another, you will not, I hope, hate me, for coupling you in my journal. It will be impossible for me to write separate accounts of any length or satisfaction, so I crave your joint permissions to address you together' (*Diary and Letters*, vol. 2, p. 356). The narrative occasion derives from the necessary conditions and negotiation of a writing space as both daughter/sister and subject.

Even early on, however, Burney is dramatizing her writing experience. On 21 May 1769 she writes that her sore throat 'tells me to leave idle and affected moralising; to leave my Journal; – to put out my candle – And hie to Bed' (*Early Journals*, vol. 1, p. 67). In those early diaries she also feels the need to draw attention to the assembly of the text which she writes in a cabin in the garden having satisfied her family with a suitable amount of reading and needlework in the morning. On 30 July 1768 she tells Nobody or more properly herself in the future: 'And so I suppose you are staring at the torn paper, & unconnected sentences – I don't much wonder – I'll tell you how it happ'd ... .' Her father has discovered one of her memoranda and this dramatic event is an opportunity to describe the process of compilation: 'You must know I always have the last sheet of my Journal in my pocket, & when I have wrote it half full – I join it to the rest, & take another sheet – & so on' (*Early Journals*, vol. 1, pp. 18–19).[8]

Perhaps even more than the address to Nobody which was prioritized in the published version in 1842, Burney's entry for a Wednesday in early July 1768 clarifies the purpose of the diary:

> I cannot express the pleasure I have in writing down my thoughts, at the very moment – my opinions of people when I first see them, & *how* I alter, or *how* confirm myself of it – & I am much deceived in my *fore sight*, if I shall not have very great delight in reading this *living proof* of my manner of passing my time,

---

[6]   *Diary and Letters of Madame D'Arblay: author of 'Evelina', 'Cecilia', &c.* (7 vols, London: Colburn, 1842–46), vol. 3, p. 347. References to material not yet available in the modern edition are to this original edition hereinafter *Diary and Letters*.

[7]   Joyce Hemlow, *The History of Fanny Burney* (Oxford: Oxford University Press, 1958), p. 49.

[8]   Joyce Hemlow describes the narrative assemblage with further examples in her introduction to *Journals and Letters*, vol. 1, p. xxxii.

my sentiments, my thoughts of people I know, & a thousand other things in future
– there is something to me very Unsatisfactory in passing year after year without
even a memorandum of what you did &c. (*Early Journals*, vol. 1, p. 14)

She draws out the sense of writing immediacy, the 'moment' which Samuel
Richardson had defined in his epistolary novels of the 1740s and 1750s.[9] Even
at the age of 15 she also wants to trace her own development in her attitudes
to people and to consider how she will benefit in retrospect. She sees the diary
as 'living' but also giving an account of the use of her time for review in the
future. She is acknowledging the traditions of the diary as a document of spiritual
progress and family chronicle but she also wants something dramatic to narrate
as her very next entry on 17 July 1768 announces: 'Alas, alas! My poor Journal!
– how dull, unentertaining, uninteresting thou art! – oh what would I give for some
Adventure worthy reciting – for something which would surprise – astonish you!'
(*Early Journals*, vol. 1, p. 15).

Burney is inevitably aware of literary models and their structure. From the
new family house in Queen's Square in London on 16 January 1773 she writes
portentously whilst continuing to insist on her audience of one: 'This is my 5th or
6th Journal Book – yet will not, I am persuaded, be my last. But it would require
very superiour (*sic*) talents to write an Annual Exordium. I must therefore content
myself with plainly & concisely proceeding with my Life and Opinions, addressed
to myself' (*Early Journals*, vol. 1, p. 229). In October 1791 despite addressing her
correspondents, she envisages a structure: 'Though another Month is begun since
I left my dearest of Friends, I have had no Journalizing spirit: but I will give all
heads of Chapters, & try to do better' (*Journals and Letters*, vol. 1, p. 72).

Her style too echoes literary content which she practises in her early diaries. In
1768, she tells how Arthur Young 'did not pollute my chamber with his unhallow'd
feet' following a family altercation. The adult Burney has then added that her half
sister Maria Allen was mortified because Young wanted to see 'her Journal' which
was 'in full sight – on her open Bureau. He said he had a right to see it as her
Uncle' (*Early Journals*, vol. 1, p. 5). This real life event is reminiscent of the full-
scale assault on written evidence by Mr B. in Richardson's *Pamela*.

Burney's attitude to journals 'in full sight' was a complex negotiation which is
part of the discussion of the published diary in Chapter 3. The shaping of a diary
for public consumption occurs in a context different from its early composition.
Burney's concerns about privacy came to compete with her responsibilities as
family chronicler when her long life brought her correspondence back to her from
the estates of the dead. This brief overview of her 'journalizing' in both private
diary and journal letters reiterates the model of received practice for the nineteenth
century.

---

[9]   Nearly twenty years after the 1768 entry she writes from Court: 'And now, good
night. I have not thus written to the very moment for a longer time than I can now recollect'
(4 January 1788, *Diary and Letters*, vol. 4, p. 9).

Emily Shore was writing her diary within that received practice. Shore was an accomplished amateur botanist who kept a diary from the age of eleven until her death in 1839 aged only nineteen. The manuscript of over nineteen hundred pages was edited by her sisters Louisa and Arabella and published in 1891; this version was only 350 pages long.[10] Emily's life as reflected in the diary is perhaps not strictly typical. Emily and her siblings were educated at home by their father, and Emily in turn taught the younger ones. She notes on 8 January 1836: 'Papa continually takes opportunities in common conversation to give us information on many subjects which we are not likely to find explained in books' (p. 135). Her role as a student and observer of life was intensified by her intellectual powers and, to some extent, by her awareness of her own impending death. The family moved to Madeira in 1838 in an attempt to arrest the progress of consumption.

Shore inherits the household accounts to administer from her sick bed (2 October 1837, p. 220) and she intertwines her various pursuits with prayer, reading and writing the journal. She writes on 19 March 1839: 'Having finished my devotions and reading, I wrote my journal and then worked at the same time learning John XV ... I had every now and then a few housekeeping interruptions ... After tea, I returned to my room, where I am now sitting' (p. 345). Her diary strives for balance. It absorbs both the spiritual and domestic-economic traditions and draws attention to the narrative occasion.

The dating process which stresses the occurrence of anniversaries is heightened for Shore by the fact that she was born on Christmas Day. Although her life is still unfolding she demonstrates a shaping continuity, a sense of authorship of herself. On 25 December 1838, which is to be her last birthday, she writes: 'For some years past every birthday has been almost an unexpected addition to my life' (p. 301). She observes that she has written in a pocket book from the age of ten and by 1836, her diary is a specially made volume for 'the use of the pen is amongst the most valuable means of improving the mind' (30 April 1836, p. 138). She acknowledges the change from volume to volume as a subsidiary anniversary, commenting on the eighth volume begun on 11 April 1837: 'The commencement and conclusion of every new volume in my journal always seems a kind of era to me' (p. 189). Shore was a published writer aware of literary models. She mentions 'the cares of authorship' (15 December 1837, p. 231).[11] After an illness in 1836 she writes with some drama and in contrast to her normal discourse of ornithological information: 'To me all this spring and part of the summer are quite lost, and it might almost as well have been continual winter' (6 June 1836, p. 139). Her encounter with the young man, H.W. who has been discouraged by her family because of her consumption has a literary style reminiscent of a novel and a re-

---

[10]   Emily Shore, *The Journal of Emily Shore*, ed. Barbara Timm Gates (Charlottesville: University Press of Virginia, 1991). All references in the text are to this edition.

[11]   She contributed two articles to the *Penny Magazine* in 1837 although the other works listed by her sisters ('Introduction', pp. viii–xii) including many poems, three novels and a Greek translation are not extant.

narrated performance: 'I was anxious to read his face but dared not look up and meet his eyes' (17 May 1838, p. 247).

Whilst illustrating the day-to-day commitment to diary-writing, Shore also takes time to consider the act of writing itself. On 6 July 1838, she muses where her new volume, the eleventh, will end. She has been reading John Forster's essay 'On a Man's Writing Memoirs of Himself' and writes of her own journal: 'I'm sure it is a memoir of my character, ... a valuable index of my mind' which she uses to peruse her own follies (pp. 261–2). She also demonstrates the struggle to express female experience such as her feelings on meeting H.W. again: 'For some other reasons, his coming rather annoys me, and very much surprises me too. But let that pass' (5 March 1838, p. 240). She is tentatively exploring her thoughts on love also in 1836: 'There is completely a world within me, unknown, unexplored by any but myself' (25 December 1836, p. 175).

Shore also indicates that the diary is well-known within the family and read by others in the style of a journal letter. Shore is thus conscious of the diary as a performed family narrative and she says that this cramps her expression so that she cannot write the most secret things. On the one hand she would like to write these things, and on the other she would not wish to deprive her family and her future children of what she can contribute. She even proposes to keep a second secret journal of which there is no extant evidence.[12] In fact, she will be dead within a year despite her entry on 28 January 1839: 'Mine has not been an eventful life, yet for a long time past every year has been rife with what would have utterly astonished me could I have foreseen it all. What strange things may fill its future pages?' (p. 327).

Shore's diary reflects the traditions which have evolved into the nineteenth-century. She evaluates her life in the manner of the spiritual diary and her record of natural history resembles the travel diary. Her household duties are reflected as well as her responsibilities as a family chronicler. There is a sense of the cloistered diarist and of the process of composition from a single perspective as well as the lack of order or hierarchy of values in the contents. She describes her own attempts to sort 'confused heaps of manuscripts' on her arrival in Madeira (6 March 1839, p. 340). She analyses her writing and the physical creation of the text as well as its frames and milestones within the events of her life. It may be shapeless but this diary is shaped by tradition, by the private space in which it is composed and by both the life expectation and life expectancy of its author. Shore writes in the knowledge that she is a woman in an extraordinary household but still a woman; she writes in the knowledge that she is going to die; she writes in the knowledge that her family will share these thoughts as a matter of course. She also, however, makes an index of this diary (p. 190), an act which must question its non-retrospective and unpublishable character.

---

[12]   Her sisters list the existence of three volumes of 'Brief Diaries' from 1835–39 'containing merely the common facts of daily family life ... carried on simultaneously with the fuller journals' ('Introduction', p. xii).

At the same period, Elizabeth Gaskell was writing a diary of only nine entries made at irregular intervals between 10 March 1835 and 14 October 1838.[13] Although brief in the context of Burney's and Shore's diaries, Gaskell's record provides other examples of the use of the diary in a nineteenth-century domestic context which are valuable in the consideration of its fictional counterpart. This diary seems to have grown out of Gaskell's experience of losing her own mother, and she begins: 'To my dear little Marianne I shall 'dedicate' this book, which, if I should not live to give it her myself, will I trust be reserved for her as a token of her mother's love, and extreme anxiety in the formation of her little daughter's character' (10 March 1835, p. 5). The diary is to be a memoir for her daughter if Gaskell too dies. Marianne is the implied reader of the diary from which it is possible to conclude that the text is tailored and aiming at an audience. Anita Wilson describes Gaskell as 'cultivating powers of observation'.[14] At one point the diary reverses its function and is aimed at memorializing Marianne who suffered with a number of childhood illnesses but in fact survived until 1920. Gaskell writes: 'I sometimes think I may find this little journal a great help in recalling the memory of my darling child, if we should lose her' (7 February 1836, p. 13).

This diary also incorporates elements of the diary models. Gaskell is offering opportunities for self-improvement and family record: 'If that little daughter should in time become a mother herself, she may take an interest in the experience of another' (10 March 1835, p. 5). She offers a family narrative concerning the 'changes in our domestic relations' (9 December 1837, p. 18) for the benefit of the book's inheritors and eventual readers. There is also an element of self-surveillance both on a domestic level and on a spiritual one. Gaskell discusses her own methods: 'I have generally begun my journal with describing the bodily progress she has, and I will keep to the proper order of things' (7 February 1836, p. 14). More coolly and managerially, she comments on a standard against which she is measuring herself: 'I put down everything now because I have thought a good deal about the formation of any little plans, and I shall like to know their success' (10 March 1835, p. 7). She invokes the authority of order and daily record even though she does not physically keep her record on a daily basis.

Gaskell also adds a spiritual dimension by concluding many of her entries with an appeal to God for Marianne's wellbeing. She expresses her own concerns that she values the baby – her 'dear little subject' – too highly and later adds: 'Teach me to love this darling child with perfect submission to thy decrees ... for thou art a God of Love & wilt not carelessly afflict' (5 November 1836, p. 18).[15]

---

[13]   Elizabeth Gaskell, 'The Diary' in *The Works of Elizabeth Gaskell*, ed. Joanne Shattock (10 vols, London: Pickering and Chatto, 2005), vol. 1, pp. 5–25.

[14]   Anita Wilson, 'Critical Introduction' to Elizabeth Gaskell and Sophia Holland, *Private Voices: The Diaries of Elizabeth Gaskell and Sophia Holland*, ed. J.A.V. Chapple and Anita Wilson (Keele: Keele University Press, 1996), p. 33.

[15]   Anita Wilson points out that the level of anxiety was higher in the diary than it was in Gaskell's letters written at the time of the later death of her baby son Willie. She observes that the letters were a public medium which may have called for more restraint than the diary abandoned some seven years before (Wilson, p. 24).

For herself, she asks: 'Oh my Father help me to regulate my impatient temper better' (28 October 1838, p. 25). At other points the moral and practical elements of motherhood and contemporary childcare manuals affect her as when Marianne begins to attend school in the mornings: 'I am sometimes afraid of becoming a lazy mother, willing to send my children away from me, and forgetting that on *me* lies the heaviest responsibility' (25 March 1838, p. 22).[16] Joanne Shattock points out that these were conduct books specifically aimed at middle class mothers, what Clement Shorter the Diary's first editor in 1923 called a 'literature of the psychology of childhood'.[17] As Anita Wilson comments, 'Her private voice complements the abundant public discourse of an era which bombarded mothers with advice.'[18]

In the case of Elizabeth Gaskell, her daughter Marianne is the implied reader of the diary, a text which is therefore conscious of its own composition and a partial rehearsal for fiction. Gaskell in fact looks back and reviews her writing like Emily Shore who makes an index of her diary for the family. Gaskell even describes one of her entries as a 'chapter' (p. 23). As a self-conscious diarist she also gives a sense of narrative occasion; she observes at one point 'I was stopped by the lateness of the hour' (8 April 1838, p. 23). This is coupled with a lyricism and immediacy which is an early indicator of her fictional writing: 'I had no idea the journal of my own disposition, & feelings was so intimately connected with that of my little baby, whose regular breathing has been the music of my thoughts all the time I have been writing' (10 March 1835, p. 7). In addition to the family memorial, this diary is a response to contemporary concepts of motherhood and child care. It functions like an advice and memory bank demonstrating retrospection and catharsis as well as acting as a spiritual monitor in conjunction with household matters. It applies dailiness to the greater moral questions which defined the role of nineteenth-century women in a private space.

In a chronological arc over the diaries of Shore and Gaskell,[19] the diary of Anne Lister represents an additional life recorded before the publication of women's diaries and within a period of development towards the diary form in the novel. Lister was a politically active landowning woman who lived near Halifax. Her diary is prized in part because of her unusual activities in the public sphere and its cryptic code has been deciphered to reveal the private life of a committed and active lesbian. Lister kept her diary from the age of fifteen in 1806 until her death in 1840. She records details of the weather and of estate business almost obsessively. Thirty four years of diary entries are contained in 27 volumes which have been variously decoded and edited firstly by her distant relative John Lister

---

[16] William Gaskell appears to have chosen not to involve himself in his wife's anxieties despite his representation as a participant in his eldest daughter's education (Wilson, p. 12).

[17] Gaskell, *Works*, vol. 1, p. 1.

[18] Wilson, p. 12.

[19] Burney keeps her diary from 1768 to 1839; Shore from 1831 to 1839 and Gaskell from 1835 to 1838.

who inherited the diaries in the late nineteenth century, and latterly by a number of historians who engage in various ways with Lister's local historical significance, her contribution to the landed gentry and her sexuality.[20]

Lister's life is clearly atypical and has tended to be mined for its contribution to debates about gender and sexual agency operating at a time when it was assumed that the lesbian identity was unknown.[21] The diaries do, however, reinforce a sense of the traditions and writing practices represented by Burney, Gaskell and Shore. Lister's role as a landowner in dispute and concerned with dynastic succession may have made her unusual but her diary-keeping also follows many of the patterns already observed.

Like Shore, Lister acknowledges the occurrence of her birthday. On 3 April 1820, she reflects: 'I thought of it being my birthday, but let it pass without notice. How time steals away! What will the next year bring? May I improve it more than the last!' (p. 119). After she inherits Shibden Hall from her uncle, she writes on 3 April 1826: 'I have completed my thirty-fourth year. I am my own master. What events have happened during the last twelve months.'[22] Lister demonstrates that sense of authorship of herself which can be observed in the other diarists. On 19 February 1819, she clearly sets out the same goals as Burney: 'Wrote in this book the journal of yesterday ... I am resolved not to let my life pass without some private memorial that I may hereafter read, perhaps with a smile, when Time has frozen up the channel of those sentiments which flow so freshly now' (p. 80).[23]

She describes the physical text on 20 March 1819: 'Called at Whitley's & got the blank book which is to form the next volume of my journal' (p. 83). She discusses its compilation, referring on numerous occasions to the act of writing and the occasion for writing up memoranda. She also discusses her editing process, regularly indexing the events of the year as on 14 January 1818: 'Before breakfast writing out the rough draft of an index to this volume of my journal' (p. 36). She thinks of the text as a conduct book of herself. On 18 June 1824, she recalls various lovers including the now married Miss Browne who is 'merely noted in the index': 'Volume three ... I read over attentively, exclaiming to myself, 'O women, women!' (p. 346). She even thinks of the potential for publication when she has produced a 96-page letter of a visit to France.[24]

---

[20]   See Lister, *I Know My Own Heart*; Jill Liddington, *Presenting the Past: Anne Lister of Halifax 1791–1840* (Hebden Bridge: Pennine Press, 1994) and *Female Fortune*.

[21]   See Anira Rowanchild, '"My Mind on Paper": Anne Lister and the Construction of Lesbian Identity' in Alison Donnell and Pauline Polkey (eds), *Representing Lives: Women and Auto/Biography* (Basingstoke: Macmillan, 2000), 199–207, and Dannielle Orr, '"I Tell Myself to Myself": Homosexual Agency in the Journals of Anne Lister (1791–1840)', *Women's Writing*, 11/2 (2004): 201–22.

[22]   Quoted by Rowanchild, p. 206.

[23]   See above: 27 March 1768, *Early Journals*, vol. 1, p. 1 and July 1768, *Early Journals*, vol. 1, p. 14.

[24]   22 December 1819: 'At least I have gained a valuable turn towards a habit of patient reference and correction which, should I ever publish, may be of use to me' (p. 111).

It seems likely that Lister's valuation of record and collation stems from a sense of dynastic responsibility related to the family chronicle tradition of the diary. This is intensified by her performance of the role of landowner and her conflicted gender representation, if not disguise, as a heterosexual woman. In 1817, at the age of only 26 she conflates the acts of recording, editing and evaluating herself as Burney did in her eighties. She looks over an 'old portfolio of papers, extracts, letters ... The general rummage among my letters & papers puts me sadly out of the way – but as I have never had my things fairly set to rights as they ought to be, 'tis high time to begin if I mean to get it done in my lifetime' (16 October, p. 16).This could of course either be a stylized pose or perhaps an acknowledgement of her task in restoring the fortunes of her improvident family; she was the fourth child of a fourth son in a family described by Jill Liddington as 'dynastically frail'.[25]

Lister also uses the diary for spiritual guidance and authorization in the manner of Shore and Gaskell. She has no problem with God's acceptance of her sexuality and writes in code on 31 December 1832 with the New Year in view: 'Who will be the next tenant of my heart? Providence orders all things wisely.'[26] On 28 July 1819 writing up from the 'pencil journal' made on a trip to France, she observes that ruin results from such borrowing of time as from borrowing money: 'May I never forget this and always profit by its remembrance' (p. 94). She addresses God even in her calculated approach to the acquisition of land through her lover Ann Walker: 'I shall not give way, come what may' is a coded entry followed by the uncoded, 'I know, O Lord, that thy judgements are right.'[27]

Like other diarists, Lister uses the diary to discuss the need for order and resolution. On 26 February 1821 she proposes a new 'plan of reading ... I have hitherto wandered over too many books with too little thought' (p. 147). This extends also to her concern to seek 'a style of dress that suits me' (17 July 1821, p. 157) which apparently led her to adopt a black costume. She was also known locally as Gentleman Jack. [28] This debate which is part of her gender/public negotiation continues at intervals and causes disputes with Marianna Lawton, a former lover now married. On 2 April 1817 she announces: 'Began this morning to sit, before breakfast, in my drawers put on with gentleman's braces I bought for 2/6 on 27 March 1809 & my old black waistcoat & dressing gown' (p. 1). On 3 September 1820 aged thirty, she records that she is 'trying things on ... Studying how to improve my chest by stuffing' and on 16 September 1823, she worries about her lack of 'proper dress ... My figure is striking' (p. 133, p. 295).

Lister also indicates another level of reading and collation which introduces familiar concepts of the diary as spiritual and confidential companion. On 24 August 1822, she spends two and a half hours over her index: 'The looking over & filling up my journal to my mind always give me pleasure. I seem to live my

---

[25]   Liddington, *Female Fortune*, p. 9.

[26]   Ibid., p. 70.

[27]   Ibid., 26 November 1835, p. 196.

[28]   Lister, *I Know My Own Heart*, p. ix.

life over again. If I have been unhappy, it rejoices me to have escaped it; if happy, it does me good to remember it' (p. 214). On 16 September 1823 in Scarborough for her health, she observes that 'writing my journal has amused me and done me good. I seemed to have opened my heart to an old friend. I can tell my journal what I can tell none else' (p. 295).

Lister thus uses the diary as part of the evolution of her own identity within the framework of public life to which she offers the challenge of being both a female landowner openly and a lesbian in private. There is clear evidence of the equivocal secrecy of the text one-sixth of which was written in a 'secret alphabet' or 'crypt hand'.[29] Lister's lover Isabella Norcliffe mentions the journal at a tea party and calls it 'peculiar hand-writing'.[30] This incident antagonizes Lister but also draws attention to the uses made of the code. It is apparent that having been originally devised with Eliza Raine, a school friend, the code was shared with a range of lovers of widely varying degrees of intimacy.[31] Lister also mentions that her partner Ann Walker with whom she went through a form of marriage 'has locked up my journal' in a passage that is itself uncoded.[32]

Critics have pointed out that Lister used the code to record not only her sexual feelings and relationships but also her financial insecurity and as Anira Rowanchild observes, 'A code both presupposes and contrives a reader.'[33] Lister was therefore regulating and privileging access to her 'second self' with the diary acting as a textual signpost of sexuality, intimacy, value and identity. The code as a mimetic document, a private showing of self, reflects the concept of performance as much as the discussion of clothing is a performance of gender, pushing the boundaries of the acceptable and exploiting that lack of a gender category which seemed also to protect Lister from notice.

If her lovers have access to the journal as substitutes for the semi public diary read within the family, the content may have been further policed and coded in anticipation of this further level of decoding. Lister writes, for instance, that she reads to Marianna who has now married Charles Lawton some memoranda on wasted love which have formed her journal entries.[34] On 29 January 1821, she affirms in dramatic style: 'I love, & only love, the fairer sex & thus beloved by them in turn, my heart revolts from any love than theirs' (p. 145). There is a complex audience relationship between Lister the diarist and her past and potential future readers, those privileged decoders in her own circle. This secrecy and authorized reading is a feature of the fictional diary when it emerges into literature in the late 1840s.

---

[29]   22 May 1817 (p. 8); 6 August 1819 (p. 96).
[30]   6 August 1819 (p. 96).
[31]   Noted by Rowanchild, p. 202.
[32]   8 August 1835 (*Female Fortune*, p. 186).
[33]   See Liddington, *Presenting the Past*, p. 19 and Rowanchild, p. 205.
[34]   4 April 1820 (p. 119).

Lister evaluates her life in the manner of the spiritual diary and records the environment and business of landowning. Her dynastic aspirations are reflected as well as her struggles with public identity. There is a sense of the attempt to impose order and to consider the creation of the text as both a friend and a discussion document. Lister's diary is shaped both by tradition and by her negotiation of her private space. Despite the extraordinary amount of material available which Jill Liddington describes as a 'dazzlingly rich mix'[35] some entries offer a concentrated insight into the evolution of a role. Thus on 29 January 1821, her entry reads: 'Cutting curl papers half an hour ... Arranging & putting away my last year's letters. Looked over & burnt several very old ones from indifferent people that no trace of any man's admiration may remain' (p. 145). The curl papers are one element of Lister's construction of her identity, a hijacked performance of gender through the signs of femininity. She is also engaged in life writing as a woman and as a family chronicler through the editing of her papers, and she enacts the secrecy of the diary writing process by destroying evidence which should not be read. In this case, of course, she is also engaged in the construction of her secret identity, another form of the 'second self', by rejecting heterosexual relationships and perhaps recoding this for the benefit of her decoding readers, past, present or future lovers.[36]

Anira Rowanchild describes Anne Lister's diary as 'a safely encoded textual space'[37] but her diary is doubly encoded both by her identity and social-financial insecurity in 'crypt hand' and by her place in the ideological code of the female diarist. Like Burney, Shore and Gaskell, she composes her diary in a tradition where the diary is an understanding friend, a repository for confidences and a place in which to debate forms of dress. Emily Shore, writing at much the same time, is no different in her obsessions and textual coding through ornithology and botany. She too proposes a secret diary which is not extant. Elizabeth Gaskell records her daughters' childhoods and questions the code of motherhood. There is a sense in which these are marginalized identities as much as Lister's is, and the diary offers a space in which negotiation for the other selves takes place. The publication of Burney's diaries highlights these negotiations in their nineteenth-century context.

The diaries of Burney and Lister, Shore and Gaskell exemplify the non-fictional traditions of the period and the received conventions for nineteenth-century diary writers and readers. The diary model which emerges demonstrates that the diary for a nineteenth-century woman has both an ephemeral and memorial function. The diarist regards herself as compelled to write by domestic duties which also shape the entries and authorize self-representation through repetition or even obsession. A woman regards the diary as a friend willing to listen to any confidence. Despite the authorization of diary writing as a non-retrospective act, the diary

---

[35]   Liddington, *Presenting the Past*, p. 9.
[36]   This is the entry which continues as above that 'I love, & only love, the fairer sex'.
[37]   Rowanchild, p. 199.

demonstrates degrees of retrospection and of structure. The privacy of the diary as a personal record is already vitiated by its circulation within the family and its potential recreation as family chronicle or spiritual autobiography. The diaries of these four women demonstrate how daily record can become what Judith Butler terms 'a strategy of survival within compulsory systems'.[38] Although ideologically denied narrative evaluation and self representation, the female diarist adapts both authorized daily record and the absence of an audience to create a text made performative through repetition and mimetic acts of creation.

---

[38] Judith Butler, *Gender Trouble: Feminism and the Subversion of Identity* (London: Routledge, 1990), p. 139.

Chapter 3
The Diary in Print

The fictional model of the diary employed by novelists is also predicated on the published diary. This chapter investigates the event of a woman's diary entering the marketplace by examining the appearance of the first diary in print, that of Frances Burney. It then considers the diaries which emerge in print within the six core texts. The private use of the diary as women's life writing and the public editorial practices of the printed diary feed directly into any analysis of the published diary acting as a fictional narrative.

The act of keeping a diary in private was a heavily encoded and loaded activity in the nineteenth century. The publication of a woman's diary required a much more complex negotiation between the self and society. The first female-authored published diary was that of Frances Burney which appeared in seven volumes between 1842 and 1846.[1] *The Diary and Letters of Madame D'Arblay* used material dating between 1778 and 1840 which Burney herself had reviewed in the last twenty years of her life and which passed into the marketplace as family chronicle, domestic memoir and spiritual autobiography. Burney's diary is both a representative example and a potential catalyst for the diary narratives which occur in nineteenth-century novels. Her diary reached the marketplace through a complex process of preservation and transmission. Its public appearance was only authorized after a renegotiation of public and private character which exposes the very tensions that the private diarist experienced in using her text for self representation.

Burney's task of preserving family history using the papers in her possession weighed on her after the deaths of her father and husband in 1814 and 1818 respectively. She produced accounts of her time in Brussels, of her mastectomy, and of her near-drowning on the cliffs at Ilfracombe, as well as her *Memoir* of her father published in 1832. The editing process was apparently a painful one particularly after the death of her son, and Burney refers to 'this killing mass of constant recurrence to my calamity' in a letter to her sister Charlotte on 20 April 1838.[2] The personal record provided by her own diary and letters was published in two stages after Burney's death. Five volumes appeared at intervals in 1842 covering the years 1778 to 1792 from the publication of *Evelina* to Burney's release from her Court duties. In 1846, a further two volumes covered 1793 to 1840.

---

[1]   Cited by Stuart Sherman, *Telling Time: Clocks, Diaries and English Diurnal Form 1660–1785* (Chicago: University of Chicago Press, 1996), p. 270.

[2]   Quoted by Joyce Hemlow, *The Journals and Letters of Fanny Burney* (12 vols, Oxford: Clarendon Press, 1972–1984), vol. 1, p. xli; hereinafter *Journals and Letters*.

Examples from Burney's diary as it was written have been included in Chapter 2. Whilst an understanding of women's diary-writing can be enhanced by the recovered diary – recovered that is from the process of editing – features of the woman's diary in print must be established from the edited version of 1842–1846. This process can consider the elements of the published diary which allows Burney's text into the marketplace together with the issues which are prioritized by both its framing memoir and selection of material. The presentational choices made for the published text also illustrate how the process of editorial modification would apply to diary material within a novel.

Charlotte Barrett, daughter of Burney's sister Charlotte and editor of the *Diary and Letters*, calls her edition 'a journalizing memoir'[3] crossed between a family chronicle and autobiography, accounting for a life.[4] Barrett engages in a number of techniques which frame the papers, insisting on both provenance and womanly reticence, and there is also a dialogic relationship between the public and private *personae* of the subject. The editor requests 'no eye but that of indulgent friendship' but also insists that Burney's reputation of sixty years' public esteem 'renders criticism and comment superfluous' (*Diary and Letters*, p. iv). This is a complex rhetoric demanding a response of cosy familial acceptance and at the same time recognition of Burney's market worth as an author. Despite her plea for a friendly fireside Barrett also wrote to her son Richard on 8 February 1840 'the very names will sell the book'.[5]

The dichotomy between the private life of Burney and her public fame is apparent from the beginning of the 'Editor's Introduction' which precedes the neatly arranged and indexed chapters. Barrett observes: 'those who have derived pleasure and instruction from her publications may feel interested in reading her private journals and thus becoming acquainted with the merits and peculiarities of her individual character' (*Diary and Letters*, p. iv), that of a shy, retiring and dutiful daughter and loyal subject of the Queen. Pleasure is balanced with instruction, the private record displaying the private person. Barrett must then negotiate the appearance of the private to public view. She continues: 'We would also hope there may be a moral use in presenting the example of one who, being early exalted to fame and literary distinction, yet found her chief happiness in the discharge of domestic duties, and in the friendships and attachments of private life' (*Diary and Letters*, p. iv–v). There is a moral purpose behind publication which is nonetheless aimed at an account of the fame which makes Burney a

---

[3]   *Diary and Letters of Madame D'Arblay: author of 'Evelina', 'Cecilia', &c.* (7 vols, London: Colburn, 1842–46), 'Editor's Introduction', vol. 1, p. iii; hereinafter *Diary and Letters*.

[4]   Linda Lang-Peralta decides on the term 'life-writing' to describe Burney's writing practices which do not put letters and journals into distinct categories ('"Clandestine Delight": Frances Burney's Life-Writing', in Linda S. Coleman (ed.), *Women's Life-Writing: Finding Voice/Building Community* (Bowling Green, Ohio: Popular, 1997), p. 40 note 3).

[5]   Quoted in *Journals and Letters*, vol 1, p. xliv.

suitable exemplar of womanhood and incidentally attaches performative agency to the diary. The published diary is specifically attuned to the tensions created between the claims of the domestic and public spheres. The very titles of Barrett's volumes illustrate the conflict between their desire to present Burney in her married character as Madame D'Arblay and in her public character as 'the author of *Evelina*'. The paradox remains that the 'moral use' of the published diary can only be exploited because of the 'fame'.

The next framing mechanism for the *Diary and Letters* is the introductory invocation to 'Nobody' which is relocated as a preface to the first volume and almost immediately denigrated by Barrett as a childish invention. Burney herself rewrote the passage and the facsimile in her hand is bound in with the other material. It seems to present Burney's acknowledgement of the existence of an audience: 'I must imagine myself to be talking – talking to the most intimate of friends.'[6] At the moment of writing in 1768, however, this was an imaginary friend, the 'Nobody' whose existence empowered the diary as a personal record. Both the addressee and audience, however, were still 'nobody'. Barrett's 'Introduction' in 1842 acknowledges a subsequent audience for Burney's journal letters in Burney's sisters and 'Daddy' Crisp and later Mrs Locke, recipients who were allowed to see 'a window in her breast' (*Diary and Letters*, p. xxi). Lars Troide points out in his edition of the *Early Journals* that the mature Burney overscored her reference on 7 February 1770 to 'Nobody – that good old friend of mine, who never refuses me her attention'[7] and Barrett too attempts to erase the original addressee and reconstruct the domestic and discerning audience for the private text in order to present it in public.

Within this frame, in the first few pages of the published text of 1842, the newly published author of *Evelina* calculates her importance as a documenter of events as she recovers from illness at Crisp's house in Chesington: 'Here I am, & here I have been this Age; though too weak to think of Journalising; however, as I never had so many curious anecdotes to record, I will not, at least *this Year*, the first of my *appearing in public* – give up my favourite old Hobby Horse' (18 June 1778, *Early Journals*, vol. 3, p. 18). Barrett must preserve still the fiction that Burney might any moment give up 'journalising'. Burney describes how she has been reading *Evelina* to her cousin Richard but cannot speak aloud 'the little introductory ode ... the sincere effusion of my Heart, I could as soon read aloud my own Letters, written in my own Name & Character' (18 June 1778, *Early Journals*, vol. 3, p. 21). In the novel, the published prefatory letter or 'ode' is addressed outside *Evelina* to 'the Authors of the *Monthly* and *Critical Reviews*'. The anonymous author asks for justice and mercy on her literary production in her own person before assuming the role of editor of the letters which make up the novel. Only

---

[6]   *The Early Journals and Letters of Fanny Burney*, ed. Lars E. Troide (6 vols, Oxford: Clarendon Press, 1988–), vol. 1, p. 1; hereinafter *Early Journals*. Barrett has silently corrected the spelling of 'imagion' to 'imagine'.

[7]   Ibid., vol. 1, p. 108.

in this public but anonymous character can she write the Preface proper which follows.[8] Despite potential editing, this incident of reading aloud is preserved within the published context of the *Diary*. Not only were readers in 1778 reading the published novel *Evelina*, readers in 1842 are reading the published but private record of this event. In the diary entry of June 1778, Burney differentiates between performing the fiction of the novel or 'History' she has written and performing her own thoughts in the editorial matter which precedes it.

This equivocation over her public character is the subject of lifelong conflict for Burney as Kristina Straub and Judy Simons have observed.[9] Its complexity is demonstrated by Burney's deference to the male figures in her life who tried to suppress or guide her writing ambition and her evident eagerness to write. While Burney ostensibly accepts this conflict there are times when she wants her father to come to terms with her literary aspirations. For instance, in spite of his apparent opposition she writes to Dr Burney on 25 July 1778 signing herself 'Francesca Scriblerus' (*Early Journals*, vol. 3, p. 51). In reality, her father's retention of Burney as his amanuensis restricts her time for her own writing. She has to produce the manuscript of *Evelina* in a disguised hand to avoid recognition because of her involvement in her father's writings. This is an instance similar to the public reading of the 'ode'.

The conflict between recognition as an author and the role of woman can be further illustrated in an incident she relates later. In the winter of 1786–1787 when recalling events without the benefit of memoranda, she writes in her journal that she has heard her own novel *Cecilia* mentioned in a scandalous play. She manages complete recall of these offending 'lines, or something like them' which yet maintain the morality of her character: 'Let sweet Cecilia gain your just applause, / Whose every passion yields to Reason's laws.' This accolade is presented exactly from memory but Burney must also, for the benefit of the journal and its audience at least, react according to the tenets of womanly modesty:

> My whole head was leaning forward, with my opera-glass in my hand, examining Miss Farren, who spoke the epilogue. Instantly I shrunk back, so astonished and so ashamed of my public situation, that I was almost ready to take to my heels and run, for it seemed as if I were there purposely in that conspicuous place – 'To list attentive to my own applause.' (*Diary and Letters*, vol. 3, pp. 354–5)

Having allowed these incidents preserved by Burney to remain in the printed text, Barrett wrestles with the public/private dilemma into the very last volume of the *Diary and Letters*: 'In conclusion, may we not find throughout these memoirs a

---

[8]   Frances Burney, *Evelina*, ed. Margaret Anne Doody (London: Penguin 1994; reprinted 2004), pp. 4–6 and pp. 7–9. The novel is subtitled *The History of a Young Lady's Entrance into the World*.

[9]   See Kristina Straub, *Divided Fictions: Fanny Burney and Feminine Strategy* (Lexington: University Press of Kentucky, 1987), pp. 1–6 and Judy Simons, *Diaries and Journals of Literary Women from Fanny Burney to Virginia Woolf* (Iowa City: University of Iowa Press, 1990), pp. 19–39.

confirmation of General d'Arblay's parting testimony, that those who knew her only from the public reputation were unacquainted with the best and most valuable part of her character. And this is no slight praise when given to the Author of *Evelina, Cecilia* and *Camilla*' (*Diary and Letters*, vol. 7, p. 385). The devoted wife is still the famous author and it is her privacy made public which gives her a value as a spiritual guide to others.

Within the equivocal incidents of privacy and performance, the diary is also that of a woman narrating her own story who adopts the codes of the anniversary, the family documentary, the narrative occasion and lack of a recording language. In the *Diary and Letters* as arranged for the 1842–1846 edition, the newly published author dramatizes herself in the proposed 'moment' which opens her published presentation of herself re-edited by Barrett and her publisher. She shows at once the role of the diary in marking an anniversary with a flourish of comic exaggeration: 'I doubt not but this memorable affair will, in Future Times, mark the period whence chronologists will date the Zenith of the polite arts in this Island!' (*Early Journals*, vol. 3, p. 1).

The element of family record is strongly marked together with a sense of documentary accuracy. There is much emphasis on the diary's being 'faithful' but this compulsion to keep a true record is combined with a need to justify the record of herself within her own diary. For instance, Burney presents an exchange between the Thrales and Dr Johnson as a play at the time when she was trying out her own dramatic composition subsequently disapproved by both her father and Crisp. She writes herself out of the action but the diary context cannot obliterate her as an observer: 'I must now have the honour to present to you a new acquaintance, who this day dined here' (20 October 1779, *Diary and Letters*, vol. 1, p. 270). Burney also keeps up the fiction of the inability to record which is notable for women's diaries. Having time to compose the diary in the context of dailiness is the paradox of female diarist lore: 'Very concise indeed must my Journal grow, for I have now hardly a moment in my *power* to give it; however, I will keep up it's Chain, & mark, from Time to Time, the *general course of things*' (10 July 1779, *Early Journals*, vol. 3, p. 333). Similarly, it is customary to emphasize that a woman can have nothing important to write as she tells her father and sister from Windsor: 'I have only to beg of Fortune some events worth recording' (November 1785, *Diary and Letters*, vol. 2, p. 356).

Subsequent critics have identified that the retrospective amendment of the *Diary* serves to reinforce a public image more suited to the era into which Burney survived than that in which she claimed to be recording 'to the moment'. She had published her first novel in 1778 and died in 1840 aged 88. The level of fictionalization in Burney's *Diary* is a complex question. She rewrote incidents from memory and from memoranda at varying degrees of chronological distance and she discusses this process. She wrote about events as dramatized scenes and she varied her persona according to an audience which was herself, her family and to an extent the unknown readers of posterity. She indicates her control over her material in June 1792: 'Let me now finish this long Month by short sentences' (*Journals and Letters*, vol. 1, p. 213).

Joyce Hemlow has identified three layers of editing unearthed in the process of recovery which has reproduced for the twentieth century the documents written at the time: layers added by Burney, by Barrett and by the publisher Henry Colburn.[10] Burney herself sought to edit ten thousand pages of manuscript journals and letters between 1817 and 1838, keeping a register, scoring out and adding remarks and symbols.[11] As Lars Troide observes, 'Her concerns in this massive undertaking were both prudential and artistic.' She excised what was seen as offensive to others or likely to cast the family in a bad light. She cut out the trivial and repetitive or anything deemed too personal and she corrected grammar as well as adding new passages to clarify or 'tighten' the narrative.[12] In fact she destroyed the whole of her journal for 1776, the year her brother Charles was sent down from Cambridge for theft. She observes in a note added during the process of excision: 'The whole of what was written of This Year was upon Family matters or anecdotes, & I have destroyed it in totality' (*Early Journals*, vol. 2, p. 199). Charlotte Barrett re-edited and added a new set of deletions and adjustments based on her response both to the demands of the prevailing ideology of womanhood and to the sensitivities of any survivors who were concerned about the appearance of family members in the published pages. Hemlow has identified tampering, composite letters and chronological rearrangement as a result.[13]

The framing of the material demonstrates some of the important considerations of the woman as author. Barrett insists on provenance and the propriety of the nineteenth century. She is keen to stress that her aunt, has 'herself arranged these Journals and Papers with the most scrupulous care' (*Diary and Letters*, vol. 1, p. xxi). Provenance is also claimed in the transmission of the papers bequeathed to Barrett in Burney's will. Burney leaves to Barrett 'the whole of my own immense Mass of manuscripts, collected from my fifteenth year, whether personal or collateral, consisting of Letters, Diaries, Journals, Dramas, Compositions in prose and in rhyme ... with full and free permission according to her unbiased taste and judgement to keep or destroy' (*Journals and Letters*, vol.1, p. v). Barrett's claims of provenance and her role as a successor to Burney in owning the papers are protested at some length. Burney is described 'in her last hours, consigning them to the editor, with full permission to publicise whatever might be judged desirable for that purpose' (*Diary and Letters*, vol. 1, p. xxi–ii).

The text presented in the first volume in 1842 thus has a traceable link to Burney. Provenance and propriety are also reflected in a discussion of editing practice which is preserved in the *Diary and Letters*. Despite her feelings of ownership of Dr Johnson and her break from Hester Thrale now Mrs Piozzi, Burney commends the process of editing when Dr Johnson's letters are published by Thrale in 1787: 'The few she has selected of her own do her, indeed, much credit: she has discarded all that were trivial and merely local and given only such

---

10   See *Journals and Letters*, vol. 1, p. v.

11   Ibid., vol. 1, pp. xxxvi–vii and *Early Journals*, vol. 1, p. xxv.

12   *Early Journals*, vol. 1, p. xxv.

13   *Journals and Letters*, vol. 1, pp. xlix–lii.

as contain something instructive, amusing or ingenious' (9 January 1788, *Diary and Letters*, vol. 4, p. 15). These are categories which Burney maintains over fifty years later close to the end of her life and in the midst of her selection process when she writes to her sister Charlotte about burning sacks of papers: 'Shall I Burn them? at once – or shall I, & can I so modify a division as to spare for future times various collections that may be amusing & even instructive? – Certainly were I younger & could here wait for the examination – but such is not the case.'[14]

Both Burney and Barrett preserve at some length a discussion with Mr Fairly at Court in which the two Court attendants disagree about destroying correspondence. He suggests that it is safer to burn letters than to preserve them and she responds with an excuse based apparently on familial devotion that too much fortitude is required 'to burn them, when they are written by those we wish to write them!'. She then preserves his appreciation of her public character as an author as well as the horror of public exposure if her letters circulate more widely at her death. His histrionic response also appears to perform Burney's own dilemma: 'Think but how they will be seized; everybody will try to get some of them; what an outcry there will be! Have you seen Miss Burney's letters? Have you got any? I have a bit! And I have another! and I! and I! will be the cry all around' (30 July 1788, *Diary and Letters*, vol. 4, p. 208).

Their interaction is further dramatized. 'Fairly' is already the fictional name of Colonel Stephen Digby, vice chamberlain to the Queen and object of Burney's disappointed love. Much of their relationship is necessarily expunged but the journal entry has been allowed to exist so that Burney can insist within this exchange that her papers will pass to her sister Susan 'in whose discretion and delicacy I had a reliance the most perfect' (30 July 1788, *Diary and Letters*, vol. 4, p. 208). Susan is, of course, also the audience for the letter when it is first written in 1788 and this coded message both authorizes the act of writing and its preservation as personal record.

The issue of the preservation and misuse of documents is only partially resolved. Burney decides, apparently in 1788, 'to take a general review of my manuscript possessions, and to make a few gentle flames, though not to set fire to the whole' (30 July 1788, *Diary and Letters*, vol. 4, pp. 208–9). This reflects too the many incidents of burning papers recorded in Anne Lister's diary.[15] The threat of discovery and indiscriminate unguided reading of these 'manuscript possessions' is a feature of Burney's preoccupations as it is of many diary-writers. The fact that she and Barrett retain this exchange despite its painful associations following 'Fairly's' marriage demonstrates the importance of Burney's negotiations with herself both at the time and in the years before her death, and by Barrett after her death.[16]

---

[14] Letter dated 20 April 1838 quoted by Hemlow, *History*, p. 486.

[15] See Chapter 2, p. 36.

[16] Hemlow discusses the 'tortured reporting' of the Fairly portions and there are extant letters between Barrett and her cousin and daughter about the preservation of this relationship in print (*Journal and Letters*, vol.1, p. xlviii).

A third layer of amendments and editorial choices can only be briefly touched upon here: those of the publisher Henry Colburn who had already published the diaries of Evelyn and Pepys in 1818 and 1825 respectively. Even the reduced material presented by Barrett could not be accommodated in the volumes allocated to it, and it is apparent from the modern day research of the Burney Centre that further choices were made. In addition, Colburn's advertising caused further demands for excision from the descendants of those expecting to be included in the printed version and he in turn curtailed the resulting manuscript for length at the publishing stage which resulted in further amendment. Attempts were also made to emphasize the domestic appeal of the *Diary and Letters* which were advertised as a 'charming diary' (*Weekly Chronicle*) with its 'charming picture' of the family of George III on the endpapers of Volume 7. Barrett herself commends 'the picture ... of domestic virtues in the most exalted rank.'[17] The very choice of the word 'diary' for the title and its iteration in the press places emphasis on the daily over the more retrospective 'journal' which Burney describes and names in her packets. The choice of 'diary' by Burney, Barrett and Colburn suggests a need to reinforce the authorization of an account written in this way.[18]

Burney's *Diary* as it appeared to a nineteenth-century audience was thus affected by editorial and textual changes. It was constructed in various ways by Burney in semi-literary journals written to convey news and in the monthly chronicle of Court journals or grouped journal letters. Letters have then been inserted, burned, curtailed, summarized and redated. The printed version was edited for propriety both by Barrett with her retuned nineteenth-century sensibilities and indirectly by those who objected to the inclusion of family members. It was then restyled for reasons of printing by Colburn. Joyce Hemlow believes this has resulted in distortion but not untruths although she draws attention to Barrett's 'fine disregard of chronology' and free use of the paste pot and scissors.[19] Barrett herself, however, insists that she received from Burney: 'no negative injunction except ONE, which has been scrupulously obeyed, *viz*: that whatever might be effaced or omitted, NOTHING should in anywise be deleted or added to her records' (*Diary and Letters*, vol. 1, p. xxii).

The editorial process requires omissions or, as D'Israeli observed, the diary is nothing,[20] and history is now in the process of investigating Barrett's deletions. Hemlow concludes: 'It was Charlotte's aim to make a smoothly running unexceptionable text such as could be safely read *en famille* in a

---

[17]   *Diary and Letters*, vol. 1, p. xxi.

[18]   The Burney Centre has preferred the term 'Journals' for the modern editions of the Burney collection.

[19]   Hemlow, *History*, p. 462; *Journal and Letters*, vol 1, p. xlviii.

[20]   D'Israeli notes, 'to write down everything, may end in something like nothing' (Isaac D'Israeli, 'Diaries Moral, Historical and Critical', *Curiosities of Literature*, Vol. 2 (New edition London: Warne, 1881), p. 215).

quiet rectory.'[21] The publishing choices made by Barrett indicate the sources of narrative adjustment which allow the diary of a woman to be made safe when it is written 'to the moment', lacks a language and is reframed as a moral lesson to others. Burney's *Diary* also demonstrates that rewriting and the use of retrospect can be accommodated within the process of journalizing. Her use of the family communication channel repositions the addressee and authorizes publication. There is a balance between the ideological effacement demanded by the conduct book and the public fame which creates an exemplar. Issues of framing, editing and provenance enter the bargain for publication and breach the permeable boundary which makes the private diary available as a non-fictional narrative.

The main contention of this study is that the publication of a woman's diary empowers the fictional diary to become a vehicle for narrative. The private diary of a woman became both publishable and publish-worthy through the appearance of Burney's diary in print. Despite its composition in the late eighteenth and early nineteenth centuries the *Diary* was revised and reconsidered by Burney, Charlotte Barrett and Henry Colburn in the light of the mid nineteenth-century concept of womanhood. It also employed complex negotiating strategies to make it worthy of print. In addition, print was cheaper and more readily available and there was a parallel market for accounts of real life within the output of court reporting, journalism and the periodical. Real stories became consumable and the boundary between the public and private was breached by changes in the role of the media and in the growth of the reading public. The growth of reading targeted at women – not just conduct books but novels, periodicals and household management advice – is also a significant factor.[22]

This network of developments puts the woman's diary into the market as a commodity for telling a woman's story and for telling a story within the context of the novel itself. Ultimately, of course, the diary as narrative draws attention to the role of diary-writing in the life of any woman who keeps household accounts or writes journal letters to send news home. It is a familiar and yet equivocal genre for the nineteenth century. The core texts for this study incorporate narratives of inclusion through which their editors negotiate as assiduously as Burney for the right to use the medium of the diary to produce the effect of daily record within a closely controlled plot.

Each of the chapters in Part 2 deals with the construction, transmission and publication of the text in order to illustrate the ways in which the woman's fictional diary acts out a role within the novel. As a prelude to this more detailed analysis, the core texts are examined here with brief considerations of the ideological position of the woman as narrator and the role of the woman's diary within the editorial practices adopted in each novel.

---

[21]   Joyce Hemlow, 'Letters and Journals of Fanny Burney: Establishing the Text', in D.I.B. Smith (ed.), *Editing Eighteenth-Century Texts* (Toronto: University of Toronto Press, 1968), p. 40.

[22]   See the wider discussion of reading and serialization in Chapter 6.

Andrew Hassam notes that a published text offers authority for the reader to read but that it also conveys an editorial message encoded by the time and context of publication. [23] From the 1840s, the Burney/Barrett coding methods were in circulation for adaptation by novelists. The woman's diary had a negotiated public status which re-coded a private document for public consumption. Writing of the fictional diary, Valerie Raoul specifically highlights the conventions of the diary and the novel, and 'the interference of each of these "codes" in the functionality of the other'.[24] The role of the fictional female diarist both echoes and subverts that of her non-fictional counterpart. When the diary performs in a public context as a fictional narrative, this defies nineteenth-century norms for women. A woman's diary is a self portrait of someone who should be invisible, silent, even erased as Laura Fairlie is in *The Woman in White*, acting on the advice of Sarah Stickney Ellis in the 'sacred privilege' of forgetting herself. At the same time, the diary in recording household accounts, family events and the spiritual life of its writer brings with it the non-fictional role of moral guide and comforter. The published diary as an advice manual might replicate the woman's place within the home but it takes on at the same time a performative role which subverts the stated ideological conditions of the time.

Diary fiction takes from actual diaries a range of received conventions and both exploits and interrogates them. A woman's diary is employed to narrate a portion of each of the six novels selected as core texts for this study. The first person cloistered narrator apparently provides unmediated and non-retrospective experience; the occasion and location for writing is dramatized with reference to the framing action of the novel; the physical shape and documentary role of the diary itself becomes part of the evolution of the plot. Within these hybrid texts there is also competition in the narrative matrix constructed by the tensions set up within consecutive narratives or extratextually created by editorial acts equivalent to those carried out on the authentic diary.

In the texts under consideration, women's diaries have been chosen to act as narrative and to form matrices of varying degrees of complexity. Elizabeth Miller describes *Dracula* as 'the story of a production of the text ... a narrative patchwork'[25] and in the six core texts there are different styles of patchwork.

In *The Tenant of Wildfell Hall*, Helen Graham's diary is framed by a long letter and occupies just over half of the overall novel. The text of the diary is relinquished to the fictional editor Gilbert Markham in 1827 and he describes the act of reading it in a letter which he writes in 1846. His access to the diary at this later date is questionable as discussed in Chapter 4. He exploits the narrative

---

[23]   Andrew Hassam, 'Reading Other People's Diaries', *University of Toronto Quarterly*, 56/3 (Spring 1987): 439.

[24]   Valerie Raoul, *The French Fictional Journal: Fictional Narcissism/Narcissistic Fiction* (Toronto: University of Toronto Press, 1980), p. vii.

[25]   Elizabeth Miller, '*Dracula*, The Narrative Patchwork', *Udolpho*, 18 (September 1994): 27.

immediacy of Helen's diary and justifies its inclusion at least to himself and to his friend Halford. The narrative of the diary's transmission is, however, outside the action he chooses to present.

A Life for a Life is narrated by means of what Dinah Craik called 'a double diary.' Dora Johnston's diary has an unknown echo in the parallel record of Max Urquhart, an army doctor whom she will eventually marry. The diary of a woman narrates about half of the novel and becomes an exchange of letters when their engagement is acknowledged. There is some sense of the provenance of the physical text and its future fate in telling a story although the diary is largely used as a vehicle for revealing feelings which can be explored in greater depth in the first person. Unlike *The Tenant of Wildfell Hall* and *The Woman in White* which provide framing edited narration, Craik's novel is a hybrid text because of the interaction of diaries and letters.

In *The Woman in White*, Marian Halcombe's diary appears in real time and in context as evidence, but it is also revisited and the process of its use is discussed within the narrative of the textual collator or extradiegetic narrator, Walter Hartright. The diary occupies one fifth of the overall novel and the text always remains in its author's possession. There is no act equivalent to the authorized reading of Helen's diary in *The Tenant of Wildfell Hall*, although Count Fosco invades and reads Marian's text when she is taken ill.

In *Armadale*, Lydia Gwilt's diary appears some two thirds of the way through the novel. The first portion is retrospective, but later entries appear in real time alternating with extradiegetic narration. The diary occupies one fifth of the narrative although Lydia also writes letters in which she debates sharing her diary with her fellow criminal Mother Oldershaw. The retrospective portion is presented on the page during this epistolary discussion but reading authorization is dramatically withdrawn. In the event, Lydia retains control over the diary and there is no discussion of its transmission into the text of the novel. Her criminality is reinforced as much by this independent stance as by her stereotypically red hair.

In *The Legacy of Cain* which is Collins's last completed novel, he returns to the concept of diary narrative using two sisters who compose diaries within the frame of a recovered narrative by a retired prison governor. The diaries occupy about two fifths of the finally published text. The entries are undated and largely written by Helena who also reads her sister Eunice's entries apparently in real time. Eunice gives up the dangerous practice of writing after recording in her diary that she has been tempted to murder her sister. For the reader of the time it is implied that this is because of a genetic inheritance since she appears in the governor's narrative as the toddler daughter of a hanged murderess. It is, however, Helena, the daughter of a clergyman and an ideologically impeccable mother, who really stoops to murder. The transmission of the text is complex and difficult to trace, a fact probably caused by Collins's increasing ill-health and writing to deadlines for newspaper serialization. The diary of Helena Gracedieu, however, is actually produced and read in court as proof of her plot against her own fiancé which grows out of her dangerous programme of novel-reading.

In *Dracula*, Mina's diary, along with the other evidence, exists in shorthand and is typed and copied, the original being burned. This process appears to give her a voice of equivalence created by her roles as both the observer of Lucy Westenra's degeneration and the transcriber of Jonathan Harker's Transylvanian travel diary. There are a number of competing diaries by Jonathan and by Doctor John Seward which appear directly on the page. The diaries, letters and newspaper cuttings overlap in the first half of the novel but become linear once the quest to destroy Dracula is confirmed. This type of hybridity shares the features of Craik's *A Life for a Life* published some forty years earlier. The assembly of the 'patchwork' in *Dracula* demonstrates also the attempts which are made to exclude Mina from the events which need to be narrated. Her actual diary occupies less than one seventh of the overall novel and unlike Helen and – to a large extent – Marian, Mina is given a role as a collator. Beyond this, there is no exterior acknowledged organizing intelligence or implied author in *Dracula*.

The role of the woman's diary within these novels attracted different levels of attention from critics at the time of publication. The diary of Helen Huntingdon which she uses to explain her position as a runaway wife to Gilbert Markham was regarded as both undramatic and unlikely by reviewers at the time. [26] Whilst Marian Halcombe was admired for her resourcefulness, Lydia Gwilt was seen as doubly designing and fallen because she reveals her poisoning plot through the daily record of her life.[27] This brief overview of the position of the diarists in *The Tenant of Wildfell Hall*, *The Woman in White* and *Dracula* demonstrates the female fictional diarist's role and relationship to the model of her non-fictional nineteenth-century counterpart.

The Tenant of Wildfell Hall uses a woman's personal domestic record authorized by Helen's role as a wife and mother to present directly the experience of marriage to an alcoholic and abusive husband. Anne Brontë's own Preface to the second edition insists that vice should be presented as it really is [28] and this seems to suggest that the real-life and, in the diary section, real-time presentation of vice as a warning and corrective justifies the device of the diary. Indeed Helen rereads and consults her diary as a text to guide younger women such as Esther Hargrave and even her married friend Milicent who are misled by their duty as daughter and wife respectively. [29]

---

[26]   See Miriam Allott (ed.), *The Brontës: The Critical Heritage* (London: Routledge and Kegan Paul, 1974), pp. 269. The response to the novel is discussed further in Chapter 4.

[27]   See Bishop Thirlwall, *Letters to a Friend*, 3rd March 1866 in Norman Page (ed.), *Wilkie Collins: The Critical Heritage* (London: Routledge and Kegan Paul, 1974), p. 146; see full text in Chapter 6, pp. 112–13.

[28]   Anne Brontë, *The Tenant of Wildfell Hall*, ed. Stevie Davies (London: Penguin, 1996), p. 4.

[29]   This illustrates Cynthia Huff's observations on the use of the diary as a reference document for female experience; see Cynthia Huff, *British Women's Diaries: A Descriptive Bibliography of Selected Nineteenth Century Women's Manuscript Diaries* (New York: AMS Press, 1985), p. xxx. Lori Paige describes Helen Graham's diary as a 'makeshift textbook on marital relations' (Lori A. Paige, 'Helen's Diary Freshly Considered', *Brontë Society Transactions*, 20/4 (1991): 227).

From her early and non-retrospective viewpoint, Helen presents the diary as Frances Burney offered hers for publication:

> This paper will serve instead of a confidential friend into whose ear I might pour forth the overflowings of my heart. It will not sympathize with my distresses, but then, it will not laugh at them, and if I keep it close, it cannot tell again; so it is, perhaps, the best friend I could have for the purpose. (p. 154)[30]

The use of the diary as an alternative confidante is established very early on to support the activity of writing authorized by this diary credo.[31] Despite her later composition of an alternative conduct guide, Helen demonstrates an adherence to the advice provided by Gisborne and Ellis when she considers her opportunity to contribute to Arthur's salvation even before the marriage. 'If he has wandered, what bliss to recall him!' she exclaims. 'Oh! If I could but believe that Heaven has designed me for this!' (p. 153). Helen often describes the narrative occasion for her long entries of reflective testimony. She also comments on the therapeutic effects of writing as a means of sifting and reviewing recent events. She emphasizes the importance of accuracy and of 'detail' which can be provided by the recording device of a diary despite the critics' reservations about the lack of drama. The spiritual dimension of the non-fictional diary is further emphasized when Helen uses it 'to meet the trials of the day' (p. 307).

The private performance within the diary read by Markham within the novel also allows the degeneration of Arthur and the erosion of Helen's life into the role of 'a slave, a prisoner' (p. 368) to be shown without the intervention of the maturer self. Juliet McMaster observes: 'Helen's diary, written in stages of experience only as she reaches them, can adequately convey the pain, the pathos and the bitterness.'[32] These stages reflect the reconstruction of events at intervals which is present in *The Tenant of Wildfell Hall* as in Burney's and Gaskell's diaries. Having this intermediate retrospect rather than the mature reflection and audience appreciation of an autobiography liberates the diary to be a starker representation of the events narrated. *The Tenant of Wildfell Hall* thus illustrates the ideological opportunities established by the immediacy and daily recording elements of the diary as narrative. It also demonstrates the potential for using a record written

---

[30]   In the address to Nobody which prefaced the *Diary and Letters*, Burney writes, 'From Nobody I have nothing to fear. The secrets sacred to friendship Nobody will not reveal' (*Early Journals*, vol. 1, p. 2).

[31]   Although there is no currently extant evidence to confirm that Brontë was specifically familiar with Burney's text, she might have had access as a reader and governess to the published version of 1842–46 or at least to references in the Macaulay essay in *The Edinburgh Review* (January 1843) reprinted in his *Critical and Historical Essays* from 1843 onwards.

[32]   Juliet McMaster, '"Imbecile Laughter" and "Desperate Earnest" in *The Tenant of Wildfell Hall*', *MLQ*, 43/4 (December 1982): 363.

at the time with its interior retrospective journalizing which is nonetheless later allowed to stand for the younger self.

Marian, the female diarist of *The Woman in White*, has a specific narrative task within a text which is controlled elsewhere. At the time of first writing, she shares the immediacy of Helen's recording processes but although the diary is presented in real time, the method of presenting evidence becomes suspect. [33] Jenny Bourne Taylor points out that this is not 'retrospective testimony' but a personal account 'crucially important as a means of observation and memory, as a means of self-control and as a way of marking and controlling time'.[34] The subject matter is justified by the recording method. With admirable insight into the structure of the overall text and the unravelling of the plot, Marian herself observes: 'In the perilous uncertainty of our present situation, it is hard to say what future interests may not depend upon the regularity of the entries in my journal, and upon the reliability of my recollections at the time when I make them' (p. 290). Her domestic records are integrated into the resourcefulness of a detective or lawyer but she also maintains elements of nineteenth-century female experience to authorize her account in its place. Thus, the 'forbidden subject' and 'unwilling words' (p. 216) of confidences about marriage indicate the topics without a language which Marian tries to normalize. She is 'nothing but a woman, condemned to patience, propriety and petticoats for life ... I must', she writes, 'try to compose myself in some feeble and feminine way' (p. 200).

This 'feebleness' means that the control of time and emotion are not always assured and the diary receives its imprint of women's powerlessness. There are brief entries about 'the confusion of small events' achievable in the diary format where the female diarist can be allowed the real-time liberty of her hysteria and alternating emotion. Thus when her sister Laura is married, she exclaims: 'They are gone! I am blind with crying – I can write no more ...' (p. 197). Like Emily Shore, Marian is driven even to vet her diary, vowing not to record 'gloom and distrust' (p. 189). She almost resolves to stop writing her journal altogether unless she can write more favourably of her sister's fiancé Sir Percival Glyde (p. 189). She is anxious that the diary promotes bad discipline rather than the approved self-surveillance but after less than three pages she is forced to add: 'In three words – how glibly my pen writes them! – in three words, I hate him' (p. 194). She wrestles with the need for more womanly reticence and passes the action of writing her hatred on to the inanimate pen but the words stay written and visible within the text. Like Helen and like Anne Lister, Marian uses the diary as a source of spiritual encouragement and resolution. She searches through 'old journals' for reassurance that she has not contributed to the error of Laura's marriage.

In *The Woman in White*, everyday actions such as a walk around the lake, writing a letter, or removing a hat provide a context for the acts of detection which

---

[33]   See further detailed discussion in Chapter 7, pp. 122–5.

[34]   Jenny Bourne Taylor, *In the Secret Theatre of Home: Wilkie Collins, Sensation Narrative and Nineteenth Century Psychology* (London: Routledge, 1988), pp. 117–18.

become the grounds of competition between Marian and Fosco in the latter half of the diary. Petticoats, themselves objects associated with propriety, are finally removed in order to execute her most daring feat of eavesdropping, thus temporarily outwitting the Count himself. Writing with immediacy from within, Marian can describe the intimate details of those petticoats (p. 326) because she is a woman and has earned by her audacity and her acts of decoding, recording and memory, the right to act like a man and not just to look like one. The effect could not be achieved and could not be as shocking without Marian's being a woman, and could not be authorized as a printed text without the apparently close proximity of event and recording. Her record is ostensibly unmediated by retrospect and apparently undiluted by any planned communication with an audience external to the diary itself.

The later use of the diary in the quest to prove that Anne Catherick and not Laura Glyde is dead distances Marian from events although it is entirely likely that a diary continues to be written. The diary becomes ideologically secure once more and Marian becomes an aunt, designated by Hartright 'the good angel of our lives' (p. 643). Outside the diary, extratextually in Duyfhuizen's terms, *The Woman in White* is a text controlled by a man making use of the recording techniques of a woman and the female experience which can thus be conveyed. The assembly of the text as evidence is at a further remove which finally undermines the diary and consigns Marian to domestic life once more.

Mina Harker describes her diary as 'an exercise book'[35] in which to practise the shorthand which will support her husband in his profession and like Marian she is ultimately confined within the role of domesticated woman. Again, despite the later date of *Dracula* at the end of the nineteenth century, Mina uses the Burney excuse for writing on compulsion but without any intention of making public. Burney's *Early Diaries* edited by Annie Raine Ellis were published in 1889 and may have rekindled interest in the younger Burney's negotiation for writing space: 'a Journal in which I must confess my *every* thought must open my whole heart.'[36] Mina's in 1897 will be 'a sort of journal which I can write in whenever I feel inclined.' She adds dutifully, 'I do not suppose there will be much of interest to other people; but it is not intended for them. I may show it to Jonathan some day if there is in it anything worth sharing' (p. 74). She proposes to be like a 'lady journalist' in a prophetic indication of her own role as collator of the text which is *Dracula*.

Mina comments on the act of writing in her anxiety for her friend Lucy and for Jonathan, 'I am anxious, and it soothes me to express myself here; it is like whispering to one's self and listening at the same time. And there is also something about the shorthand symbols that makes it different from writing' (pp. 96–7). She continues the Burney theme of self analysis and positions herself as a reader of her own thoughts which again reflects the reconstruction of the narrative which is

---

[35]   Bram Stoker, *Dracula*, ed. Maurice Hindle (London: Penguin, 1993), p. 74.
[36]   *Early Journals*, vol. 1, p.1.; see Chapter 9, p. 170.

the overall novel. She echoes the activities of another published diarist, Samuel Pepys, by suggesting that shorthand is another language or form of writing, one of many in a novel which records its narrative on a phonograph and a typewriter and produces facsimiles in support of the daily record of evidence which aims to decode the monstrous actions of Dracula. [37] The novel in turn is a narrative about the construction of a text in which Mina herself becomes a text written on or replicated by Dracula.[38] The final act of horror is, of course, to install her as a matriarch and domesticated woman following a whole range of gender struggles which take place in the novel. These are equivalent in many ways to the struggles for control of the narrative and the diary itself.

Lydia in *Armadale* and Helena in *The Legacy of Cain* do not suffer the fate of domestic containment, and this is partly because the textual transmission of their diaries is made direct and not subject to editorial reconstruction. Lydia escapes by dying to save her husband Ozias Midwinter although it is clear that her reintegration into society would have been impossible. Helena, thirty years later, serves only a brief prison sentence and then founds a religious movement in the United States although her diary is made public and circulates within the justice system. Dora in *A Life for a Life* still has a secret diary which may offer a form of family history to future generations, although Max suggests that she should 'write an end' and so close the diary with her marriage. She maintains some kind of independence by marrying an older man of her choice but she has to live in Canada to escape the taint of Max's past.

The absence of language within the diary of a nineteenth-century woman to describe abuse, fraud and vampirism draws a suggestive veil over the dark elements which all the novels wish to narrate. The reticence exploited within the texts is a significant feature of their use of the diary 'code'. Mina, as textual collator, often uses the ellipses which denote both temporal and linguistic gaps. Marian perhaps comes nearest to understanding that private experiences should not be denied a language and that outward propriety does not guarantee safety. It is she who recognizes that Fosco's control over his wife is 'a private rod, and is always kept upstairs' (*The Woman in White*, p. 225). Laura's lack of language for her marital experiences is contrasted with Marian's observation after losing her temper with Sir Percival. She notes: 'It did me good – after all I had suffered and suppressed in that house – it actually did me good to feel how angry I was' (p. 298).

The fictional diaries also display their traditional credentials. The household account book is never far away from the 'grave and sweet responsibilities' (*Dracula*, p. 139) of all the diarists. Marian describes 'the new machinery of

---

[37]   *Dracula* was first published in 1897. The transcript of Anne Lister's diary was also published in the *Halifax Guardian* between 1887 and 1892 as 'Some Extracts from the Diary of a Halifax Lady' but John Lister walled the papers up in Shibden Hall when he deciphered the code; see Jill Liddington *Female Fortune: Land, Gender and Authority: The Anne Lister Diaries and Other Writings 1833–6* (London: Rivers Oram, 1998), p. xiv.

[38]   See Jennifer Wicke, 'Vampiric Typewriting: *Dracula* and Its Media', *ELH*, 59/2 (Summer 1992): 476; 485.

our lives at Blackwater Park' (*The Woman in White*, p. 212) and Helen employs herself 'amply' with 'the direction of household concerns' (*The Tenant of Wildfell Hall*, p. 211). Even Lydia describes her journal as her 'customary record of the events of the day' (*Armadale*, p. 474). Helen in particular uses the diary as spiritual autobiography with frequent addresses to God and to the duty of redeeming Arthur. Marian contributes to the family chronicles of the Glydes and the Fairlie-Hartrights, whilst herself having no inherited place within them.[39] Mina echoes the travel diary in her descriptions of Whitby and she also uses Jonathan's account of Transylvania to guide Van Helsing.

The diary model used in Part 2 of this study, depends thus on the non-fictional diary; on the woman as a diarist and on the stylized gender role of a woman in the nineteenth century. This model also reflects the published diary and the nature of publication for a non-fictional diary of the period. The imprint of the real diary in fiction produces elements of structure which are shared with its fictional counterpart and others which reflect the exterior action of collation, editing and publication. The dailiness, language and transmission of the woman's diary are plot characteristics in themselves, and the interaction with other documents and narratives is a particular feature of the hybrid novels to be discussed.

From the evidence of the core texts, the female diarist within the nineteenth-century novel is allowed the opportunity to discuss her ideologically suspect narrative impulse firstly because the diary purports to allow personal expression in the context of home duties. The diarist also uses the narrative occasion to position her accomplishment of the duties of memory and accounting which motivate the non-fictional diary. Helen describes her diary as 'this secret paper' (*The Tenant of Wildfell Hall*, p. 243) and Marian's contains 'secret pages' (*The Woman in White*, p. 219); Dora's is locked. There are many comments on the process of composition and Mina often records that she sits writing on the graveyard seat in Whitby or that she 'sit[s] here thinking' (*Dracula*, p. 241).

The diary has the advantage of being able to operate even when its compiler is 'moated' or imprisoned by circumstances or indeed hampered by her social role. All six fictional writers are cloistered to some extent by marriage or duty and the urge to protect either a child or a sister. Even Lydia is confined by the difficulties of operating as a criminal within the ideological constraints of womanhood which she exploits along with the narrative opportunities of the diary. Her successor, Helena in *The Legacy of Cain*, is particularly adept at maintaining a household but she writes under the constraint of being a dutiful daughter. Marian is a resourceful woman who writes in her diary even as she succumbs to fever. After eavesdropping on Glyde and Fosco, she still writes in the vigour and authority of her cloistered state: 'I recall the impulse that awakened in me to preserve those words in writing, exactly as they were spoken, while the time was my own, and while my memory vividly retained them' (*The Woman in White*, p. 341). She is ultimately,

---

[39]   This is reminiscent of the dutiful female biographers cited by Isaac D'Israeli in *Curiosities of Literature*.

however, the silenced 'angel of our lives' just as Mina with New Womanhood on the doorstep must be rescued from the influence of Dracula and reinstated for Victorian domesticity by Van Helsing and the men.

These fictional diarists are permitted to narrate. The use of the female diarist is also an opportunity for the novelist and his/her controlling editor within the novel to exploit facets of female diary writing. There can be no model for Helen's diary because alcoholism and abuse have no shared nineteenth-century language to be utilized by women. [40] She adapts instead the model of the female daily record and the conduct book. The diary offers an escape, an imaginary addressee, which in turn becomes oneself and an opportunity to reflect on the 'narrative occasion.' The diary purports to immediacy and accuracy from its daily composition, non-retrospection and lack of revision. It is a repository without judgement or value system and it is a genre made safe for women's performance by its privacy and by its role as the source of routine record. The dailiness of female experience which has made the diary a feminine form exonerates the editor/author of the hybrid text of the novel from accusations of triviality, and the editorial process elevates the experiences of women to a status of influence which they are not accorded in real life.

The fictional diary, however, only comes into existence as a means of telling a story that cannot otherwise be spoken. This diary may be read within the narrative by another character or reframed by an editor to give that story provenance, credence and propriety. A mimetic record apparently made at the time – one which shows as well as tells – is allowed to be published and becomes performative for the very reason that it was not written for performance. Its mimetic and gender-specific qualities allow it to be admitted into the hierarchy of texts which present the truth.

Paradoxically, it appears from the evidence of the diary in print in the nineteenth century that the diarist must return to domesticity to regain autonomy over her text. The role of competing texts and of the collators or editors of the fictional diaries is a significant part of the 'patchwork' and its assembly which is discussed in the following chapters. It is by means of an edited text that a story may be told or untold depending on the female diarist's viewpoint, her accessibility to the action and her ability to say 'I'. [41]

---

[40]   See Siv Jansson, '*The Tenant of Wildfell Hall*: Rejecting the Angel's Influence', in Anne Hogan and Andrew Bradstock (eds), *Women of Faith in Victorian Culture: Reassessing the Angel in the House* (Basingstoke: Macmillan 1998), p. 33.

[41]   See Chapter 1, p. 15.

PART 2
The Diary and Literary Production

Chapter 4
The Diary and Women Writers

The seventh and final volume of Frances Burney's *Diary and Letters* appeared in 1846; in 1847, Anne Brontë's eponymous heroine and first person narrator of *Agnes Grey* concluded her own story: 'Here I pause. My diary, from which I have compiled these pages, goes but little further. I could go on for years: but I will content myself with adding, that I shall never forget that glorious summer evening ... .'[1] This is the first reference to such a document, a daily record which contributes to the memorial reconstruction of Agnes's story. The novel was equally lost in the furore which accompanied the reception of *Wuthering Heights* with which it was published. In the following year, Brontë's next novel concerned a diary very much rediscovered and presented directly within the text of *The Tenant of Wildfell Hall*.

This chapter considers the role of the diary as a narrative device used by women writers in *The Tenant of Wildfell Hall* and in Dinah Mulock Craik's *A Life for a Life* (1859). The critical reception of the novels reflects an equivocal view of the place of women's writing whether by established authors or by their fictional female creations. The chapter discusses that critical reception and also considers both *Wuthering Heights* (1847) and Craik's earlier *Bread Upon the Waters* (1852). The processes of transmission which preserve women's fictional diaries within women's fictional writing reflect attempts to make a text safe through male framing or collusion. The reaction of contemporary critics suggests, however, that the gender-orientated response of the reviewers extended to women writers internal to the novel. It also becomes clear that neither the reconstruction by a male persona in *The Tenant of Wildfell Hall* nor the absorption of the male persona into an equivalent narrative voice in *A Life for a Life* increased the diary's authority or cultural significance.

When Anne Brontë's *The Tenant of Wildfell Hall* was first published in 1848, the role of the diary attracted adverse reviews. These related both to the reading experience of a diary embedded within Gilbert Markham's narrative and to the dangers of a direct engagement with the diary as a preserved text. *The Examiner* complained that being 'thrown back' from the diary to the framing narrative of Gilbert's letter reduced the intensity of the reading experience: 'after so long and minute a history, we cannot go back and recover the enthusiasm which we have been obliged to dismiss a volume and a half before.'[2] *The Rambler*, reviewing 'Mr Bell's New Novel', was particularly concerned that the attraction between Helen

---

[1]   Anne Brontë, *Agnes* Grey, ed., Angeline Goreau (London: Penguin, 1988), p. 250.

[2]   *The Examiner* (29 July 1848); Miriam Allott (ed.), *The Brontës: The Critical Heritage* (London: Routledge and Kegan Paul, 1974), p. 255.

and Gilbert engaged the unwary reader's sympathies in the early chapters so that approval was effectively being sought for adultery. Its reviewer complained of a 'disgusting and revolting species' of scenes concerning Arthur's behaviour: 'her diary is the record of what she endured ... and details with offensive minuteness the disgusting scenes of debauchery, blasphemy and profaneness in which ... he delighted to spend his days.'[3] The diary becomes part of a critique of female writing despite the fact that the reviewer believes the author of the novel to be male.

In her Preface to the second edition, Anne Brontë insisted: 'when we have to do with vice and vicious characters, I maintain it is better to depict them as they really are than as they would wish to appear' but *Sharpe's London Magazine* protested that the novel was not fit to be read by those who needed its warnings.[4] Charles Kingsley felt that Helen herself would not have the heart or decency to write down such oaths and drunken scenes. He also picks up the issues of language and reticence in his review in *Fraser's Magazine* when he observes: 'there are silences more pathetic than all words'. He senses the danger of the diary's performativity but he also allies the objections of narrative technique with the experience of the reader: 'Dramatic probability and good feeling are equally outraged by such a method.'[5]

The critics stress that their outrage is about the probability of a woman writing a history of abuse and of a writer employing a diary to tell that story. In *The Tenant of Wildfell Hall*, the narrative is dominated by a male epistolary transaction with the woman's diary at the most interior point of its transmission. Analysis of the woman's diary telling that story and of the inclusion of that text demonstrates how the diary model reiterates the role of ideologically policed writing whilst creating a language or lack of language to convey the immediacy of marital abuse within a masculine and domestically authorized framework.

This analysis considers three elements of the diary model which interrogate the role of the woman telling her own story in print: firstly, immediacy and lack of retrospection which allow the story to unfold without the apparent benefit of an overseeing consciousness; secondly, and in part opposing the element of immediacy, the action of the diary as spiritual adviser; and finally the silence or reticence which emphasizes the inability to record and itself authorizes a female account of abuse from within.

When Helen's diary opens, it demonstrates its non-retrospective viewpoint by adopting a sunny approach to the task of rescuing Arthur from his vices. It is in fact doubly retrospective as it is written looking back on the London season from the vantage point of Staningley in the country. Helen's reconstruction of events seems to borrow from the journalizing methods of Burney's *Diary*. It is at moments of crisis that Helen records on a daily basis, but she also looks back at various stages

3   *The Rambler* (3 September 1848); Allott, pp. 267–8.
4   Anne Brontë, *The Tenant of Wildfell Hall*, ed. Stevie Davies (London: Penguin, 1996), p. 4; *Sharpes's London Magazine* (August 1848); Allott, p. 265.
5   *Fraser's Magazine* (April 1849); Allott, p. 269.

using longer periods of time excused by her inattention and neglect. Thus she includes an ominous conversation with her aunt about her marriage prospects but she accounts for it by observing: 'I am not sure her doubts were entirely without sagacity; I fear I have found it much easier to remember her advice than to profit by it' (p. 135). This entry indicates that a review was possible, but it negotiates between both a maturer viewpoint and an emotion at the time.

The diary at this stage is a new amusement which ranks with painting, walking and music but it is notable that Arthur is discussed within the diary's pages and not with her aunt 'for I never mention his name' (p. 151). Helen has no language for her love but is instead in love with the role of moral manager or angel in the house. She considers it 'bliss' to deliver him from vice and 'wicked companions' (p. 153). Meghan Bullock has observed that the language of abuse within marriage was not written down or transmitted from one generation to another and, moreover, that Helen speaks to her diary and not to Milicent, her otherwise 'confidential friend.'[6] Helen's aunt at least tries to advise her niece logically until she concludes in reported exasperation: 'you little know the misery of uniting your fortunes to such a man!' (p. 150).

The diary, however, proves to be an unsafe method of secret recording because of the existence of other texts such as Helen's imperfectly erased drawings 'witnesses of my infatuation' (p. 156), the painting of the 'amorous turtle doves' (p. 159) and also some letters which Milicent later wants burned to destroy proof of her distrust of Hattersley (p. 227). According to Helen's account, Arthur finds his likeness sketched, although partially erased, on the back of a painting (p. 156). He uses this as a pretext for stealing a kiss and, after going hunting, he climbs back in through the window. He is described as 'poring so intently over the seeming blanks ... [and] in half a minute he came back, and, setting his gun against the wall, threw up the sash, sprang in, and set himself before my picture' (p. 159). These acts of violation are mirrored later by his reading the diary and destroying the paintings designed to be Helen's livelihood.

Helen thus appears to be writing within the silences of nineteenth-century womanhood which lacks a language to deal with either infatuation or abuse. As discussed in Chapter 3, she proposes to 'pour forth the overflowings of my heart' although she expects no returning sympathy. Then again, a diary cannot apparently betray her which makes it 'the best friend ... for the purpose' (p. 154).

On a number of occasions, however, the diary fulfils a *quasi* interactive function, stressing Helen's isolation and the absence of a confidante. The entry for 9 October 1824, for instance, describes the narrative occasion and the therapeutic effects of writing as a means of sifting and reviewing recent events. Helen realises that Arthur's adulterous relationship with Annabella is still going on, a fact she learns from her maid Rachel. She cannot herself narrate the awful realization that Arthur's loving greeting in the shrubbery (p. 296) was not for her:

---

[6]   Meghan Bullock, 'Abuse, Silence and Solitude in Anne Brontë's *The Tenant of Wildfell Hall*', *Brontë Studies*, 29 (July 2004): 135–41;137.

lighting my candle, ... [I] got my desk and sat down in my dressing-gown to recount the events of the past evening ... I have found relief in describing the very circumstances that have destroyed my peace, as well as the trivial little details attendant upon their discovery. No sleep I could have got this night would have done so much towards composing my mind and preparing me to meet the trials of the day. (p. 307)

Arthur believes that her confidantes are actually the scheming Mrs Hargrave and her own aunt to whom she cannot turn out of pride (p. 306), but Helen explains to him – and tells the diary – that she has complained to no one: 'I have struggled hard to hide your vices from every eye, and invest you with virtues you never possessed' (p. 306). It seems that up to a point she continues to rewrite her husband for public view and in the terms of the conduct books but the reader's evidence comes from the diary and what Helen learns in the process of writing it. Tess O'Toole observes that: 'The text ... produces an effect on the reader that mimics the entrapment Helen experiences in her marriage.'[7] The diary combines many of the elements of the 'second self' as a friend and adviser, and as the woman herself.

The missing language or reticence required by women's writing causes the omission of key events. Helen never confides directly to her diary that she is pregnant. On 8 May, Arthur is reported as saying 'remember your situation, dearest Helen; on your health, you know, depends the health, if not the life of our future hope' (p. 218). In August she writes that she will not overindulge a child, 'If ever I am a mother' (p. 226), at which point she must be at least five months pregnant. The baby is born before their first wedding anniversary in late December; on her annual entry to mark that date, she thanks heaven that she is a mother: 'God has sent me a soul to educate for heaven' (p. 239). The apprehension of this narrative event within the novel is complex. Halford, the reader of the framing letter, knows that Helen is a mother and the reader of the novel knows that she is a mother because of young Arthur's involvement in Gilbert's narration of events at Wildfell Hall.

The event of becoming a mother is omitted from the diary along with the event of being married. This is included after a gap which is of Helen's own making. On 18 February 1822, when Arthur rides to hounds, Helen writes: 'He will be away all day; and so I will amuse myself with my neglected diary – if I can give that name to such an irregular composition. It is exactly four months since I opened it last' (p. 202). A narrative retrospect is opened up, a sense that marriage has failed in its anticipated role of replacing the diary as a 'confidential friend'. This is in complete opposition to *Agnes Grey* whose diary does not continue after marriage. Lydia Gwilt too expects to find her diary redundant as a confidante once she is married but two months after her wedding she breaks her 'resolution' and returns to her 'secret friend.'[8]

    7   Tess O'Toole, 'Siblings and Suitors in the Narrative Architecture of *The Tenant of Wildfell Hall*', *SEL*, 39/4 (Autumn 1999): 715.

    8   Wilkie Collins, *Armadale*, ed. Catherine Peters (Oxford: Oxford University Press 1989; reprinted 1991), p. 532; see Introduction, p. 1.

The Tenant of Wildfell Hall thus enacts the diary model in its reticence, retrospective spiritual guidance and immediacy. Critics like the novelist George Moore have suggested that the explanation of her conduct provided by Helen's diary should have been given to Gilbert in person to maintain dramatic impact.[9] Aside from the problem of sustaining a face-to-face narrative, the reading of the diary allows the non-retrospective accumulation of details and accommodates the development of Helen's character, presenting her early optimism at firsthand within summary moments. Like Burney and Elizabeth Gaskell, she uses anniversaries to reflect on a portion of time and it is only at crucial moments that the diary becomes a daily piece of writing as it does for Emily Shore and for Marian Halcombe in *The Woman in White*. Contradicting previous reviewers, Juliet McMaster observes that 'a deteriorating relationship is recorded with dramatic immediacy'.[10] This private performance within the diary can be more direct than personal interaction precisely because the woman can speak as an unmediated self; unmediated by that current state of flight and of attraction to Gilbert; unmediated also by the propriety of telling and using the words necessary to describe Arthur's behaviour. Elizabeth Langland points out that this is also possible because the narrative was fixed before Helen met Gilbert; he is not the intended audience.[11] Having no autobiographical overwriting liberates the text to be a starker and more direct representation of the events narrated which could have no other voice for a nineteenth-century woman. If a woman is to tell of her relationship from the inside, then a diary is a suitable narrative device.

It is not, however, the main narrative device of the novel. *The Tenant of Wildfell Hall* is classified by Garrett Stewart with brutal attention to the text as 'a letter about a read journal' and Jan Gordon describes it as 'the longest single-narrative enclosing epistolary novel of the nineteenth century.'[12] Indeed Gilbert's letter to Halford ostensibly envelops Helen's diary, literally providing her publicized narration with a pre-text. The place of the diary as narrative in women's writing is reflected by the transmission of the diary within this novel. Analysis of the novel's overall architecture considers the writing of the letters and then traces the overall construction of Gilbert's narrative with its implications for patriarchal control of the family chronicle.[13]

---

[9] See Allott, p. 35. Moore championed Brontë as 'a born storyteller' in his *Conversations in Ebury Street* (1924; reprinted 1930) but objected to the diary as cumbersome.

[10] Juliet McMaster, '"Imbecile Laughter" and "Desperate Earnest" in *The Tenant of Wildfell Hall*', *MLQ*, 43/4 (December 1982): 363.

[11] Elizabeth Langland, *Anne Brontë: The Other One* (Basingstoke: Macmillan, 1989), p. 123.

[12] Garrett Stewart, 'Narrative Economies in *The Tenant of Wildfell Hall*', in Julie Nash and Barbara A. Suess (eds), *New Approaches to the Literary Art of Anne Brontë* (Aldershot: Ashgate, 2001), p. 75; Jan B. Gordon, 'Gossip, Diary, Letter, Text: Anne Brontë's Narrative Tenant and the Problematic of the Gothic Sequel', *ELH*, 51/4 (Winter 1984): 719.

[13] See also the discussion in Chapter 5, pp. 94–6.

There are two letter-writing events. Gilbert prefaces his peace offering to his brother-in-law with an introduction and an opening chapter which are part of an initial undated letter. This is designed to be a foretaste of what is to come. This first letter appears to restore them to a friendly footing and the second chapter rejoices 'that the cloud of your displeasure has passed away' (p. 22). Gilbert has already reminded Halford that he is 'as great a stickler for particularities and circumstantial details as my grandmother' (p. 10) and the further encouragement he has received in the gap between chapters is enough to stimulate a 200–page letter framing his copied version of Helen's diary. There is only one date for the letter which appears at the very end. We are reminded of that other presence when Gilbert addresses Halford within the text as 'old boy' and there is a direct appeal at the end of the diary section: 'Well Halford, what do you think of all this? And while you read it, did you ever picture to yourself what my feelings would probably be during its perusal?' (p. 397).

Gilbert refers to the practicalities of reading and his impatience for dawn when 'with intense and eager interest, I devoured the remainder of its contents' (p. 397). He apparently fails either to note a previous 'devourer' of Helen's diary or to grasp the implication of his own – at that point – adulterous love. It is his act of reading which will clear Helen's name of the accusation of fallen womanhood which has sparked his behaviour and in 1847 he is transmitting this text to Halford with a number of purposes. As Elizabeth Langland observes: 'It is only by incorporating Helen's diary into his own narrative that Markham can reinterpret the Fallen Woman and runaway wife of Victorian convention as the model of excellent womanhood that the novel proposes.'[14]

The physical fate of the diary is also framed by the fact that Gilbert is composing with the assistance of 'a certain faded old journal of mine' (p. 10) which he is using as a family chronicle and source of his letters. It is not clear whether either diary is among 'certain musty old letters and papers' he has been 'looking over' in the library (p. 10) and in any case we have only his word that this apparently casual action is proof of provenance. He had authority to read Helen's diary in 1827. Helen has handed him 'a thick album or manuscript volume' (p. 129) and asks him later, 'Have you looked it over?' (p. 399) echoing his own actions of 1847. In 1827, he 'cast the manuscript on the table' at Wildfell Hall (p. 399) but further transmission of the diary is not explained.

Twenty years on, Helen's diary is competing with the musty papers and is also framed by another journal. The authority to read it given to Halford and to the reader has passed to Gilbert while the family is away. The dubious status of the resulting narrative, which contemporary critics seem to have preferred to the text of a woman, emanates from that dubious authority. Helen's voice is contained within what Stewart calls a 'narrative recess' [15] where she is physically distanced both by Gilbert's framing letter and by her own social obligation to pay a visit during Gilbert's act of transcription in June 1847.

---

[14]   Langland, *Anne Brontë*, p. 123.

[15]   Stewart, p. 75.

This extratextual situation raises concerns that Helen has not authorized the wider reading of the diary. The readers of the novel, at the point most distanced from the narrative recess, seem to have the authority of Anne Brontë's Preface but there is an un-narrated gap between the return of the album and Gilbert's offering the diary as a debt of honour to his brother-in-law.

Intertextually, when Arthur is drawn into the circle of readers with Gilbert and Halford, the role of Helen's diary in a masculine value system is explored further. Arthur believes that Helen is writing her troubles in 'long letters to aunt Maxwell' (p. 306) not that she is inscribing them in a private diary. In a scene which parallels Gilbert's authorized access, Arthur is controlled enough 'and actuated by some base spirit of curiosity' (p. 364) to overlook the writing of a diary entry in the drawing room and to 'wrest' the diary itself from Helen to give himself a reading occasion. At this point Arthur sees Helen's new, commercially targeted canvases as the competing texts which signal her rebellion, and they are destroyed at once. This mirrors his abuse of the private, domestic canvases during their courtship when he ascertained the personal value placed on them by Helen. In this scene the performativity of the canvases is prioritized over that of the diary which escapes destruction partly because it does not represent the external commercial freedom of Helen's paintings. Diary writing is an act of self-representational defiance, but a diary does not have the power to give her economic independence.

Arthur spends half an hour with a candle upstairs reading the diary and then comes back to examine Helen herself by the same light, before leaving the manuscript on the drawing room table, an action also mirrored by Gilbert at Wildfell. She writes of her 'humiliation':

> I could not bear the idea of his amusing himself over my secret thoughts and recollections; though to be sure, he would find little good of himself therein indited, except in the former part – and oh, I would sooner burn it all than he should read what I had written when I was such a fool to love him! (p. 367)

Arthur does not value the diary as evidence or as an opportunity to improve himself through its spiritual guidance, [16] but he acknowledges its role as a repository for information peculiar to women: 'It's well you couldn't keep your own secret – ha, ha! It's well these women must be blabbing – if they haven't a friend to talk to, they must whisper their secrets to the fishes, or write them on the sand or something' (p. 367). The diary as text may connote female rebellion, but its threat is neutralized now he has discovered it. It is the knowledge of Helen's plan which he values rather then the fact of her private text. He has missed the opportunity, offered Gilbert later, of using it as a source of self-knowledge and amendment.

In 1827, Gilbert Markham is an authorized reader but his motives in *The Tenant of Wildfell Hall* have come under scrutiny in the years since the novel has received greater critical attention. He takes bold control of his material in the epistolary

---

[16] There is a discussion of the self-improvement value of reading personal narratives in Melody J. Kemp, 'Helen's Diary and the Method(ism) of Character Formation in *The Tenant of Wildfell Hall*', in Nash and Suess (eds), pp. 195–211.

frame by contrast with the childish and spiteful behaviour which he re-enacts using his own contemporaneous journal. Other than claiming his journal as a memory bank (p. 10), he does not refer to it again until he starts using it to record Helen's letters in the final section of the novel (p. 439). Elizabeth Signoretti identifies his interest in Helen's diary as 'predatory': 'In his narrative, he incorporates Helen's past, edits it, calls it his own, then pays a debt with it.'[17] There is much critical debate about the impact on Gilbert and his role as a fit second husband.[18] Helen's silence in the framing narrative of inclusion renders the sharing of the diary's contents a highly questionable act.

Gilbert's role as an editor making the diary public reflects some of the techniques observed in non-fictional diaries. Helen has said of her diary 'you needn't read it all; but take it home with you' (p. 129) and Gilbert moves back to his 1847 act of rereading to explain his purpose to Halford when he claims: 'I have it now before me.' Having observed that Halford will not 'peruse it with half the interest that I did,' he tells his friend: 'I know you would not be satisfied with an abbreviation of its contents and you shall have the whole, save, perhaps a few passages here and there of merely temporal interest to the writer, or such as would serve to encumber the story rather than elucidate it' (p. 129).

It is the classic diary editor's claim of truthfulness to his subject as well as an indication of his omission of the 'temporal' or daily which might not suit his project.[19] Walter Hartright will offer a similar explanation in the first footnote to Marian Halcombe's diary; Charlotte Barrett claims that she has 'effaced ... NOTHING'. Gilbert assumes a masculine editorial stance which allows him to choose the immediacy of personal evidence whilst disowning the domesticity which authorizes it. This statement of intent sounds a note of caution. As so often in controlling the reader's access to the story, he draws attention to himself. He is not only unreliable but naïve in believing himself a neutral overseer of the information in his library. He is engaged in self-promotion and intends to forge a bond with Halford by giving him 'a full and faithful account of certain circumstances connected with the most important event of my life – previous to my acquaintance with Jack Halford at least' (p. 10).

He demonstrates his editorial responsibilities through the literary orderliness and critical faculty he attempts when introducing the diary: 'It begins somewhat abruptly, thus – but we will reserve its commencement for another chapter, and call it,' (p. 129) – using the over-page chapter heading – 'The Warnings of Experience' (p. 130). Gilbert has taken on the role of dramatizing the diary and giving it a plot, another task appropriated by editors.[20]

---

[17] Elizabeth Signoretti, '"A Frame Perfect and Glorious": Narrative Structure in Anne Brontë's *The Tenant of Wildfell Hall*', *Victorian Newsletter*, 87 (Spring 1995): 22–3.

[18] See O'Toole, p. 722.

[19] Wilkie Collins, *The Woman in White*, ed. John Sutherland (Oxford: Oxford University Press, 1996; reissued 1998), p. 163; Frances Burney, *Diary and Letters of Madame D'Arblay* (7 vols, London: Colburn, 1842–46), vol. 1, p. xxii.

[20] Barrett divides Burney's material into chapters. See also the discussion of modern editorial concerns in Suzanne L. Bunkers, 'Whose Diary Is It, Anyway? Issues of Agency,

Unlike authorized editors, Gilbert is not allowed to see every piece of material after all, particularly when Helen's own editorial act of removing 'a few leaves from the end' (p. 129) deprives him of her first unmediated opinion of him. These leaves are never restored. They are not available for Halford's perusal twenty years later, and Gilbert endeavours to fill this gap by briefly rewriting his own early chapters from her point of view: 'I would have given much to have seen it all ... to have seen how much of love ... had grown upon her in spite of her virtuous resolutions and strenuous exertions' (p. 396). The parallels between the two husbands are perhaps most poignant when Helen describes Gilbert just once, by the pure accident of textual survival, as '[t]he fine gentleman and beau of the parish' (p. 396). These words echo Regency terms which might liken him to Arthur as a rake, a throwback to pre-Victorian manhood. Gilbert's opening words of the following chapter also seem to class him with the insinuating Hargrave when he wants Helen to accept him only in terms of Arthur's fall from her 'good graces' (p. 397).[21]

Once the diary excerpt closes, Helen's letters are subsequently relayed to Gilbert through Helen's brother, Lawrence whose intentions he continually misreads. He edits and extracts from letters he was allowed to keep. For instance, he transcribes a letter word-for-word 'otherwise, Halford, you could never have become so thoroughly acquainted with its contents' (p. 431) and on the next page he comments: 'I was permitted to keep this ... perhaps as an antidote to all pernicious hopes and fancies' (p. 432). He provides documentary evidence and exercises a woman's care in entering extracts from other letters in order to explain the logistics of their inclusion: 'I devoured those precious letters with my eyes, and never let them go till their contents were stamped upon my mind; and when I got home, the most important passages were entered in my diary among the remarkable events of the day' (p. 439).

His 'devouring' still echoes the actions of Arthur whose sufferings he almost gleefully records. He has revalued the events of Helen's life 'among the remarkable events of the day' and given them a provenance which reflects the editorial role, although in this he also assumes some of the characteristics of the feminized family chronicler. He also tries to maintain control by reflecting editorially on Helen's narrative gaps: 'for I was persuaded she had not hinted half the sufferings she had had to endure' (p. 449). The fact that we never read a letter to Gilbert from Helen re-emphasizes her textual silence in the latter part of the frame. When he is unable to interpret the gift of a Christmas rose which signals the 'emblem of my heart' (p. 483), the reader must suspect Gilbert's ability to read a diary. He narrates himself

---

Authority, Ownership', *A/B: Auto/Biography Studies*, 17/1 (Summer 2002): 11–27; and Linda Peterson's view of autobiography as a hybrid genre itself, the product of a first-person narrator and the amplifications or excisions of an editor (Linda H. Peterson, *Traditions of Women's Autobiography: The Poetics and Politics of Life Writing* (Charlottesville: University Press of Virginia, 1999), p. x).

[21] See Juliet McMaster who describes a 'period commentary' on the Regency (McMaster, pp. 352–3).

into his new social position and seems to stress by his version of family events that he was invited to marry above him and so to banish the stigma of adulterous love.

In the final section of the novel, letters have replaced the diary as a narrative device and become a further recess. Open-ended entries and questions over editorial method or indeed the acts of memory required are rekindled in a more complex documentary intertextuality. Helen's textual silence may be an indication that she has married for love again and again regretted it.

The reviewers of *The Tenant of Wildfell Hall* in 1848 were reviewing a novel by Acton Bell, ostensibly a man. Nonetheless, their concern is about a woman writing within the framed text. A narrative matrix is created by Gilbert as family chronicler which reflects both the model of diary writing and the appropriate use of family papers. These were models created by the publication of Burney's diaries between 1842 and 1846.

Sources closer to Anne Brontë's own creative life are also reflected in *The Tenant of Wildfell Hall. Wuthering Heights*, published in 1847, is a man's journal dated 1801 narrating an oral presentation by a woman and forming another matrix which intersects with Anne Brontë's writing. When the Brontës were published under their own names, Emily's name was associated with *The Tenant of Wildfell Hall* in error. [22] The woman's diary in *Wuthering Heights* is barely a page of writing by Catherine Earnshaw inscribed as a form of rebellion on the printed pages of a religious tract. It is another narrative recess within Emily Brontë's novel and forms part of the haunting of Lockwood when he has to spend the night at Wuthering Heights. In fact Catherine has written her diary on the blank sheets of 'a Testament, in lean type, and smelling dreadfully musty'; she has dated the fly leaf and named it 'her book'.[23] She dramatizes the characters of the house on an 'awful Sunday', appropriates Yorkshire dialect for Joseph and throws the Bible into the dog kennel. A greater rebellion against religious texts and patriarchal control comes with her description of the narrative occasion: 'I reached this book, and a pot of ink from a shelf, and pushed the house-door ajar to give me light, and I have got the time on with writing for twenty minutes' (p. 22).

Access to this girlhood journal is limited by Lockwood's reading capabilities in a similar way to Gilbert's. He falls asleep and a combination of 'bad tea and bad temper' (p. 22) stimulates his bad dreams and the supernatural experience of Catherine's ice-cold hand. He blocks the hole with a pyramid of books, symbolically cutting off the past for the diary writer who is appealing to him. Losing access to the diary, he turns to Nelly Dean and it is her cosier narrative with 'a smoking basin' for him and 'a basket of work' for her (p. 35) which unfolds the history he is seeking. This is a device which overlays the further recesses of the narrative with

---

[22]   See for instance *The Spectator* (15 October 1859): 1067 when it was advertised by Smith Elder alongside a notice of the new (and untitled) *Cornhill Magazine* and Elizabeth Gaskell's *The Life of Charlotte Brontë*.

[23]   Emily Brontë, *Wuthering Heights*, ed. Pauline Nestor (London: Penguin, 1995; reissued 2003), p. 20. For a discussion of the diary element see Rebecca Steinitz, 'Diaries and Displacement in *Wuthering Heights*', *Studies in the Novel*, 32/4 (Winter 2000): 407–19.

its second-hand first-person narrators. In addition, the journal must accommodate the reporting reliability of both Nelly and Lockwood and it also presents a contrast between the framing fireside tale and the extraordinary events it narrates.[24] Both *Wuthering Heights* and *The Tenant of Wildfell Hall* present female narratives in a masculine framework and overall this suggests a concern amongst the novelist sisters about narrative method and its authorization.

If Catherine Earnshaw's diary written on the blank pages of an existing text is at the innermost narrative recess, its outermost point must be Charlotte Brontë's 'Biographical Notice' of her sisters. The new edition of *Wuthering Heights* and *Agnes Grey* appeared with some of the sisters' poetry in 1850 and the accompanying 'Notice' is specifically dated 19 September 1850. Of *The Tenant of Wildfell Hall*, Charlotte writes: 'the choice of subject was an entire mistake. Nothing less congruous with the writer's nature could be conceived.'[25] She attributes the novel to Anne's brooding over the fate of Branwell Brontë and then attempts to recuperate both Anne and Emily into Victorian womanhood: 'In externals, they were two unobtrusive women; a perfectly secluded life gave them retiring manners and habits ... they always wrote from the impulse of nature, the dictates of intuition, and from such stores of observation as their limited experience had enabled them to amass.'[26] Anne in particular is described as in the shade, her mind and feelings covered by a 'nun-like veil, which was rarely lifted.'[27]

Charlotte's memorial agenda and *post mortem* control of her sisters is the subject of long-running debate.[28] Her role as custodian of the family papers might rank with that of Gilbert, recreating women in an image which suits the status of the editor; she might equally be following the path of Frances Burney in offering a re-creation for a new era and for the society in which she herself wanted to enact the life of an identifiably female author.

At the end of the next decade, another woman writer adapted the device of a woman's diary to authorize the story of a family in turmoil. In the wake of her runaway success *John Halifax Gentleman* (1856) and her collected essays *A Woman's Thoughts About Women* (1858), Dinah Craik used the interlocking journals of a young woman and a doctor in her novel *A Life for a Life* first published in 1859. She describes this narrative method, which she strenuously defended, as a 'double diary.'[29]

---

[24] Bernard Duyfhuizen offers an extended discussion of these framing devices in *Narratives of Transmission* (London: Associated University Presses, 1992), pp. 32–8.

[25] *Wuthering Heights*, p. xlvii.

[26] Ibid., p. xlix

[27] Ibid.

[28] See for instance Juliet Barker, *The Brontës* (London: Weidenfield and Nicholson, 1994), pp. 654–7 and Nicola DianeThompson, *Reviewing Sex: Gender and the Reception of Victorian Novels* (Basingstoke: Macmillan, 1996), pp. 42–65.

[29] Dinah Mulock Craik, *A Life for a Life* (London: Hurst and Blackett, n.d), 'Preface to the New Edition', p. iii.

On 6 August 1859, *The Athenaeum* both advertised and reviewed the novel, and it headed the main list of Mudie's circulating library along with *Adam Bede* and Tennyson's *Idylls of the King*. On the next page a new work was announced by 'the author of *John Halifax Gentleman*'. The advertisement quoted from the *Morning Post* which described *A Life for a Life* as: 'a picture of human joys and human sufferings ... set before us by a sympathising mind ... [with] a clearly defined moral ... [and] that strong reflective mind visible which lays bear the human heart and the human mind to the very core.'[30] The novel is thus being positioned within the context of both the newspaper's endorsement of its moral position and the success and reputation of the author's previous work.

The review printed on an earlier page of this issue of *The Athenaeum*, however, criticizes a 'want of freedom in the action of the story.'[31] This was attributed to the narrative device of the diary which Craik uses to tell alternately 'her story' and 'his story'. The reviewer, now known to be Geraldine Jewsbury,[32] objects that: 'all the events, emotions, incidents and consequences in the story are reflected not transacted ... The characters are never presented to the reader alive, only told about in the private journals of Max Urquhart, Esq., MD and of Miss Theodora Johnston.'[33] The 'discrimination' between the three sisters is praised but the journals are deemed self-conscious with 'an air of artificialness inseparable from that form of composition. Of course,' Jewsbury adds, 'it is free to all who choose to expand their egotism in a journal but, if given as a novel, the reader will be apt to feel bored'.[34] The distinction was clearly being drawn between the private diary authorized both by its privacy and by its representation of the individual, and the printed version which has no place in the transmission of narrative.

In its review of three novels of 1859, *The Christian Remembrancer* approaches the question more obliquely; its readership would expect the rhetoric of a sermon. The reviewer considers women to be 'moral' writers because of their 'feminine mode of viewing things in the particular rather than the general'. He describes women writers as wishing to assert 'the woman's side of every question ... framing the story to set it off'.[35] The review goes on to dispute the presentation of the story in journal format: 'The construction of the story is peculiar, and certainly not the best for giving the reader a general idea of what is going on, which must be most effectually done by simple narrative.'[36] The review concedes, however, that 'the authoress has more than a story to unravel; she has opinions and convictions

---

30   *The Athenaeum* (6 August 1859): 188–9.
31   [Geraldine Jewsbury], '*A Life for a Life*', *The Athenaeum* (6 August 1859):173.
32   See Monica Correa Fryckstedt, *Geraldine Jewsbury's Athenaeum Reviews: A Mirror of Mid-Victorian Attitudes to Fiction* (Studia Anglistica Upsliensia 61 (Uppsala: Uppsala University, 1986), pp. 68–70).
33   Jewsbury, p. 173.
34   Ibid.
35   Ibid.
36   Ibid., p. 310.

which she knows will not be taken for granted by her readers'[37] namely her views on courtship and on society's attitudes to criminals. This firmly sites Craik as a novelist with an agenda and, unlike Anne Brontë, she was known to be a woman. The 'authoress' herself, however, fails to appear:

> in her own person: a plan which admits of an amount of reflection, comment and impassioned protest, which could hardly be tolerated in any other form, and which, as it is, must try the patience of the ordinary novel reader, intent on the progress of a really interesting and forcibly told story, rather than on the profound questions it is designed to illustrate.[38]

The Athenaeum was a publication of high culture which often used women reviewers such as Jewsbury. *The Christian Remembrancer* was a publication of the High Church which did not regularly review novels. The cultural and religious outlook of these two reviews from contrasting periodicals creates a paradigm against which Craik's methods and subject matter are measured. The tenor of their opinions is that diaries cannot tell stories and women writers both absent and visible cannot be trusted to maintain a legal or narrative framework without undermining the laws of society and even of Nature. In the cultural context of the late twentieth century, J. Russell Perkin has observed of *A Life for a Life* that: 'The narrative effects a feminisation and domestication which lacks the perspective ... Victorian reviewers tended to value in male novelists.'[39] The narrative and cultural impact of *A Life for a Life* can be interpreted through an assessment of the double diary narrative against both the model of the female-authored journal and the reception of the female-authored text.

Dinah Craik is bringing with her to the presentation of *A Life for a Life* the reputation of 'the author of *John Halifax Gentleman*', a hugely popular novel of 1856 which celebrated middle class values and the virtues of self help. Sally Mitchell suggests that the success of *John Halifax Gentleman*, however, gave Craik the power to speak more directly and to write the series of articles in Chamber's *Edinburgh Journal* which were published in 1858 as *A Woman's Thoughts about Women*.[40] *John Halifax Gentleman* owes its narrative to the use of a diary in much the same way as that sudden reference at the end of *Agnes Grey*. The narrator, Phineas Fletcher, is a disabled only son who writes an account of John Halifax from their earliest meeting aged fourteen and sixteen. Gender roles are firmly embodied by the noble Halifax and his strong but ultimately stereotyped wife Ursula. Those gender roles are questioned, however, in the character of Phineas who finds himself an observer of the family history and is often endowed with female characteristics. When Phineas is taken ill he comments of Halifax: 'If I had

---

[37]   Ibid., p. 311.

[38]   Ibid.

[39]   J. Russell Perkin, 'Narrative Voice and the "Feminine" Novelist: Dinah Mulock and George Eliot', *Victorian Review* 18/1 (Summer 1992): 34.

[40]   Sally Mitchell, *Dinah Mulock Craik* (Boston: Twayne, 1983), p. 53.

been a woman, and the woman he loved, he could not have been more tender over my weakness.'[41] When they visit a country cottage together, Phineas is deterred by Halifax from seeking information about their host family: 'I felt quite guilty, and began to doubt whether my sickly, useless dreaming life, was not inclining me to ... small vices which we are accustomed – I know not why – to insult the other sex by describing as "womanish"' (Chapter 11, p. 108).[42] After their initial meeting, Phineas explains that he has 'compiled the present history' from two sources; his memory made vivid by a 'long and introverted life' and a diary kept at intervals. He describes the habit of diary writing as 'very useless, sometimes harmless, and incredibly foolish' (Chapter 3, p. 19) perhaps in an attempt to maintain some masculine credentials but 'the thread of narrative' is thus given a provenance although no other evidence of its daily record is discernible.

If the success of *John Halifax Gentleman* did increase Craik's confidence, the diary method may have been an offshoot of this. If Phineas and, to an extent, Halifax himself display feminine traits,[43] this is replicated by the device of the corresponding diary of a man in *A Life for a Life*. The specific interaction between the actual diary entries which offer a female as opposed to a feminized perspective in the later novel appear not to have been valued by Craik's early readership despite or perhaps because of this incorporation of the male diarist into the personal diary format. Perkin points out that her method 'gives the experiences of its protagonists equal weight ... in a manner which does not privilege the male point of view.'[44] Against the stern Old Testament 'life for a life', this is a domestic transaction of life writing for life writing rather than a domestic history based on a family chronicle as in *John Halifax Gentleman*. When *A Life for a Life* was reissued in 1860 as a response to the adverse critical feedback, described by Craik as 'that salutary rod of correction', ('Preface to the New Edition', p. iii) she added a new preface. In it, she responded to criticism of the unjustifiable remorse of her hero – and second diarist – Dr Max Urquhart but she resolutely refused to change the diary narrative. She coolly reiterates that it is 'the best mode of evolving the two characters in whose inward development and outward history lay the principle of my book' (p. iii). Readers would have approached *A Life for a Life* with expectations created out of the approved morality for women writers and the religious code of the Old Testament. The model of women's diary narrative in its immediacy, reticence and spiritual guidance operates within the field of these tropes of reading and performance.

In the novel, plain, twenty five year-old Dora Johnston, a middle sister like Burney, writes a diary out of loneliness and is drawn to the military surgeon, Max Urquhart who has returned to home duties after serving in the Crimea. This battlefield service is in part reparation for the killing of a young soldier in a moment

---

[41]   Dinah Craik, *John Halifax Gentleman* (London: Hurst and Blackett, n.d. 29th edition), Chapter 6, p. 58.

[42]   See Mitchell, p. 48.

[43]   Ibid., pp. 47–8.

[44]   Perkin, p. 34.

of fury, and in the course of the novel his victim is identified as Harry Johnston, Dora's elder half brother. There is a parallel plot concerning Dora's sister's fiancé who has fathered a child by a family servant, Lydia Cartwright. These stories are narrated by the diaries of Dora and Max although they take on the character of journal letters when the narrators become addressees for their texts. Max must eventually serve three months in prison, and with Dora's help Lydia becomes a schoolmistress to women prisoners. Dora defies her father by marrying Max and going with him to Canada although there is a last- minute reconciliation. Her sister calls off her engagement and her former fiancé reforms and marries Lydia.

Chapter 1 of *A Life for a Life* begins with a classic statement of diary writing intent:

> What a treat it is to get home and lock myself in my own room – the tiniest and safest nook in all Rockmount – and spurt out my wrath in the blackest of ink with the boldest of pens! Bless you! (query: who can I be blessing, for nobody will ever read this?) what does it matter?...this 20th September 1856, I begin with my birthday a new journal (capital one, too, with a first-rate lock and key, saved out of my summer bonnet, which I didn't buy). (Chapter 1, pp. 1–2)

These opening lines spell out the elements of the personal diary's non-fictional model. The diarist is 'cloistered' and writing from an autobiographical stance. There is a tension between the time of the events portrayed (Dora is preparing for a ball), the time of writing (Hassam's 'narrative occasion') and the potential time of discovery of the text. As discussed in Part 1, the diary exists because of a socially created impulse to write which is itself reflected by comments within that text. The role of the addressee or outside reader is a subject for debate. The occasion for writing is part of the diarist's subject matter. Within it, the female value system of daily events is apparently not ordered; an un-purchased bonnet can be mentioned within the context of wrathful rebellion.

Dora insists on her 'plan of keeping this journal accurate and complete' (Chapter 21, p. 209) despite travel and illness. She is also, however, aware of the dangers of a complete record and leaves gaps which are not just forced by the lack of a 'narrative occasion': 'Where I take up the thread of my journal, leaving the whole interval between a blank. I could not write about it if I would' (Chapter 16, p. 151). A change in her life stimulates a new interest in the diary: 'I mean to write regularly at my journal ... so that it may be a complete history ... if at a future time, I, or anyone, should ever read it' (Chapter 17, p. 169). She is questioning the value of her 'history' specified in the text as 'her story' and becomes concerned about its forced publicity when she continues: 'Will anyone ever have the right? No; rights enforced are ugly things; will anyone ever come and say to me, "Dora" or "Theodora" – I think I like my full name best – "I should like to read your journal"?' (p. 169). In the outermost recess when Geraldine Jewsbury published her disapproving comments in *The Athenaeum*, she too couched her remarks using the diarists' full names and titles.[45]

---

[45] Jewsbury, p. 173.

Dora both acknowledges and fears the possibility of an audience. The belief in a judgmental recipient returns after her illness when she writes a complicated explanation of her relationship with a young man called Colin Granton whose offer of marriage she refuses because she is already in love with Max: 'It was at first not my intention to mention it here at all, but on second thoughts I do so, lest, should anything happen to prevent my destroying this journal during my lifetime there might be no opportunity, through the omission of it, for any misconstructions' (Chapter 21, p. 203). She is clearly wrestling with the difficulties of performance and self-projection. This text is not intended to survive but the evidence of published diaries like Burney's suggests that it could and she must therefore protect her reputation.

When she refers to the spiritual diary model in Chapter 8: 'Writing a journal is a safety-valve for much folly; yet I am by no means sure that I ought to have written the last page' (p. 82) the entry nonetheless stays written. Urquhart, in his public sphere, is following a similar path when he justifies the merging of a professional scientific document into the record of his more personal reflections: 'Faith, I must be very hard up for occupation when I thus continue this journal of my cases into a personal diary of the worst patient I have to deal with', that is, himself (Chapter 2, p. 12). He also draws attention to the physical text: 'I shall tear out this page – Or stay, I'll keep it as a remarkable literary and psychological fact – and go on with my article on Gunshot wounds' (p. 12).

He discovers the diarist's dilemma of addressee which is made doubly ironic by the fact that the diary is fiction which is also published:

> A journal should be fresh, complete, and correct – the man's entire life, or nothing. Since, if he sets it down at all, it must necessarily be for his own sole benefit – it would be the most contemptible form of egotistic humbug to arrange and modify it as if it were meant for the eye of any other person. (Chapter 3, p. 20)

He is not planning an edited autobiography or memoir in the manly style of a Boswell but identifies more with Dora's feminine approach. Later he hails 'my correspondence with an "airy nothing" ... Pardon, fond and faithful Nobody, for whose benefit I write, and for whose good opinion I am naturally anxious' (Chapter 7, p. 64). This is a specific echo of Burney's published rationale for diary writing which is extracted from her earlier diaries to preface those published in 1842: 'To NOBODY, then, will I write my Journal! The secrets sacred to friendship Nobody will not reveal.'[46]

The diarists in *A Life for a Life* thus share many concerns about writing and its existing and potential audiences. Once, however, Urquhart's long-regretted act of manslaughter is in the open,[47] the diaries grow together like the diarists.

---

[46]   *The Early Journals and Letters of Fanny Burney*, ed. Lars E. Troide (6 vols, Oxford: Clarendon Press, 1988–), vol. 1, p. 2. See discussion in Chapters 2 and 3.

[47]   The 1860 edition was amended to make Urquhart guilty of killing Harry deliberately rather than by accident. Sally Mitchell explains that this was a response to critics including Jewsbury who suggested that Urquhart's guilt and suffering were out of proportion with his offence (Mitchell, p. 57).

The journals come to have addressees because their writing merges into letters and finally into marriage and emigration to Canada. Dora writes in Chapter 23: 'It is not likely I shall keep this journal much longer – but, until closing it finally, it shall go on as usual. Perhaps it may be pleasant to read over some day when I am old – when *we* are old' (p. 216). Burney's aims are much the same: 'To have some account of my thoughts, manners, acquaintance and actions when the hour arrives at which time is more nimble than memory.'[48]

Burney's debates about the preservation of her text are also echoed in the debate over the diary's physical fate in Craik's novel. Marriage ultimately contains the diarists but England cannot contain the act of forgiveness required to reinstate Urquhart into respectable society. As the couple depart for a new life in Canada, Dora concludes, 'Max says I am to write an end to my journal, tie it up with his letters and mine, fasten a stone to it, and drop it over the ship's bulwarks into this blue, blue sea' (Chapter 37, pp. 357–8). The occasion of writing, the fact of an end and the transmission of the text are all compounded here. It is proposed that the physical and textual evidence be destroyed as a function of plot although that evidence already survives as the novel itself. At that moment it is apparently assumed that the diary is a lower form of literature and a male order for its destruction, however loving, is to be obeyed.

Craik regarded *A Life for a Life* as her best book[49] and the preface to the new edition demonstrates the extent to which she upheld its narrative method. Using the title of her most commercially successful novel, Craik and her publishers preserved her semi-anonymity as a published writer under the pseudonym 'the author of *John Halifax*', in many cases dropping the word 'gentleman'. This commodity was known in public to be female, but was also associated with a manly model of goodness and integrity. This suggests an ostensibly effaced self put into the market with a commercial value, a parallel with the commercially published private diary. Anne Brontë, identified at the time of publication with the authors of *Jane Eyre* and *Wuthering Heights*, was part of the debate about the gender of the Bells and did not have the same presence in the market despite Charlotte's attempts to justify her subject matter after her death.

In *A Life for a Life*, the transmission of the text is apparently thwarted but the diary as a narrative has already been put into the marketplace as a commodity. In fact, Dora takes Burney's course and preserves her text for the family since the story it contains will be the same whether it is a family chronicle or lodged on the sea bed. The text's composition was part of the progress of the narrative and the plot it has accommodated cannot now be unwritten.

Before the fame of *John Halifax Gentleman* defined her market, Craik had already used the fictional diary in an earlier work, *Bread Upon the Waters* (1852),

---

[48]　*Early Journals,* vol. 1, p. 1. Chapters 2 and 3 discuss Burney's methods of composition and reliance on memory. Anne Lister makes a similar statement; see Chapter 2, p. 33.

[49]　See Mitchell, p. 58.

and it is instructive to explore this rehearsal for the 'double diary' because it is itself doubly edited. This novella, in a similar format, albeit a single diary, was a contribution to the Governess's Benevolent Institute,[50] and the situation of the independent heroine Felicia is similar to Craik's own.

Felicia's diary, like Dora's, operates on the mid nineteenth-century diary model. It is, however, offered to the reader in an edited format. It is the diarist herself who is significantly acting as both narrator and retrospective collator, and the work of editing is further reframed by an overall consciousness which comments on the editing process. Early on Felicia explains that reflection is possible because the text is completed and under review. A further voice then comments: 'Mem. [that is memorandum] inserted, as are several others, evidently of a much later date than the original diary' (square brackets in the original; p. 13). This is a complex textual device applied to a slight story but its methods are reminiscent of the re-presentation of family papers attempted by Burney only a few years before. The final framing device of Craik's novella pre-empts the acts of recovery made by diary critics in the twentieth century attempting to reconstruct original, non-retrospective texts. The invisibility of the author criticized by *The Christian Remembrancer* is intensified by this third round of editorship and apparent recovery of a retrospective act within an originally contemporaneous diary entry. Charlotte Barrett's plan to re-present family papers with an authorized provenance and Craik's fictional reconstruction both represent a selection of commodities in the marketplace in good domestic causes; Barrett balances the private and public faces of her aunt; Craik raises money for indigent governesses.

Felicia's immediate observations in *Bread Upon the Waters* adopt the nineteenth-century received traditions. Like Dora and like Elizabeth Gaskell, Felicia takes a spiritual and family chronicler's viewpoint: 'I wish to write all the particulars clearly, that I may at no future period have to meet an accusing conscience, or the reproaches of my brothers' (p. 24). In her introduction, Felicia is 'obliged to break off' (p. 9) in her account of her father's new wife and later there is a telltale ellipsis after a difficult interview: 'He answered, what I shall not write' (p. 25). There are necessary gaps caused first by hard work and then by relative happiness. Felicia works as a governess to support her brothers and refuses to marry either of the two men who offer to rescue her from this plight, one because she cannot love him, the other because he is loved by another woman, the sister of one of her pupils. Although she is authorizing her account of this life by pleading its immediacy, she is also looking back 'now in my old age' and even at the time 'weeds' her life like a garden (p. 47). She delays the introduction of her life-changing accident with a reflection on her fictional powers: 'How long I am in coming to my story' (p. 51).

The printed text becomes an authorized narrative by exploiting immediacy both for its dramatic impact and for its veracity as evidence of the nobility of governesses. Felicia is horribly disfigured in an accident by a garden swing which

---

[50]   [Dinah Mulock Craik], *Bread Upon the Waters: A Governess's Life* (Leipzig: Tauschnitz, 1865) Collection of British Authors vol. 807, pp. 7–86.

had seemed to represent a release of her joy and sexuality. Her last diary entry from this fateful period concludes, '[I] will finish my journal in the afternoon' and is followed by fourteen asterisks which are a vivid non-verbal portrayal of the events she later tries to describe:

> 'in the afternoon' – these are the last words I find written down in the journal so long put aside ... I think it will do me good to write down a plain account of the strange things which happened ... which the sight of these pages cause to seem fresh as yesterday, – when I laid them safely by, the ink scarcely dry. (pp. 73–4)

The forensic immediacy and deliberate retrospection of this entry reiterate the use of the diary as a narrative device; its inclusion in a missionary work of social engineering once more emphasizes the private/public boundaries which are being breached by the published diary in the marketplace.

The reception of *The Tenant of Wildfell Hall* and *A Life for a Life* demonstrates a reaction to women's writing which occurred despite their authors' attempts to dramatize their writing within a model of authorized women's record. *The Examiner* objected that it was impossible to analyse and so to review *The Tenant of Wildfell Hall* because of its 'faulty construction.'[51] *The Christian Remembrancer* observes: 'The writer, in her courageous desire to make real women, does not always make them ladies – not but that ladies can do and say, now and then, very odd things, but they will not bear print and ought not to have its sanction.'[52] The reviewer suggests that it is modern 'print' which sanctions a true representation and this ought not to be supplied for a manuscript diary. *The Christian Remembrancer* also tries to create another model for women in print. It suggests that Dora's writing to Urquhart despite her father's objections 'is not after the Hannah More school of morals.'[53]

A review of Craik's published works in 1866 made the distinction between the narrative method and her 'marvellous purity of moral tone'.[54] Harriet Parr in *The British Quarterly Review* distinguishes between the telling of the story and the known cultural value of Craik as a female and therefore moral author: 'the story is told twice over; and as there is very little of it, we don't care to read it once in a man's diary, and once in a woman's ... These faults, however, lie on the surface, whereas if we look beneath the surface, we see the abiding excellence of the author.'[55] Just as Charles Kingsley described the diary in *The Tenant of Wildfell Hall* as an outrage to 'dramatic probability', Parr observes that 'the use of

---

51 *The Examiner* (29 July 1848); Allot, p. 25.

52 'Our Female Novelists': 315.

53 Ibid., p. 320.

54 [Harriet Parr], 'The Author of *John Halifax*', *British Quarterly Review*, XCVII (July 2 1866): 58, 49.

55 Ibid., p. 49.

a diary is the most utterly improbable way of getting a story told, and to use two diaries instead of one, is to convert the improbable into a direct impossible'.[56]

The diary as a narrative device was thus criticized because of its lack of print-worthiness and its abuse of dramatic probability. The authorship of women also devalued its position despite the use of those tropes which validated the diary as a domestic document. The fictional diary occupies a position in the conflict between the private and public document, print and manuscript, and in the gender categories of literature. The public/private debate allocates to the diary a fluctuating role in the marketplace for storytelling through the printed text. It is devalued as a manuscript – a musty paper, a bundle thrown overboard – and yet the inclusion of the text becomes a critical feature of the narrative.

The diary has a commercial value as a token of masculine exchange for Gilbert Markham, as a source of fundraising for governesses, and overall, as a trading opportunity for the marketable commodity which is 'the author of *John Halifax*.' It is the reading and writing acts of men which allow the texts to be transmitted although the impact of their mediation differs. Max Urquhart is written into a female narrative which follows a linear pattern and ultimately dissolves into journal letters with addressees. Gilbert Markham largely remains outside as an unreliable controlling consciousness whose methods re-enact the abuse narrated by the diary.

In their different ways, *The Tenant of Wildfell Hall* and *A Life for a Life* bear the imprint of Frances Burney's documentary approach to the family chronicle. Craik's novel contains direct allusions; Burney and Barrett's plan for a private life in print is echoed in the exterior recess of Charlotte Brontë's renovation project to recreate her sister's image for a new era and for herself.

The contribution of the textual transmission of the narrative to the construction of the woman writer is complex. *The Tenant of Wildfell Hall* demonstrates the contemporary concern that a text is unsafe if women are invisible. Helen's absence from the framing narrative of 1847 is itself the ultimate textual reticence but the diary is preserved after all as evidence and it functions in her absence to warn the reader of the unauthorized male appropriation of the text. Despite calls for its destruction, the diary remains part of the visible published text of *A Life for a Life*. It receives further endorsement from the 'moral' authoress in her Preface to the New Edition of 1860 and Craik relies on clearly described immediacy as an authority for the balanced female/male diary approach. Although she fails to comment in *A Life for a Life* on the transmission of the text, the evidence of *Bread Upon the Waters* nonetheless suggests her consciousness of a technical documentary requirement.

Anne Brontë has been rescued from the 'nun-like veil' of the 1850 'Biographical Notice' and Dinah Craik has been described by a major female critic of the twentieth century as a 'peculiar combination of didacticism and

---

[56]   Ibid.

subversive feminism'.[57] Craik herself wrote in 1858 that: 'there probably never is written an absolutely true life of any woman.'[58] Both Craik and Anne Brontë can be read in ways which challenge their society's assumptions about women writers. Both offer male transactions to justify the role of print in transmitting women's manuscript diaries 'in the blackest of ink with the boldest of pens!'[59]

---

[57]   Elaine Showalter, 'Dinah Mulock Craik and the Tactics of Sentiment: A Case Study in Victorian Female Authorship', *Feminist Studies*, 2 (1975): 6.

[58]   *Chambers Journal* (21 August 1858); reprinted in Dinah Mulock Craik, *Studies from Life* (London: Hurst and Blackett, [1861]), p. 244.

[59]   Craik, *A Life for a Life*, Chapter 1, p. 1.

Chapter 5
The Diary and the Epistolary Form

Diaries and letters as personal records share characteristics which have been exploited within the emerging diary novel genre. Lorna Martens describes the diary novel as 'a form that the system of fiction has borrowed from the system of letters in general'. She likens diary to epistolary narrative within 'the fiction of periodic writing.'[1] There is a suggestion of the shared origins of the two forms in the word 'journalizing', the daily record which becomes a conversation with the self in a diary or with a named recipient in a letter. Both forms might ultimately be adapted as life writing in a memoir built retrospectively out of dailiness. This chapter revisits the model of the non-fictional diary, its traditions and practice by female writers, in order to establish the diary/letter linkages, and posits an evolutionary process which brought the personal diary into a narrative role within the nineteenth-century novel. That evolution can be identified in two of the core texts, *The Tenant of Wildfell Hall* and *A Life for a Life*.

Journals and letters were not distinct categories in the nineteenth century and merged into one another as forms of authorized life writing for women. Introducing his selection from the writings of Frances Burney, the critic John Wain observes that: 'since she was well aware that her Letters were much prized in her circle and since her Diary was written ... to be passed from hand to hand, Miss Burney would pick up her pen after an interruption with no very clear idea of whether she was writing Letter or Diary.'[2] As demonstrated in Chapter 3, Burney's re-assemblage of her materials presents a conscious and calculating choice of voice and audience, and this chapter also considers how her novel *Evelina* uses the techniques of both letter-writing and 'journalizing', accounts written on different occasions within the same 'letter', to control the narrative.

The traditions which fostered the diary as a writing space for women also promoted the letter. The circulation of family news was a woman's responsibility, something that Jane Austen called 'our concerns in distant quarters'.[3] The whole might be viewed in the light of a family chronicle and indeed revisited and mined to produce that chronicle. The travel journal and consequent letters home describing a journey are closely associated as daily record which might build into a more considered account when circumstance allows. Private correspondence on spiritual subjects might circulate like the published spiritual diary, and conduct

---

[1] Lorna Martens, *The Diary Novel* (Cambridge: Cambridge University Press, 1985), p. 77; 24.

[2] John Wain (ed.), *Fanny Burney's Diary: A Selection from the Diary and Letters* (London: The Folio Society, 1961), p. xxi.

[3] Letter to Cassandra Austen, 5–6 May 1801.

books were also written in epistolary format.[4] It is their form of fragmentation and daily record which authorizes letters and diaries as forms of life writing for women. There is also a process of inclusion which tells its own story.

The private news of the family was associated with the domestic life of trivial incident which might fall to the narration of a wife, mother or sister. The woman might be seen to revalue domestic issues within the ephemeral context of the letter, out of date before it is read, and also to have the leisure in which to compose the document itself. If the diary could be an authorized serial autobiography for a reticent nineteenth-century woman, the letter too represented a fragmented opportunity for life writing circumscribed by the domestic role and by its presumed subject matter. Both forms, however, provided opportunities for selectivity, recording and potentially reconstructing its author through the chosen topics and style of writing.

Many letters, of course, circulated far more widely than their allotted addressee and would have had to conform to standards which were transmitted within society's rules of etiquette. Letters were deemed to belong to the author rather than to the recipient despite the transfer in possession entailed by the process of posting and paying for receipt. Groups of letters like Burney's 'packets' might take on a retrospective appearance as life writing but their possession and transmission by another would only allow the narrative to progress as a serial by means of common authorship and the conscious recounting of ongoing experience. The letter, unlike the locked and pathologically secret diary, is already sent. In its semi-permeable public domain and in terms of the non-fictional artefact, it cannot apparently be unsent. Nineteenth-century fiction exploits the gap between the letter sent but unread, and manipulates the idea of the reader's access to the letter at the point of composition or the point of reception.[5] This parallels and also refracts the un/authorized reading of the fictional diary which both exploits immediacy and reconstructs the inquest which is the realistic novel. The nineteenth-century texts which feature a diary as part of their narrative bring into question the role of the reader and her access to the physical diary. The novels question whether that reader is reading with the diarist or rereading with the un/authorized editor. The physical text of the letter within a novel generates similar questions of sincerity, forgery, sequential recovery and preservation.

---

4   See for instance Hester Chapone, *Letters on the Improvement of the Mind* (1772). Lord Chesterfield's *Letters to His Son* (1737) were seen as the epitome of advice and clearly influenced Richardson's *Pamela* (1740). Burney knew Chapone and admired another semi-fictional set of letters between Elizabeth Griffiths and her husband Richard entitled *A Series of Genuine Letters between Henry and Frances* (1757 and 1766); see *The Early Journals and Letters of Fanny Burney*, ed. Lars E. Troide (6 vols, Oxford: Clarendon Press, 1988–), where she announces on 30 May 1768 that they are 'genuine' and 'interesting' and that she likes them 'prodigiously' vol. 1, p. 12; p. 7.

5   There are incidents of deferred reading in fiction such as the letter from Evelina's mother read sixteen years after it has been written and a letter from Lucy Westenra in *Dracula* which only comes to light after her death.

The diarist's private use of literary forms has also been identified as part of writing practice and of potential performance within an ostensibly unshared text. The letter offers further potential for shared allusion to reading and types of writing and, of course, the possibility of practising a writing style. Many manuals providing letter-writing advice circulated in the later eighteenth century. Samuel Richardson's *Pamela* was expanded as a creative response to conduct literature using the situation described in letters 138 and 139 of *Letters Written to and for Particular Friends, on the Most Important Occasions* (1741).[6] Ian Watt asserts that 'the cult of familiar letter-writing ... provided Richardson with a microphone already attuned to the tones of private experience' and Bernard Duyfhuizen observes that 'epistolary novels are secondary modelling systems derived from the primary modelling system of everyday letter writing'.[7] The letter thus evolved into a device for narration in the eighteenth century from its place as a mode of communication stimulated by increased literacy and the opportunity for circulation via the public mail.

Attempts to regulate letter-writing through the provision of templates and models grew out of classical models and developed into the conduct literature which Richardson in turn used as a stimulus for fiction. The letter manuals were structured around fictional background stories and offered models and specific wording for 'all occasions'. *The British Letter-Writer: or Letter-Writer's Complete Instructor* presented 'Letters to and from *Illuſtrious Perſons*, *Parents*, and *Children*, *Brothers*, *Siſters* and other *Relations*'.[8] The models predicate situations such as advice on marriage and messages of condolence and they also discuss the nature of correspondence. *The Complete Letter-Writer* (1776) includes an example of a rejected proposal of marriage which could easily have been written by Mr Collins in *Pride and Prejudice*: 'I am exceedingly concerned, that I cannot be as acceptable to you, as I have the good fortune to find myſelf to your honoured parents.'[9]

Despite her avowed admiration of Richardson's novels and particularly *Sir Charles Grandison*, letters were subject to satire in Jane Austen's earliest attempts at fiction such as 'Love and Freindship' and 'Lesley Castle'.[10] Austen chooses the name of Eloisa for one of her correspondents in the unfinished 'Lesley Castle'

---

[6]   See Samuel Richardson, *Pamela; or, Virtue Rewarded*, ed. Thomas Keymer and Alice Wakely (Oxford: Oxford University Press, 2001), pp. xiii–xiv.

[7]   Ian Watt, *The Rise of the Novel* (London: Chatto and Windus, 1957; reprinted Pimlico: Random House, 2000), p. 193; Bernard Duyfhuizen, *Narratives of Transmission* (London: Associated University Presses, 1992), p. 64.

[8]   *The British Letter-Writer: or Letter-Writer's Complete Instructor* (London: J. Cooke, 1760). The copy held by the British Library is inscribed 'Jane Wells her Book 1771' and again 'Miss Smith July 14th 1815' which suggests the continued circulation of models into the nineteenth-century.

[9]   *The Complete Letter-Writer containing Familiar Letters on The moſt common Occaſions in Life* (Edinburgh: Paterson, 1776), p. 155.

[10]   Jane Austen, *Catharine and Other Writings*, ed. Margaret Anne Doody and Douglas Murray (Oxford: Oxford University Press, 1993; reissued 1998), pp. 75–133.

alluding to the famous female writer of letters depicted in Pope's 'Eloisa to Abelard'.[11] 'Lesley Castle' consists of only ten letters and devotes much of its time to the discussion of how letters are forwarded to women on visits and how correspondence arises, its subject matter – or the lack of it – and the interest derived from rival accounts of the same events. Emma Marlowe begins Letter the Ninth:

> Need I say my dear Eloisa how welcome your Letter was to me? I cannot give a greater proof of the pleasure I received from it, or of the Desire I feel that our Correspondence may be regular and frequent than by setting you so good an example as I now do in answering it before the end of the week – But do not imagine that I claim any merit in being so punctual; on the contrary I assure you, that it is a far greater Gratification to me to write to you, than to spend the Evening either at a Concert or a Ball.[12]

Letter XX from a young lady in *The British Letter-Writer* exhibits a similar tone: 'Though from your laſt I had Reaſon to think you approached the indiſſoluble Bond, I could not apprehend the Change would have been ſo ſudden ... However, as I have no Doubt of your Happineſs, I ſincerely rejoice in the Event.'[13] One sequence in this manual concerns two separated young ladies. Miss Seymour writes to Miss Drury from 'Bartlett-Grove, Sunday Evening': 'News, the Life of Correſpondence has no Exiſtence here.'[14] Events offstage cause Miss Seymour to revise this view of her place of residence which she introduces by drawing attention to the narrative occasion and the performance of her own state: 'The whole Day do I dedicate (for my Eyes are ſcarcely quite open) to the Pleaſure it always give me to write to my dear *Charlotte*.'[15] She dramatizes this act of letter-writing in the context of two fictional correspondents from Richardson's *Clarissa* whilst at the same time denying the applicability of the fictional model: 'But the Bell rings, dear Charlotte, and I muſt run down to Dinner – You and I write like Clariſſa Harlowe and Miſs Howe, only not totally in the ſame ſtrain – but in this, I believe we all four agree, that next to the Converſation of a Friend is her Correſpondence.'[16] The non-fictional guide to the epistolary which itself generated the fictional Clarissa recycles her as an exemplary letter-writer. Miss Seymour or rather the manual's compiler nonetheless attempts to control the response of readers by drawing out a trite commonplace whilst at the same time offering a risqué allusion to the tragic situation of Richardson's second novel.

By the late eighteenth century, the letter as a narrative device both fictional and non-fictional was in wide circulation. It had classical antecedents and was an everyday means of communication. It was being situated as a writing

---

[11]   Charles Johnson quotes from Pope's poem on the title page of his *The Complete Art of Writing Letters* (1779).

[12]   'Lesley Castle', p. 128.

[13]   *British Letter-Writer*, p. 60.

[14]   *British Letter-Writer*, p. 30.

[15]   Ibid., p. 34.

[16]   Ibid., pp. 36–7.

mechanism which demanded control, but could always evade that control through its circulation amongst sympathetic recipients. The letter was open to public misperception and unauthorized reading, and could be forged and manipulated out of sequence. Its forms could be used to hide secrets and lies whilst purporting to open communication. It could be misread or used to construct a persona based on its intended audience.

A comparison with the model of diary fiction discussed in Part 1 illustrates the points of contact between the two forms. Since the epistolary novel appears to predate the use of the diary as a narrative device such an analysis both links the two forms and offers some reflections on the evolutionary process.

The cloistered diary writer parallels the cloistered letter writer. Dutiful communication between Pamela and her parents, and between Burney's Evelina and her guardian Mr Villars, is a semi-public act although both female letter-writers are effectively besieged by their situations. Since they have audiences of at least one person, their writing is already consciously shaped for that audience, whereas the diary writer writes only for herself. Once the texts produced are in circulation, however, the role of editor and final reader becomes equally significant to both forms of narration. Despite the illusion of immediacy, the inclusion, juxtaposition and final sequencing of diary entries and letters is controlled elsewhere.

Both letters and diaries are used as fictional devices to exploit their apparent sincerity and the lack of mediation of content. Their link with domestic everyday records allows the presentation of women's writing directly within a text and authorizes scenes such as Mr B.'s attempted rape of Pamela and Evelina's accidental association with prostitutes. Likewise, the diary and the letter narrate the immediacy of the writer's situation. Any substantial attempt at retrospection or dissociation from the self within the written text will disrupt the reality of the everyday document. The placement of a letter or diary within a fictional narrative draws attention to the document itself. The physical reality of the text which should bolster the purposes of formal realism actually interrupts the presentation of the real. The realistic effect of actual documents undermines that sense of reality. The appearance of the document questions the role and authority of the reader whether invited into the text or eavesdropping on it. The transmission of such texts into a fictional situation becomes part of the narrative itself. The reaction to *Pamela,* for instance, forced Richardson to attempt regulation of the response to the story which was reconstructed by critics contrary to his original educational project. Pamela's objectives were widely reinterpreted and satirized most notably by Fielding in *Shamela.* James Carson observes that there was 'a conflict between potential communal authorship by his readers and correspondents and his own attempts to assert control.'[17] The gaps between the message conveyed and its execution by a single narrator caused quite literally 'reading between the lines'.

The letter and the diary are, of necessity, fragmented forms dated and produced at intervals. Both Pamela in Richardson's novel and Frances Burney in her own

---

[17]   James Carson, 'Narrative Cross-Dressing and the Critique of Authorship in the Novels of Richardson' in Elizabeth C. Goldsmith (ed.), *Writing the Female Voice: Essays in Epistolary Literature* (Boston: North Eastern University Press, 1989), p. 97.

Diary demonstrate that the journal is not always a bound document. They frequently refer to memoranda which contribute to the final written product which is in the form of a journal letter. A distinction may nonetheless be made about the level of fragmentation. The diary could be broadly characterized as a bound volume which remains in the possession of its author and builds into the record of a year. A series of letters is composed on separate sheets sent in fragments which are themselves complete records to a recipient or multiple recipients over a period of time. The reconstruction of a correspondence is thus a different task from that of reproducing a personally-authored single work.

Both forms discuss their narrative occasion and location. Letter-writing etiquette encourages the writer to explain those situations which generate a letter; either to justify gaps in correspondence or to explain the length or paucity of the communication. Diaries seek authority for their composition from the writer's situation and reflect on the opportunity afforded by privacy to tackle difficult or unresolved questions. For women writers, it is necessary to explain that writing does not cause them to neglect domestic tasks. They can claim in letters that news circulation and advice to others is a worthier occupation. The location for the act of writing and the status of that writing within the hierarchy of women's work is a necessary discussion whether with the self in a diary or with others who will receive the letter. Both forms also share the extratextual activity of narrating their assembly so that acts of writing and reconstruction generate their own plot.[18]

A specific by-product of the use of diaries and letters as narrative devices is the manipulation of their open-endedness. The non-fictional versions may be composed using topics chosen by the writer for herself or on the basis of the recipient. They will unfold some sort of story over time. The non-fictional diary or letter provides a limited structure or awareness of its outcome and of its ongoing contribution to the shape of a life or family history. It may, of course, fictionalize to the extent that it will assume a role for different audiences. The fictional versions, however, reflect the choices of the editor or author of the fictional text and so will be read as building into a story with a fixed outcome. Elizabeth MacArthur derives her specific viewpoint from Richardson when she claims that the epistolary novel is 'a series of present moments of letter writing ... the future is yet to be decided'.[19] The editor/author tries to maintain the illusion of the transmission of the text by indicating omissions from an original manuscript where choices about the inclusion of material have been made. There might also be an indication that matter remains private because it has been reclassified as unimportant or unauthorized for publication. This in turn reflects the practices of editors shaping real lives into manageable works who themselves make choices in order to package a subject for publication and who are taking a judgmental stance over that subject.[20]

---

[18] See Duyfhuizen, *Narratives of Transmission*, pp. 45–6 for a discussion of this 'double narrative'.

[19] Elizabeth J. MacArthur, *Extravagant Narratives: Closure and Dynamics in the Epistolary Form* (Princeton, New Jersey: Princeton University Press, 1990), p. 3.

[20] An example with contemporary applicability is Elizabeth Gaskell's *Life of Charlotte Bronte* particularly as discussed by Deirdre D'Albertis, *Dissembling Fictions: Elizabeth*

The letter and the diary might also be compared through their technique of 'writing to the moment', the phrase coined by Richardson to describe his use of epistolary narrative.[21] Both forms question the nature of composition and its use of retrospect. Both raise issues about chronology in terms of time of writing and the reflection inherent in the retrospective narration of events. The time frame of the 'moment' is further questioned by time passing and by real time, the time required for a movement in the plot and the time taken for composition. The letter also demands time for transmission and reading by the recipient which must be accommodated by the plot and scripted within the time frame.

There is a sense in which the personal letter for women can be seen as authorizing the personal diary. Permission to keep a record progresses from household accounts to a narrative of household events and thence to a reflection on self worth. It is a stage on the way to personal record just as the use of a letter as a fictional device predates first-person realistic narrative. This evolutionary process of the fictional letter becoming diary can be illustrated by Samuel Richardson's *Pamela* (1740) and Frances Burney's *Evelina* (1778). This process is also visible in Mary Shelley's *Frankenstein* (1818), *The Tenant of Wildfell Hall* (1847) and *A Life for a Life* (1859) where diaries and letters interact under the terms of nineteenth-century novel-writing.

Richardson's 'Introduction' to *Pamela* creates the exterior fiction of an editor for '*this little Work*' with a long list of 'Recommendations' to the reader. This Preface is a grand frame for the letters of a serving maid and it already contains the seeds of Richardson's future contest over the meaning of the text once it circulates to others. In the outermost frame with himself as Editor, he sets up his authority as collator of the physical documents '*which have their Foundation in* Truth *and* Nature', observing that '*[A]n* Editor *may reasonably be supposed to judge with an Impartiality which is rarely to be met with in an* Author *towards his own Works*' (italics in original p. 4).

A secondary frame of complimentary letters from readers of the manuscript version of the Letters[22] excuses in part the use of uneducated style by Pamela herself: 'let us have *Pamela* as Pamela wrote it, in her own Words without Amputation or

---

Gaskell and the Victorian Social Text. (London: Macmillan, 1997). See also, Suzanne L. Bunkers, 'Whose Diary Is It, Anyway? Issues of Agency, Authority, Ownership', *A/B: Auto/Biography Studies*, 17/1 (Summer 2002): 11–27.

[21] He first uses the phrase in a letter to Lady Bradshaigh quoted by Joe Bray, *The Epistolary Novel: Representations of Consciousness* (London: Routledge, 2003), p. 55. The public statement was coined in the Preface to *Sir Charles Grandison* (1753–1754) 'The nature of familiar letters written, as it were, to the moment, while the heart is agitated by hopes and fears, on events undecided must plead an excuse for the bulk of a collection of this kind.'

[22] The writers of these 'puffs' have been identified as associates of Richardson (Tom Keymer, *Richardson's 'Clarissa' and the Eighteenth-Century Reader* (Cambridge: Cambridge University Press, 1992). Keymer points out in his edition that Fielding may have been correct in claiming that Richardson wrote them himself as yet another fictional framing device (*Pamela*, p. 526, note 10).

Addition' (p. 9). The frame also provides the voice of another correspondent to propose the value of 'writing to the moment': 'the Letters being written under the immediate Impression of every Circumstance which occasioned them' (p. 5). This apparatus of immediacy, veracity and other '*good Ends*' in itself questions the nature of Richardson's approach because he later violates it by editorial interventions in the text and extratextual efforts to insist on his moral meanings against the interpretation of critics. Its first aim, however, is one shared by later users of the diary as narrative, that of allowing a woman to speak and to perform in her own voice. The project is perhaps complicated by Richardson's experience as a publisher who pays attention to the physicality of a text's production and later finds it necessary to intervene when the story and its narration begin to strain credibility.

Pamela thus begins its life as a commodity in the marketplace using the multiple fictions of letter writer, correspondent, author and editor. Pamela's letters to her parents dramatize the narrative occasion and the act of writing. At the death of her mistress, Pamela must write to her parents in secret and trust her letters to a fellow servant, the perfidious John. The means of narration she employs blurs writing and reading occasions and is punctuated by her explanations: 'I Was forc'd to break off; for I fear'd my Master was coming' (p. 46). An early confrontation with her master provokes her exit on a moralizing note: 'And so saying, I went up Stairs to my Chamber, and wrote all this' (p. 67). She is accused of 'always scribbling' (p. 22) but insists 'I work all Hours with my Needle ... and am besides about flowering him a waistcoat' (p. 22). She justifies her writing activity as the duty of a daughter and closes a later entry 'having a little Time, I went up, and wrote thus far' (p. 211). Events and the opportunity to write about them pile up and she has to observe: 'I have wrote a vast deal in a little Time' (p. 275).

However justified, the acts of writing and of sending are precarious in the B. household and a number of letters are lost. There is a gap between Letters IX and X which is never recovered (p. 22) or presented to the reader. Letters XIX–XXXI which can be read in sequence on the page are withheld from the Andrews by Mr B. (pp. 75–91). This is explained through editorial intervention in order to dramatize Pamela's apparent escape which leads to her incarceration in Lincolnshire; it is by this means that the reader learns of the illicit reading of letters transmitted by the treacherous servant and reads the substitute letter sent by Mr B. (pp. 92–4).

Despite the suspicions aroused, Mr and Mrs Andrews are powerless against the wealthy squire and their inability to act produces a change in narrative style. The Editor announces:

> We shall now leave the honest old Pair, praying for their dear *Pamela*; and return to the Account she herself gives of all this; having written it Journal-wise, to amuse and employ her Time, in hopes some Opportunity might offer to send it to her Friends, and, as was her constant View, that she might afterwards look back upon the Dangers she had escaped ... and that then she might examine, and either approve of or repent for, her own Conduct in them. (p. 98)

This effectively echoes Pamela's own letter written in the very throes of setting off for her parents' home which she must write for the purposes of the plot although it seems unlikely to have been written in reality: 'I Will continue my Writing still, because, may-be, I shall like to read it, when I am with you, to see what Dangers God has enabled me to escape; and tho' I bring it in my Pocket' (p. 86). The letters are thus undermined as a means of communication firstly because in this case unsent and secondly because they are exposed as a form of pseudo conduct book composed through life writing.

Pamela claims that her 'writing Time will soon be over' (p. 38) but it is now prolonged and takes the journal form. She adjusts her writing pattern: 'I will every Day now write my sad State' (p. 99) and 'I will close this Day's writing' (p. 156). She reflects the diary's fictional role as an understanding friend when she tells her text and her parents 'I can write to ease my Mind, tho' I can't send it to you' (p. 100). She also professes to find difficulties in language which are applicable to the diary writers of the later novels: 'How shall I find the Words to paint my Griefs and his Deceit?' (p. 225). Critics of the time, of course, saw deceit in Pamela which is here highlighted by her lack of language.

The acquisition of writing materials to create the physical text is an integral part of the plot once Pamela is under supervision in Lincolnshire and paper supply is a frequent topic for discussion. Mr Longman provides supplies (p. 100) which are later distributed around her Lincolnshire closet (p. 112). She stores the journal 'in my Under-coat, next my Linen' and fears discovery of her papers 'for they grow large!' (p. 131). When Mr. B. demands to read them he describes them as a fabrication, a 'pretty Novel' (p. 232), and Pamela requests the opportunity to edit them for his perusal. When he demands to see the papers 'uncurtail'd' (p. 235) she pretends they are hidden in the equivocally private space of her closet and once there she cannot bear to give them up: 'Besides, I must all undress me in a manner to untack them' (p. 235). In this way Pamela comes to be her own journal and she reluctantly edits what she 'untacks' in case it is never available for her parents again, although the summary remains in the text for the reader before it becomes two parcels.

The novel is in part about access to Pamela through her journal. There are signs that she is becoming a self-conscious writer. She performs for her parents the role of the virtuous daughter and demonstrates her awareness of this: 'What one writes for one's Father and Mother is not for everybody' (p. 229). She claims not to be aware of her letters being intercepted and suffers the voyeuristic attentions of both Mr B. and his sister.[23] The record, however, is written from her point of view and her writerly capabilities may perhaps match her 'Counter-plottings' once Mr B.'s unauthorized reading becomes the norm. It is surely a double bluff when she writes, 'I shall have but little Heart to write if he is to see all' (p. 237).

At her marriage, Pamela announces with plain diary-writing intent: 'I am glad of the Method I have taken of making a Journal of all that passes in these first

---

[23]   Lady Davers besieges Pamela in her own home after the marriage and explains 'I should take great Pleasure to read all his Stratagems, Attempts, Contrivances, Menaces, and Offers to you ... and all your pretty Counter-plottings, which he much praises' (p. 454).

Stages of my Happiness, because it will sink the Impression still deeper; and I shall have recourse to them for my better Regulation, as often as I shall mistrust my Memory' (p. 448). She expects to reread her own words as spiritual guidance and her habit of record is vital for the continuation of the novel, but the final presence of her addressees, which is to be satirized later by Jane Austen in *Lady Susan*, brings about a degree of closure reframed by lessons on virtue inserted by the editor.

The link between women's diaries and letters becomes more explicit nearly forty years later in Frances Burney's first published novel *Evelina*. The author's own difficulties with writing as a woman in the late eighteenth century have been discussed in Chapter 3. Evelina writes letters to communicate with her guardian Mr Villars whose ostensible role is to advise her on matters of etiquette in the wider world which he has reluctantly allowed her to join. He bases this advice on Evelina's accounts of her experiences, relying on both her naïve point of view and the information she chooses to tell him. [24] In true epistolary style she suggests that she has barely time to write to Villars because of all the pressure of events. His sheltered life, however, fails to qualify him as an adviser and in fact his interpretation of public conduct delays the outcome which reunites Evelina with her biological father and produces the match with Lord Orville.[25] The plan to write to her guardian is, however, the authorization for writing. Even at the crucial moment of Orville's declaration she adds: 'I have a conversation to write.'[26]

Like Burney herself, Evelina sees her letters building into a narrative whole. On leaving town she describes her writing which is now in Villars's possession as 'my London letters' (p. 53) and the group is named, like Burney's later Worcester or Teignmouth journals, Evelina's 'town journal' (p. 116). She 'shall shortly have no more adventures to write' and so will complete this journal and she asks for Villars's 'thoughts and observations on it' (p. 116). The narrative occasion and the narrative opportunity are part of her communication and set the scene for the events she describes: '*1 July 5 o'clock* O, Sir, what an adventure have I to write! All night it has occupied my thoughts, and I am now risen thus early to write it to you' (p. 258). The pressure both of events and of time justify her irregular habit and create breathless naïvety. She shows her self-consciousness of the issue of time frame and chronology which caused the epistolary form to be ridiculed. Early on she identifies a mismatch between the time to live the events and the time required to narrate them: 'As to my plan of writing every evening the adventures of the day, I find it impracticable; for the diversions here are so very late, that if

---

[24]	See the discussion of Evelina's control of information in Julia L. Epstein, 'Evelina's Deceptions: The Letter and the Spirit' in Harold Bloom (ed.), *Fanny Burney's 'Evelina'* (New York: Chelsea House, 1988), pp. 111–29.

[25]	Susan Greenfield suggests that the lack of paternal control gives Evelina the space for her authorship (Susan C. Greenfield, '"Oh Dear Resemblance of Thy Murdered Mother": Female Authorship in *Evelina*', *Eighteenth Century Fiction*, 3/4 (July 1991): 301–20.

[26]	Frances Burney, *Evelina*, ed. Margaret Anne Doody (London: Penguin 1994; reprinted 2004), p. 383.

I begin my letters after them, I could not go to bed at all' (p. 31). She comments later: 'how many long letters has this one short fortnight produced' (p. 127).

The dates and the headings '*in continuation*' which Austen will also use in her early fiction maintain the sense of periodic writing as well as the sense of a composition building into a whole. As early as 2 April Evelina exclaims: 'I can write no more now. I have hardly time to breathe ... *Saturday Night* ... I shall write to you every evening all that passes in the day' (p. 28). The speed of events is juxtaposed with the control imposed by daily letter writing 'journal-wise' as Richardson described it in his editorial intervention in *Pamela*. Evelina admits to Maria Mirvan, 'I cannot journalize; cannot arrange my ideas into order' (p. 285) indicating that the function of her writing is not only communication but orderly transmission.

Evelina recognizes alternative modes of authorship for audiences other than Villars and she adopts a different style of writing to her female friend indicating consciousness of the styles of letter-writing exemplified in the manuals. [27] She echoes *The British Letter-Writer*'s Miss Seymour and Miss Drury on 14 July: 'Maria will be much surprised ... when instead of her friend, she receives this letter;- this cold inanimate letter, which will but ill express the feelings of the heart which indites it' (p. 283). She later complains, like the model letter-writers, of the paucity of material at Berry Hill. Her silence of ten days is caused by a lack of 'sufficient matter for a letter': 'Narrative does not offer, nor does a lively imagination supply the deficiency' (p. 292). In fact within the same letter, she finds matter enough to report a conversation with Villars in which he transforms Evelina into 'a book that both afflicts and perplexes me' (p. 294).

At this moment there are also narrative complexities. Evelina is translating her thoughts for Maria and in turn transmitting a letter purported to be from Lord Orville which has actually been forged by his rival Clement Willoughby. The whole scene calls into question the action and permeability of the epistolary communication reconstructed as narration. Evelina is making an ostensibly innocent and direct communication to both Maria and Villars, which she wants her two correspondents to receive in very different ways. Villars is being invited to act as judge and guardian and to be introduced to the concept of Orville through the social construct of Evelina's journal and the written construct of his own – Orville's – letter. Maria has been present at Evelina's meetings with Orville and as a result of their separation has received a letter from her friend describing the lord as a brother. Within the code of feminine communication, Maria is actually being invited to consider Orville as Evelina's suitor. The whole, however, is undermined by the letter's being a forgery, a manipulation of the epistolary code which questions the nature of the documentary evidence on show.

Like the female diary writers, Evelina's lack of a language can be used to suggest narrative omission when she writes to Maria Mirvan: 'no words, no language can

---

[27] Epstein points out that their correspondence would produce another very different novel (Epstein, 'Evelina's Deceptions,' p. 119).

explain the heaviness of heart with which I made the journey ... but let me pursue my journal' (p. 283), the journal here becoming another understanding friend who is embodied in an actual woman. This reticence is used to special effect following Orville's proposal when authorship must be cautiously essayed for the sake of propriety and safety of publication: 'I cannot write the scene that followed, though every word is engraved in my heart' (p. 390). Like Burney and Shore with their secret diaries, Evelina cannot write the proposal within this equivocally private narrative but the novel reader is invited to write her own words constructed from the scene and the words which surround it.

Burney did not use the letter form in her succeeding novels. It has been suggested, however, that Mary Shelley used the convention of epistolary narrative forty years later in *Frankenstein* (1818) because she was a young writer as Burney was in 1778. Mary Favret believes that the novel demonstrates a 'desire to make sense of communication.'[28] *Frankenstein*, written by a woman, uses a man's journal letters to frame oral narrative. This record is initially made in the knowledge that it may never be transmitted. The journal writer will either present himself in person or the narrative will be lost. There are multiple narrative enclosures which contain journals and letters. Walton is writing to his sister Margaret under a compulsion even though she will see him in person before the letter arrives: 'So strange an incident has happened to us that I cannot forbear recording it, although it is very probable that you will see me before these papers can come into your possession.'[29] He later believes that she will never receive his communications when he writes he is 'encompassed by peril' and 'ignorant' of the final outcome of the expedition (p. 215). His words here are almost identical to the earlier passage: 'A scene has passed of such uncommon interest, that although it is highly probable that these papers may never reach you, yet I cannot forbear recording it' (p. 216). The remarkableness of the story can be contained within a recognizable formula. At the same time, despite the threats to the record of Walton's journey, the novel reader has access to 'these papers', a fact which contradicts the doom foreseen in the framing journal.

Effectively, there is no means of transmission as there is no postal system, and therefore Margaret becomes a diary addressee as 'Nobody' is both for Burney in her *Diary* and for Max Urquhart in *A Life for a Life*. Walton writes like a diary-writer justifying the preservation of the story: 'This manuscript will doubtless afford you the greatest pleasure: but to me, who know him and hear it from his own lips – with what interest and sympathy shall I read it in some future day!' (pp. 31–2). Four letters introduce Frankenstein's story which he begins to tell on 20 August and concludes on 26 August when Walton's journal letter recommences. Frankenstein has also 'corrected and augmented' Walton's 'notes concerning

---

[28] Mary A. Favret, *Romantic Correspondence: Women, Politics and the Fiction of Letters* (Cambridge: Cambridge University Press, 1993, p. 178). Favret links the novel with *Emma* also published in 1818. Shelley began writing *Frankenstein* in 1816 aged only 19.

[29] Mary Shelley, *Frankenstein*, ed. Maurice Hindle (London: Penguin, 2003), p. 25.

his history' (p. 213) which accretes another layer in the transmission history of the documents and itself opens up doubts about the immediacy of his account and its inclusion in a letter.

Within this competing narrative economy of texts, there is also Frankenstein's journal of the progress towards creating the monster 'this history ... mingled with accounts of domestic occurrences' (p. 132) as well as Clerval's journal (p. 159) and letters from Elizabeth (pp. 65–8, 191). In parallel with the monster's exposure to language the novel reflects the efforts of others to make sense of the use of records. Despite Frankenstein's personal narrative and editing, it is the supporting documents which make his 'hideous narration' (p. 201) more real to Walton. Favret points out that the novel is itself 'a patchwork monster'[30] just as Pamela becomes her own journal by sewing memoranda into her petticoats and Evelina becomes a book. When the expedition turns back, Walton returns to his journal to write his account of the death of Frankenstein dating his record 12 September and wishing his sister good night in real time when he hears the monster arriving. He then records the narrative occasion offering both his lack of a language and his attempt at closure: 'Great God! What a scene has just taken place! ... I hardly know whether I shall have the power to detail it; yet the tale which I have recorded would be incomplete without this final and wonderful catastrophe' (p. 221).

This discussion of *Frankenstein* illustrates an important point in the evolution of diary narrative for it indicates the future tendency to hybrid narrative forms in which a woman's diary will occupy a place. The novel uses the techniques of the journal letter to contain its Gothic tale in a style which will be developed by Wilkie Collins and later by Bram Stoker in a more overtly nineteenth-century context. Despite the narrators of *Frankenstein* being male, the recipient of the story is female and so is the author of the novel who was known to be female in the edition of 1823, five years after the original composition.

Like Burney, Shelley professed herself unsure about literary fame gained in the public arena. Her introduction to the 1831 standard edition of the novel is at pains to stress her private persona:

> It is true that I am very averse to bringing myself forward in print; but as my account will only appear as an appendage to a former production, and as it will be confined to such topics as have connexion with my authorship alone, I can scarcely accuse myself of a personal intrusion.' (p. 5)

This sentence goes into contortions to avoid accusations of authorship and the introduction itself tries to retain a sense of domestic propriety. Shelley claims that as a child 'I was not confined to my own identity' (p. 6) and that she was encouraged to write by her husband because of her literary antecedents. Like Pamela, like Burney and like Walton, she describes writing as a compulsive act: 'As a child I scribbled' (p. 5). The 1831 introduction explains that it was Percy Shelley who wrote the novel's Preface in 1818 where what Mary Shelley now calls her 'hideous

---

30 Favret, p. 184.

progeny' is deemed to have arisen from 'casual conversation', 'the amiableness of domestic affection' and the 'playful desire of imitation' (pp. 11, 12) rather than the competitive authorship described. In 1831 with her husband and children dead, the tale of the monster has become the 'offspring of happy days' (p. 10).

A woman's literary use of a journal has thus been adapted to the purpose of contesting her own authorship. The patchwork story using interacting narratives of diary and letters must flout its own creation and present a safely domesticated tale of composition. The exterior apparatus, like that of *Pamela* and *Evelina*, attempts to reconcile the private and public persona of a female authored text. *Frankenstein* itself is regularized by the actions of journalizing performed by Walton as a domestic duty, and the fractured text is part of the evolutionary process from letter to diary.

The Tenant of Wildfell Hall presents another male author framing a domestic communication. It is a patchwork under strict if equivocal control. It effectively stands at a crossroads where the epistolary novel can no longer go but where the idea of a woman's diary telling a story has been promoted in the 1840s by Burney's *Diary* and promulgated by Macaulay's review of that text. Walton, as narrator, is gifted the story of the monster and is told it in a remote place with some doubt of his ever living to tell the story over. Gilbert Markham looks back from a place of safety to trade his wife's diary as a homosocial bond framed within a letter and bounded by his own journal. Victor Frankenstein's narrative is freely given although reported under the pressure of events, but Gilbert's physical access to Helen's diary has a more circuitous provenance.

Chapter 4 considered the extent to which the diary of a woman comes to occupy a more distant narrative recess. The act of enclosing the diary within a letter and drawing attention to the acts of reading reflects the epistolary tradition, but also invests the diary with a new distance where the fictional female author must stand outside the frame to allow its transmission.

Gilbert's letter supplies only one date which appears at the end but like Walton he imagines the impact of his words on the recipient, asking Halford to imagine his – Gilbert's – feelings as a reader in 1827.[31] As in *Frankenstein* there are other competing records including that 'certain faded old journal' (p. 10) which Gilbert is using as a family chronicle and source for his letter. There are musty papers in the library where Gilbert dramatizes his narrative as there are physical letters which Walton finds more convincing than the narration of the monster's actions (*Frankenstein*, p. 213). Gilbert, however, may no longer be an authorized reader of the text but effectively a violator of it. Terry Castle has observed that the letter is a 'mark of absence'.[32] *The Tenant of Wildfell Hall* is generated by twin absences in 1847; firstly, that of Halford who is Gilbert's correspondent and secondly that

---

[31]   Anne Brontë, *The Tenant of Wildfell Hall*, ed. Stevie Davies (London: Penguin, 1996), p. 397.

[32]   See Terry Castle, *Clarissa's Ciphers: Meaning and Disruption in Richardson's 'Clarissa'* (Ithaca, New York: Cornell University Press, 1982), p. 45.

of Helen who is fulfilling a social obligation. Her absence is rewritten into the text of 1847 by contrast with her presence in Gilbert's authorized reading of the diary in 1827.

The novel itself becomes an edited epistolary narrative when Gilbert narrates Helen's return to Grassdale to nurse Arthur Huntingdon in his last illness in 1827. The reception history of the letters reinforces some of the impressions of the narrative of inclusion from the earlier part of the novel. Gilbert communicates his hunger for details and copies letters brought by Lawrence in a style similar to that of epistolary heroines like Pamela and Evelina; these letters appear to have been preserved in his journal and then returned to Helen's brother as the recipient. In the final text of the letter to Halford, it thus appears that he is reinforcing both his qualifications as family chronicler and the provenance of the documents given in evidence.

Gilbert's actions construct a feminized role of exclusion and outsider status. Initially he differentiates clearly between his activity of 'inditing some business letters' (p. 419) and his mother and sister 'on household cares intent' (p. 419) in apparently casual allusion to Eve in *Paradise Lost*.[33] His attempt to maintain manly distance is undermined, however, when news of Helen's departure reaches him through the medium of the female gossip which has pressed Helen into offering him the diary in the first place. When he confronts Lawrence, the letter explaining her actions in leaving Wildfell Hall demonstrates that Helen has found an addressee in her brother. Gilbert snatches the letter and then offers to return it unread until Lawrence reluctantly permits him to 'read it if you like'. Gilbert then turns outward in 1847 to tell Halford 'I read it and so may you' (p. 421). Lawrence in turn authorizes Gilbert to keep this letter which entangles the chain of possession since Helen has not agreed to its transmission and nor can she as a married woman.

Gilbert, however, continues his project of reconstructing the fallen woman: 'she has never once mentioned me throughout – or made the most distant allusion to me; therefore there can be no impropriety or harm in it' (p. 430). Again he can turn aside to offer his provenance: 'And so I kept it; otherwise, Halford, you could never have become so thoroughly acquainted with its contents.' (p. 431) When the next letter arrives his actions appear to be cross-gendered. He takes Lawrence out to inspect his corn as a pretext for seeing the letter, but his language knits propriety and a feminine yearning when the letter is 'submit[ted] to my longing gaze' (p. 432).

The subsequent letters are translated by Gilbert for the purposes of record. Lawrence allows access rather than retention and the letters are appropriated and reclassified as attempted masculine discourse within Gilbert's diary: 'the most important passages were entered in my diary among the remarkable events of the day' (p. 439). He provides the actual text, however, of the letter which communicates Arthur's death, the death which will restore the propriety of his relationship with Helen. Starkly, in his role as editor, he allows it to end a chapter

---

[33] See note in *The Tenant of Wildfell Hall*, p. 530.

without further comment leaving just the bald confirmation of her real name in conjunction with an appeal for Lawrence's help and 'HELEN HUNTINGDON'. Despite this verbatim report, he claims to return the letter to Lawrence and then embarks on his gloomy analysis of their relative social states. He is excluded from further letters and later corresponds with Lawrence himself without any information passing between them about Helen.

This sequence of letters reproduced in Gilbert's journal represents further struggles with access and control which question Gilbert as a reader and family chronicler. His act of communication with Halford is a prelude to his presence on an annual visit and reminiscent of other epistolary narrators who write under unlikely circumstances such as Pamela on her imminent departure to her parents' home or Evelina to Berry Hill. [34] This use of a letter to restore friendly relations reproduces the distance which Helen imposed on her own narrative by handing Gilbert the diary to read in 1827. Gilbert is acting in feminine subservience to Halford as he did to Lawrence in maintaining communication with Helen during Arthur's illness.

The diary and the epistolary in *The Tenant of Wildfell Hall* act as narrative devices which give Gilbert the opportunity to introduce voices into his 180,000-word letter of excuse. He attempts to write immediacy into his story by appropriating the texts of a woman but the epistolary style which overlays other meanings on the lives of Pamela and Evelina allows the novel reader in 1848 access to un-narrated gaps in both textual transmission and in the intended message of the editor. Arthur's reading of the diary after he has spied on its composition reproduces the role of Mr B. in *Pamela* as unauthorized reader of a female-authored text and Gilbert is an editor for the nineteenth century seeking documentary authority in a new but recognizable social context. Like Pamela and Evelina justifying their entrances into higher society by marriage, Gilbert must make a case for his elevation as a man.

Where *Frankenstein* is a journal letter with a named addressee, but temporarily without a destination, *A Life for a Life* comprises two journals in search of addressees. The records of Dora and Max demonstrate connections between the diary and letter forms. Max begins his diary within the framework of hospital reporting which has been cut back by the peacetime relocation to an army camp. The first instalment of 'His Story' is linked with patient details and his article on gunshot wounds until he finds himself scribbling his name and debating 'the sort of circumstances under which people commit journals'. [35] His use of the word 'commit' is an early indicator of his own crime and of Craik's narrative dilemma in using the format to withhold the information about his act of murder. He must 'commit' his thoughts to paper and also 'commit' his time as he has committed the criminal act in his past. He immediately decides that his composition must have a title and recalls a 'Diary of a Physician' which is a storybook for which he has neither time

---

[34]   *Pamela*, p. 86; *Evelina*, p. 386.

[35]   Dinah Mulock Craik, *A Life for a Life* (New Edition, London: Hurst and Blackett, n.d), Chapter 2, p. 12.

nor inclination: 'Besides, all fictions grow tame compared to the realities of daily life' (Chapter 2, p. 13).[36] He is afraid that writing will bring back 'the old horror' (Chapter 3, p. 15), unidentified at this stage although he recognizes parallels with his consulting methods for patients. His second instalment nine days later emerges because he has no cases to write up. He receives 'the evening post – but only business letters ... I have no one to write to me – no one to write to' (Chapter 3, p. 16). Having previously designated his record a '*Hospital Memoranda*' (Chapter 2, p. 12), he invents an 'imaginary correspondent' for his journal.

That first entry which is already committed to the page is an involuntary one which retells part of Dora's account of the ball. In the second, evolution from the letter is demonstrated when his writing migrates from memorandum to article to journal: 'To begin at once in the received epistolary form' (Chapter 3, p. 17). His diary is a text with an unnamed addressee, that 'fond and faithful Nobody' (Chapter 6, p. 64) with whom he debates in the early part of the novel. Dora in 'her story' of course retains the female diarist's conceit that 'nobody will ever read this' (Chapter 1, p. 1). She later reiterates 'I ought, properly, to tear this leaf out, and begin again afresh. No, I will not. Nobody will ever see it, and it does no harm to any human being.' (Chapter 12, p. 112) The link between them through this 'Nobody' is established from the beginning. A female diarist, however, need not excuse her writing despite all the debate about continuing and potential discovery, and Dora has already accepted the therapeutic effects which make Max wary with her very first words about hating soldiers: 'I can't help writing it – it relieves my mind' (Chapter 1, p. 1).

The connection between the two diaries allows them to renarrate events, a factor which critics deplored in reviewing the novel on first publication.[37] It is, however, these potential connections which chart the migration towards more recognizable epistolary narrative. The journals are in correspondence as much as the letters and these links are also an element of Max's feminization as a diary-writer which is explored in his earliest involuntary entries. He cannot write an approved and manly memoir because this would spoil the plot but also because he is still not able to confront what he has done and needs Dora's approval to do so. The journal is thus an alternative to the more public acts of writing – letters and biography. The diarists not only share subject matter but also questions about the validity of their recording acts. Dora, for instance, accuses herself of 'scribbling such trivialities ... I shall give up my journal' (Chapter 10, p. 97) and almost immediately Max announces 'I had almost given up writing here' (Chapter 10, p. 98). Max reflects on his encounter with a soldier in the Crimea who ordered his journal letters addressed to an unknown woman to be burnt because he believed that he was dying. The name of the woman was visible in the conflagration and

---

[36]   This is an allusion to Samuel Warren, *Passages from the Diary of a Late Physician* serialized between 1830 and 1837 in *Blackwood's Edinburgh Magazine* and often reprinted in collected editions.

[37]   See Chapter 4, pp. 70–71, 77–8.

Urquhart had to bury it with the poker. Like Dora's mute desk, he says 'the fire and I told no tales' (Chapter 14, p. 123).

Initially, he follows this same course and when he recognizes that he has an addressee in Dora after all, his first letters are unsent. His journal becomes himself: 'the only record that will exist of the veritable me' (Chapter 14, p. 123), but he announces 'The form of Imaginary Correspondent I henceforward throw aside. I am perfectly aware of the person to whom and for whom I write; yet who, in all probability, will never read a single line' (Chapter 14, p. 123). He may still burn the letters but 'in the mean time, there shall be no name or superscription on them – no beginning or ending' (Chapter 14, p. 124). They will be encoded as 'mere statement' although occasionally he reverts to a discussion of his overall narrative which remains secret: 'There are some things I cannot explain, till the last letter, if ever I should come to write it' (Chapter 15, p. 139). Dora's illness while still writing her journal and nursing her father causes the couple to come together despite Max's scruple that he must offer his life in reparation for the life he took ; thus on New Year's Eve 1855: 'I am not young; my life is slipping away – my life which is *owed*' (Chapter 18, p. 186). His special entries for Christmas and New Year are dated journalizing though still unsent and he reflects Shore and other diarists when he writes, 'I have faith in anniversaries' (Chapter 18, p. 186). He is concerned that he writes 'strong words – dare I leave them for eyes that may, years hence, read this page' (Chapter 18, p. 182).

By Chapter 20, the letters are becoming physically separate from the diaries. Max describes his part in Colin Granton's proposal before Dora narrates her refusal of his offer of marriage and he again recalls the Crimean soldier with his packet of letters (Chapter 20, p. 200). Dora and Max become engaged soon afterwards and Dora narrates in her own diary the receipt of the first sent letter from Max which she preserves and records 'between the locked leaves of my journal' (Chapter 24, p. 223). Max, however, reintroduces the concept of an unsent letter in which he provides an account of his harrowing return to the site of the murder. There he discovers that he did indeed kill Dora's half brother whose family connections are recorded on his tombstone in Salisbury. Max starts out with the intention of non-sending when he begins to write the account of this discovery as a 'preventive measure' (Chapter 25, p. 232). He knows that he is a murderer but does not want to believe that Harry Johnston was the victim. At the beginning of the letter he tells Dora of her role as a non-reader: 'I trust we may burn it together, and that I may tell you its contents at accidental times, after the one principle fact has been communicated' (Chapter 25, p. 232). His search narrated within this letter destined for the unreading addressee is reported with chronological gaps indicated in the text by asterisks so that Max apparently reads the inscription on the tombstone in real time. The reader of the novel thus appears to know the outcome of Max's mission pior to Dora. She describes the reading occasion for this letter in her next journal entry where she indicates the need for writing the secret down: 'now his name is written, and I can tell it ... I write this down calmly now; but it was awful at the time' (Chapter 26, p. 249), the time when she received a letter which would otherwise have been burned. And with this she is released to mention Harry and to remember him as the brutal and spoilt son.

The fiction of potential destruction paradoxically allows the story to be told and this raises the question of its interaction with readers of the printed text. Can the letters be read because Dora is now permitted to read them and so has not married someone else?

Dora herself commissions what Urquhart describes as the last, probably, of those '"letters never sent" which may reach you one day' (Chapter 27, p. 257). She requests 'an accurate written record' of that day *'February 9th 1857'* when he confessed to Mr Johnston. This is separate from his 'ordinary' or 'Dominical letters' (Chapter 27, pp. 266–7) which the reader comes to understand he exchanges with Dora. Her first letter is not produced and the novel then plunges into the midst of their correspondence with the understanding that they are now in regular contact. Like the model letter-writers and like Evelina to Miss Mirvan, Dora must apologize 'If I write foolishly, and tell you all sorts of trivial things, perhaps some of them twice over, it is just because there is nothing else to tell' (Chapter 28, p. 267).

The most important event she must reassess in letter format is the discovery that her elder sister's long-standing fiancé has a child by a village girl. Her role as female correspondent in the nineteenth century requires her to be still, moated by her recovery from illness, and to provide Max with the information he needs to save Charteris. She can also offer herself as a copyist for his research on reformatories (Chapter 28, p. 272). When Max's trial is precipitated by rumours around the prison in Liverpool where he is working, this domestic task acts as a catalyst for her father's appearing in his defence. Although her letters have a performative agency, Dora herself must remain still at home as a dependant daughter and as an invalid.

A Life for a Life has not the timbre of an eighteenth-century epistolary novel, but the testamentary evidence of a nineteenth-century one. Letters are migrating and mutating in and out of the journal form, and women's writing is debated through both Max and Dora's reasons for writing. In the latter section, letters are edited and presented out of order, representing the recognition of novelists that the letters' meanings must be controlled and that the exhaustive presentation of epistolary evidence which Richardson advocated no longer has a place in the narrative matrix.

If letters act as substitutes for action by a female diarist, the male correspondent in Craik's novel can work and act in the wider world. As a substitute for the destructive and purgative fire proposed by Max's earlier encounter with the Crimean soldier, the couple discuss the potential destruction of their joint record, a packet tied up with a ribbon to be cast into the sea on their journey to Canada. The final chapter of *A Life for a Life*, however, proves that Dora is still writing her journal in which she can describe this proposed act. She no longer needs to write secretly to Max or for practical reasons of recordkeeping; having negotiated her diary's existence as spiritual guidance, she must now invoke the family chronicle diary tradition. Preservation either in person or at the bottom of the sea is regarded as equivalent to a family narrative, that private text which can be preserved by a female diarist since 'the record ... can never be lost' (Chapter 38, p. 358).

It has been suggested that the decline in the 'pure' epistolary novel was caused by nineteenth-century 'fascination with closure' as opposed to an eighteenth-century preoccupation with the creation of meaning.[38] The role of the diary as a document juxtaposing meaning with lack of closure is explored in Chapter 7. Nicola Watson observes that 'the epistolary would remain a surreptitious but troubling ghost in the fiction of the nineteenth-century.'[39] Critics were apparently troubled by that 'ghost' in emergent diary narrative throughout the century. This chapter contends that the application of the diary as fiction was an evolutionary process in which the established epistolary tradition was reinvented to open up the possibilities of personal narrative within the nineteenth-century novel.

The two forms of narrative are elided in *The Tenant of Wildfell Hall* and *A Life for a Life*. Late on in Craik's novel the addressee becomes a second and separate self. There is then an echo of both D'Israeli's definition of the diary as a conversation with oneself and Frances Burney's intention in the address to 'Nobody' of 'talking to the most intimate of friends'.[40] Dora seeks permission for letter-writing from her correspondent and future husband: 'I may write thus, Max, may I not? It is like talking to myself, talking to you.'[41]

---

[38]   MacArthur, *Extravagant Narratives*, pp. 15, 20.

[39]   Nicola J. Watson, *Revolution and the Form of the English Novel, 1790-1825: Intercepted Letters, Interrupted Seductions* (Oxford: Clarendon Press, 1994), p. 193.

[40]   Isaac D'Israeli, 'Diaries Moral, Historical and Critical', *Curiosities of Literature*, Vol. 2 (New edition London: Warne, 1881), p.206.; *Early Journals*, vol. 1, p. 1.

[41]   Craik, *A Life for a Life*, Chapter 34, p. 322.

Chapter 6
The Diary and Serial Narrative

The diary and the letter re-present fragments building into a life or narrative of the self. Many novels of the nineteenth century also existed as fragmented or unfolding narrative as part of their publication process. This chapter therefore investigates the intersection between the serialized novel and the serialized life characterized by the diary. In the process, women are discussed as both readers and writers of diary narrative.

The woman reader was identified in the nineteenth century with both periodical reading and diary writing. The concept of the serialized narrative can thus be analysed against the model of the woman's diary. This can be illustrated through a reconstruction of the reading experience of serialized diary narrative in two of Wilkie Collins's novels of the 1860s: *The Woman in White* which was serialized weekly in *All the Year Round* and *Armadale* serialized monthly in *The Cornhill Magazine*. This approach pays particular attention to the clashing chronologies of diary time and periodical time and also provides a commentary on the consumption of the miscellany which was part of the original periodical reading experience. Collins's last completed novel, *The Legacy of Cain*, was first published in a range of northern newspapers; it uses a double diary format and also offers a critique of women's reading.

The growth in the community of readers targeted by the periodical in the nineteenth century has been widely investigated. In 1957, Richard Altick's book *The English Common Reader* identified the social and economic factors which created this new readership. His survey established the parameters for all subsequent investigations of the 'mass reading public' armed with their 'literacy, leisure and a little pocket money'.[1] In 1993, Kate Flint, approached the specific issue of gender difference in nineteenth-century readers, addressing the 'discrete category' of the woman reader whose 'special characteristics, as well as her presumed needs and interests, affected the composition, distribution and marketing of literature'.[2]

In August 1858, Wilkie Collins himself attempted to assess the 'Unknown Public' in a leading article for *Household Words*. He presented the evidence of his own encounters with the penny journal as a would-be customer and used five of these weekly publications as a sample of the genre. He concluded with a mixture

---

[1]   Richard D. Altick, *The English Common Reader: A Social History of the Mass Reading Public, 1800–1900* (Chicago: University of Chicago Press, 1957; revised 1983), p. 306.

[2]   Kate Flint, *The Woman Reader 1837–1914* (Oxford: Clarendon Press, 1993; reprinted 2002), p. 13.

of wariness and excitement that 'the future of English fiction may rest with this Unknown Public which is now waiting to be taught the difference between a good book and a bad'. [3]

Collins wrote his article before he himself became a household name and there are elements in his approach to the subject of readerships which illuminate those novels of the 1860s which secured his success as a novelist. The 'public' was acknowledged specifically to include women who could speak for themselves in the correspondence columns of his sample journals: 'Married women who have committed little frailties consult the editor ... Ladies whose complexions are on the wane, and who wish to know the best artificial means of restoring them consult the editor.'[4] Men who consult the advice columns ask about personal and domestic issues such as the 'manly confidence' required to control blushing in the presence of a lady and the best method of removing corns. The editor or 'referee' metamorphoses into the required adviser: 'Now he is a father ... now a young lady's confidante ... now a lecturer on morals, and now an authority on cookery.'[5] Collins's tone is mocking but he is also an admirer of the penny journals' discovery of the new public, an audience of three million potential readers.[6] His article reflects on the composition of a fragmentary reading experience built into a whole and on the role of an editor who manipulates his own persona to produce readable and entertaining text.

The woman reader and the periodical reader have been widely researched since Altick's ground-breaking study.[7] It has been demonstrated that women's literary interests were firmly linked to the domestic arena by the publishers and marketers of periodical output and that the reading of the periodical was a feature of the fragmented and home-based life of the nineteenth-century woman. The woman reader is an identifiable commodity and her presence in the market is seen as both a restriction on subject matter and an opportunity to address a family audience. Thackeray's famous prospectus for *The Cornhill Magazine* in which *Armadale*

---

[3]   Wilkie Collins, 'The Unknown Public', *Household Words*, XVIII (21 August 1858): 222.

[4]   Ibid., p. 219.

[5]   Ibid.

[6]   Lorna Huett describes how a middle class audience for the journal is created by identifying one social group against another (Lorna Huett, 'Among the Unknown Public: *Household Words*, *All the Year Round* and the Mass-Market Weekly Periodical in the mid Nineteenth-century', *Victorian Periodicals Review*, 38/1 (Spring 2005): 61).

[7]   See for instance Louis James, 'The Trouble with Betsey: Periodicals and the Common Reader in mid Nineteenth-century England' in E.J. Shattock and Michael Wolff (eds), *The Victorian Periodical Press: Samplings and Soundings* (Leicester: Leicester University Press, 1982), pp. 349–66; Flint, *The Woman Reader*; Hilary Fraser, Stephanie Green, Judith Johnston, *Gender and the Victorian Periodical* (Cambridge: Cambridge University Press 2003) and Jennifer Phegley, *Educating the Proper Woman Reader: Victorian Family Literary Magazines and the Cultural Health of the Nation* (Columbus: Ohio State University Press, 2004).

was serialized insisted on the domestic scene of a family dinner: 'At our social table we shall suppose the ladies and children always present.'[8]

The woman reader was characterized as both voracious and leisured in the cultural codes of the nineteenth century but the reading of fragmented text within the periodical matched the domestic structure of time within the home.[9] Space for reading would thus be organized within, or snatched from, the domestic and wifely duties which were always her first priority. The absorption of periodical reading into daily routine which did not disrupt the schedule of the home meant that an opportunity for education could be authorized within the domestic context. This aligns periodical discourse with the moral management advice of the day. Wives were counselled by conduct books to acquire enough knowledge only to entertain their husbands and male guests and not to aspire to command a subject.[10] In terms of scientific knowledge, Sarah Stickney Ellis informed the 'Daughters of England,' 'Neither is it necessary that you should sacrifice any portion of your feminine delicacy by diving in too deep.'[11] She pointed out that there was no need to learn Greek and Hebrew to understand the Bible; it was more important to act out its precepts.[12]

Twentieth-century critics have also identified a specifically female response to reading the periodical. Margaret Beetham observes that the resistance to closure which characterized the serial publication encouraged an 'open' and so feminine reading. Other commentators regard the serial novel as presenting 'structures attuned to actual female experience'.[13] This sense of the 'open' entry and of the fragmented reading model relates clearly to the feminine practice of diary-writing. The periodical has thus been attributed with specifically female characteristics of both consumption and reception. Within the framework of domestic duty, the periodical both structured input and at the same time restrained the rate of consumption in its weekly or monthly appearance. Women were commercial targets for a publication which was at once a policing mechanism and an educative and philosophical tool for the time.

The diary and the periodical as forms of writing and reading practice shared an ability to be accommodated within the domestic space. The personal diary

---

[8]   Quoted in J. Don Vann, *Victorian Novels in Serial* (New York: Modern Language Association of America, 1985), p. 8.

[9]   See Fraser *et al.*, p. 48.

[10]   See Sarah Stickney Ellis, *The Women of England* (London: Fisher and Son, 1839), p. 163.

[11]   Ibid., p. 69.

[12]   Ibid., p .65.

[13]   Margaret Beetham, 'Open and Closed: the Periodical as a Published Genre', *Victorian Periodicals Review*, 22/3 (Fall 1989): 98; Linda K. Hughes and Michael Lund, 'Textual/sexual Pleasure and Serial Publication', in John O. Jordon and Robert L. Patten (eds), *Literature in the Marketplace: Nineteenth-Century British Publishing and Reading Practices* (Cambridge: Cambridge University Press, 1995; reprinted 2003), p. 147.

occupied a place in the regulation of nineteenth-century life. It had emerged from the record of household events into a personal record and from the account and examination of spiritual events into a shaped life.[14] It was written in fragments as the periodical or serial novel appeared to be and unfolded over a period of time. Crucially, the diary was, of course, authorized as a piece of writing by its immediacy and lack of retrospection whereas the periodical and particularly the serial novel was deconstructed for reintegration into a preordained whole. Charles Dickens used Wilkie Collins as an example of expertise in this writing format when writing to the novelist, Charles Lever.[15] Six years later, Dickens explained to a female correspondent and would-be author 'how patiently and expressly the thing has to be planned for presentation in these fragments, and yet for afterwards fusing together as an uninterrupted whole'.[16]

When Wilkie Collins turned to the woman's diary as a narrative device within the periodical in the 1860s, the woman's diary had become a publishable if not publish-worthy text. The common reader who could read newspaper reports of court cases and society scandal could also read the diaries of actual women.[17] As illustrated in Part 1, the personal diaries of real Victorian women became part of print culture with the publication of Burney's *Diary and Letters* between 1842 and 1846.[18] Charlotte Barrett as editor insists that these are private family documents with a detailed provenance but her 'Introduction' draws immediate attention to the dichotomy between the private life of Burney and her public fame. Barrett proposes 'a moral use' of Burney's example whilst insisting that 'fame and literary distinction', here revisited by the published text, were always secondary to 'the discharge of domestic duties'.[19]

The diaries of Frances Burney were largely composed in an earlier age but their publication presented her and her nineteenth-century editors with the dilemma of the marketplace. Her diary might draw its validity from a home-based narrative, but the act of editing for wider circulation demonstrated the permeability of the public/private boundary; a boundary exploited also by the periodical. The periodical itself represented a commercial arrangement, a commitment to purchase and to consume, its price often flagged on every page as in *Household Words* and *All*

---

[14]   See Chapter 1, pp. 9–10.

[15]   Letter to Charles Lever, 6 October 1860 (*The Letters of Charles Dickens*, ed. Graham Storey (12 vols, Oxford: Clarendon Press, 1965–2002), vol. 9, p. 321); the correspondence concerned *A Day's Ride* which was the serial due to succeed *The Woman in White* in *All the Year Round*.

[16]   Letter to Mrs Brookfield, 20 February 1866 (*The Letters of Charles Dickens*, vol. 11, p. 160).

[17]   See Kathryn Carter, 'The Cultural Work of Diaries in Mid-Century Victorian Britain', *Victorian Review*, 23/2 (Winter 1997): 251–67.

[18]   See Chapter 2. The diary of Samuel Pepys had first appeared in 1825 and that of John Evelyn in 1818.

[19]   *Diary and Letters of Madame D'Arblay* (7 vols, London: Colburn, 1842–1846), 'Editor's Introduction', vol. 1, pp. iv–v.

the Year Round. Although Dickens's periodicals did not, many others contained advertising and the promise of fashionable acquisitions. *Cassell's Magazine* and *The Graphic* which serialized Collins's novels of the 1870s contained a high proportion of illustrations, and the topical articles surrounding the serialized novel represented reading opportunities which brought the hearth into communication with the wider world.

Twentieth-century reinterpretations also stress the relationship between the text and the reader as consumer. Linda Hughes and Michael Lund describe the serial as 'a continuing story over an extended time with enforced interruptions' and Margaret Beetham observes that regular publication of the periodical 'both affirms the reader's place in a time-regulated society and promises that ... there will be another number'.[20] These definitions might apply equally to a diary and within the terms of periodical publication, the distinctive tropes of the diary model can be compared with the serialized novel. The first person cloistered narrator apparently provides unmediated, non-retrospective and therefore validated experience; the occasion and location for writing is itself dramatized; the physical shape and preservation of the diary become part of the diarist's evaluation of her life. The editor's actions in diary transmission allow the text to permeate the public/private boundary. In the novels, editing in *The Woman in White* is performed by Walter Hartright, although the diaries in *Armadale* and *The Legacy of Cain* offer no clue to their editorial reconstruction.

Looking at these conventions from the viewpoint of the periodical, it too is a dated work produced regularly and in portions. Anonymous contributors offer opinions at a fixed point in time, authorized by their deployment or selection as reviewers and article writers. In *All the Year Round* that authority is highlighted on every page by the dominant heading words 'conducted by Charles Dickens'. The periodical itself has both an ephemeral and memorial function. Its date apparently expires with acquisition but it will still build into a satisfying whole. It is an eagerly awaited production which could be deemed to be read simultaneously by a fixed community of readers acting as one.[21] That readership is implicated in the production firstly of an organic unit created by the reading of one issue and then of a linear construction linking the serial across multiple issues. This echoes the reading practice of the diary accommodated within domestic life.

Like the diary, a serial might bear the imprint of the writing situation or narrative occasion and Andrew Maunder concludes that the study of the periodical discloses 'a world of competing, as well as complementary, discourses'.[22] John Sutherland

---

[20] Linda K. Hughes and Michael Lund, *The Victorian Serial* (Charlottesville: University Press of Virginia, 1991), p. 1; Beetham, 'Open and Closed': 99.

[21] See Laurel Brake, *Print in Transition, 1850–1910: Studies in Media and Book History* (Basingstoke: Palgrave, 2001), p. 11.

[22] Andrew Maunder, '"Monitoring the Middle- Classes": Intertextuality and Ideology in Trollope's *Framley Parsonage* and *The Cornhill Magazine* 1859–60', *Victorian Periodicals Review*, 33/1 (Spring 1999): 45. This sense of competition echoes Duyfhuizen's competitive narrative matrix (Bernard Duyfhuizen, *Narratives of Transmission* (London: Associated University Presses, 1992) p. 123).

has traced Wilkie Collins's writing 'emergencies' and the amended time frame of *The Woman in White* which responded to contingencies of composition. At the time, Collins demonstrated his awareness of the competing discourses within his market when he commented rather testily in a letter to his publisher that 'readers are not critics who test an emotional book by the base rules of arithmetic'.[23] It has also been noted that the serial could be 'compromised by the mediation of its new productive frame' if audience feedback disrupted its linear progress.[24] Dickens thus wrote alternative endings for *Great Expectations*, and Collins himself reacted to complaints like those about Madgelan Vanstone's 'happy ending' in *No Name* by having Lydia Gwilt commit suicide in *Armadale*.

The diary and the periodical also share a sense of inferiority in cultural terms. The volume edition of a novel bound on the shelf is prioritized over the serialized version[25] as autobiography is over the diary. This emphasizes and reiterates the role of women as consumers. Miscellany reading is suited to women in the nineteenth century acquiring their knowledge in fragments just as diary writing is their chosen record because it can evolve and be authorized by dailiness. A creative tension, however, arises when these complementary discourses – reading a private diary within a published novel – are interrogated by the serial form. The following commentary attempts to recover some of that reading experience.

The fictional diary of a woman had first appeared in a periodical in 1712 when Addison introduced his readers to the diary of Clarinda.[26] *The Spectator* has been described as 'the greatest of the weeklies' with a circulation of over eleven thousand copies in 1712.[27] It was composed at least in part in the form of letters purporting to be from real correspondents. Women were brought into the sphere of the periodical through male exchanges of information within an educated gentlemanly frame. This first published female diarist predates Frances Burney by 130 years. In 1712, the 'frivolous' Clarinda submits to the editor of *The Spectator*

---

[23]   John Sutherland, 'Two Emergencies in the Writing of *The Woman in White*', *Yearbook of English Studies*, 7 (1977): 148–56 and Wilkie Collins, *The Woman in White*, ed. John Sutherland (Oxford: Oxford University Press, 1996; reissued 1998), pp. 662–702; *The Letters of Wilkie Collins*, ed. William Baker and William M. Clarke (2 vols, Basingstoke: Macmillan, 1999), vol. 1, 31 October 1860, p. 191.

[24]   Bill Bell, 'Fiction and the Marketplace: towards a study of the Victorian Serial' in Robin Myers and Michael Harris (eds), *Serials and their Readers 1620–1914* (Winchester: St Paul's Bibliographies, 1993), p. 128.

[25]   See Robert L. Patten, 'Dickens as Serial Author: A Case of Multiple Identities', in Laurel Brake, Bill Bell and David Finkelstein (eds), *Nineteenth-Century Media and the Construction of Identities* (Basingstoke: Palgrave, 2000), pp. 137–9 and Hughes and Lund, 'Textual/sexual Pleasures,' p. 144.

[26]   *The Spectator*, CCCXXIII (11 March 1712): 418–23; cited by Lorna Martens, *The Diary Novel* (Cambridge: Cambridge University Press, 1985), p. 67 as the first woman's fictional diary.

[27]   See J.M. Price, 'A Note on the Circulation of the London Press 1704–1714', *Historical Research*, 31 (November 1958): 219.

five days' worth of her newly begun diary. This is a 'response' to an essay the week before calling for diaries to be employed as an assessment of character and worth. The spoof is prefaced: 'My following correspondent is such a Journalist as I require ... Her Journal is only a picture of a life filled with a fashionable kind of Gaiety and Laziness.'[28]

The diary was preceded on 8 March by a review commenting favourably on the fourth book of *Paradise Lost*. [29] This was itself in serial following on from reviews of the other three books. The account of Milton's work contains particular references to the domestic felicity of Adam and Eve, the latter 'our general Mother' in Milton's phrase although clearly the outcome of the woman's role in the Garden of Eden would be anticipated. The position of another fallen woman is made public in the 10 March issue in a letter from 'Octavia' presented by Steele. This piece describes a woman who has been abandoned after a sham marriage.[30]

Against these two models, women in general and women in particular are inscribed for the consuming reader of the eighteenth-century daily periodical. The diary of the 'journalist' Clarinda is also presented in serial as a response to the mundane and prosaic diary of a man published the week before on 4 March.[31] Addison is assuming a correlation in the mind of his reader. The brief entries of the fictional male demonstrate his concern with eating, drinking and bemoaning the delay in payment of his annuity. Addison proposes on 4 March that a week's diary entries should provoke the review of a whole life and on 11 March he claims to have received 'accounts of many private lives cast into that form'. He declines, however, to publish the male authored responses which he has received from a 'sot' and a 'whoremaster'. He frames Clarinda as harmless in parallel with the diaries of men both published and unpublished. The reader might also, however, see her position within a wider interpretation of womanhood through both the biblical model of Eve and the contemporary social isolation of 'Octavia'.

In terms of the diary, Addison is suggesting in his juxtaposition or serialization of diary articles that the daily record is likely to be as prosaic or frivolous as the diarist. Additionally, *The Spectator* is itself a daily record. This earlier manifestation of the diary within periodical discourse demonstrates how a network of associated form and content builds up in the context of serial reading which has become a much more widespread practice by the 1860s. An investigation of the reading practices of these consumers can be undertaken through a reconstruction of novels narrated by diaries and in serial form. Categories of literary production interact with one another, and this was made possible by the print culture and society of the mid nineteenth century.

Wilkie Collins's first use of the female fictional diarist occurs in his two-part short story 'The Diary of Anne Rodway' published in *Household Words* in July 1856.

---

28 *The Spectator*, CCCXXIII (11 March 1712): 419.
29 *The Spectator*, CCCXXI (8 March 1712): 413.
30 *The Spectator*, CCCXXII (10 March 1712): 416–18.
31 *The Spectator*, CCCXVII (4 March 1712): 395–7.

In the same year, he also used 'Leah's Diary' as a framing device for the collected short stories *After Dark*.[32] These are the diaries of poor struggling women, Anne a seamstress and Leah the wife of a travelling portrait painter. Three years later, *The Woman in White* was narrated for nearly twelve of its forty instalments in the form of a diary by its unusual heroine, the sexually alluring but ugly Marian Halcombe. Like Anne Rodway the working woman, Marian is a detective. Crucially, however, and despite her equivocal appearance, Marian represents the middle class educated female readers of Dickens's target audience for his periodicals, writers of diaries and readers of nineteenth-century serial narrative.

The Woman in White was Collins's first novel to be published after his *Household Words* article on 'The Unknown Public' and the second novel serialized in *All the Year Round*. Its narrative method demonstrates that Collins has to some extent taken up the challenge of the penny journals which formed the basis for his earlier piece. In the article, he describes his sample publications with their 'miscellaneous contributions ... in the most orderly manner, arranged under separate heads, and cut up neatly into short paragraphs'.[33] In the novel, first person narrative is firstly supplied by the artist Walter Hartright acting as witness to a putative court inquest. Within this frame, however, Collins uses other devices such as reported narrative, dictated testimony, letters, an inscription on a tombstone, a death certificate and an extended extract from a woman's diary. This range of 'miscellaneous contributions' suggests the influence of those penny journals and the place of the diary in Collins's development of his novel technique.

In terms of the novel's publication, *The Woman in White* followed on immediately from the thirty one-part serialization of *A Tale of Two Cities*, in Dickens's terms occupying its 'station'. The first appearance of Collins's novel was significantly used to illustrate the boundaries and intentions of *All the Year Round* as a periodical. In his linking paragraph between the two serials, Dickens makes particular reference to the chronological implications of the appearance in the 'first place' within the periodical of 'a continuous original work of fiction, occupying about the same amount of time in its serial publication as that which is just completed'.[34] Dickens had himself chafed against the periodical format for *A Tale of Two Cities* when he wrote to Mary Howitt 'you can better perceive my design by seeing it all together, instead of reading it in what Carlyle ... calls "Teaspoons"'. He draws attention to the illusion of time created by serialization when he describes a serial in one of his later letters as 'a story nine or ten months

[32]   *Household Words*, CCCXXX–XXXI (19 and 26 July 1856); see Wilkie Collins, 'The Diary of Anne Rodway' in *Mad Monkton and Other Stories*, ed. Norman Page (Oxford: Oxford University Press, 1994), pp. 129–64; Wilkie Collins, *After Dark*, ed. W.A. Brockington (London: Gresham, n.d.).

[33]   Collins, 'The Unknown Public': 221.

[34]   *All the Year Round*, XXXI (26 November 1859): 95. Subsequent references in the text as *AYR*.

long'.[35] He appears to have trusted Collins with the responsibility of both 'fusing' the whole and leading *All the Year Round* for forty weeks. He wrote to Collins in January 1860 of the novel in proof, 'it grips the difficulties of the weekly portion and throws them in a masterly style'.[36]

The very first instalment of *The Woman in White* in serial thus carried the weighty burden of both fulfilling Dickens's plan for his new periodical, and of moving the reader on from Sydney Carton's speech at the guillotine. Collins describes his effort in completing the novel as 'solitary confinement under a female turnkey'[37] as if he is in prison like Carton, incarcerated by a regime composed of the novel, the periodical format and his readership. Carton's closing speech was both transplanted within the plot of *A Tale of Two Cities* and spoken within an historical recess more than sixty years distant from the reader of the 1859 serial. Collins's novel is firmly located in the near past of 1849–50 which positions it in a closer chronological relationship with the reader, allowing the later fluctuation of timescale between periodical publication and diary entry to be manipulated.

At the level of intradiegetic diary narration, 'The Narrative of Marian Halcombe. Taken from her diary' begins in the tenth instalment of *The Woman in White*. This was 28 January 1860 in periodical time and 7 November 1849 in diary time. The diary and the serialized novel interact in a number of ways. The validity of the diary as a published document is maintained by the immediate appearance in *All the Year Round* of a footnote punctiliously referencing a row of asterisks in the text. The footnote explains that the asterisks will indicate gaps or ellipses in the diary but the anonymous compiler also wishes, like Charlotte Barrett, to stress the authenticity of the text: 'The passages omitted, here, and elsewhere, in Miss Halcombe's Diary, are only those which bear no reference to Miss Fairlie or to any of the persons with which she is associated in these pages' (p. 163). The diary narrative closes because Marian succumbs to typhus on 6 July (or 21 April in periodical time).[38] She can no longer write the entries and the editor must physically intervene in parentheses to describe the text and the feeble blots which conclude it (pp. 342–3). The postscript by Fosco reading the diary on 7 July 1850 reminds the readers on 21 April 1860 that they are reading a private text whose violation is confirmed by the Count's sentimental praise and self-aggrandisement (pp. 343–4).

This final entry in number 52 of *All the Year Round* is not privileged within that instalment since Marian's record is not the closing text. It is in fact a brief entry with three sets of three asterisks denoting editorial gaps. Instead, the 1860

---

[35]   Letter to Mrs William Howitt, 28 August 1859, *The Letters of Charles Dickens,* vol. 9, p. 113; Letter to Mrs Brookfield, 24 January 1866, Ibid., p. 144.

[36]   Letter to Wilkie Collins, 7 January 1860, Ibid., p. 195.

[37]   Letter to Anne Procter, 23 July 1860 (*The Letters of Wilkie Collins*, vol 1, p. 183).

[38]   These dates were amended in the 1861 volume edition following the errors identified by E.S. Dallas (*The Woman in White*, pp. 662–3). References to the diary in this section use the dates from *AYL* and page references from Sutherland's Oxford edition.

reader would read the narrative of the feeble Marian rounded off by an anonymous editor who uses a footnote to postpone his explanation of the method by which the narratives have been assembled (p. 345). This editor then juxtaposes the actual words of the villainous but energetic Fosco with an account of Fosco's visit to Limmeridge House presented and apparently composed by Laura's uncle, Frederick Fairlie an effete, malingering hypochondriac. The original appearance of the diary thus incorporates elements of a biographer's editorial role. Collins allocates to a fictional character the type of commentary which Dickens himself makes within the periodical. This is a sophisticated manipulation of a range of reading conventions mediating the diary into a consumable text within a serialized fragmented work which is reinterpreted by an editor.

Diary and serial interact on a variety of levels. Within the plot of *The Woman in White*, chronology is vital. The development of the novel hinges on the date of Laura Glyde's departure from Blackwater Park and dating operates as a constant reminder of the progress of the story both in the life of Marian and in the life of the reader of the periodical. The accurate record of a date is one of the authorizing characteristics of a household diary, but that date eludes all three women who know it: Laura because she is substituted for Anne Catherick and taken to an asylum; Marian because she is dangerously ill; and the housekeeper Mrs Michelson because her household memoranda are unaccountably incomplete partly as a result of the disruption caused by illness. The women whose diaries might yield the information – Countess Fosco and the nurse Mrs Rubelle – are part of the Glyde/Fosco plot. The inability to fix any valid account produces a conflict. The diary's role as a vehicle for the truth presented as evidence loses its validity and is undermined or confused within a series of other dates supplied by letters, written accounts and the periodical itself. Frederick Fairlie protests, 'I am told to remember dates. Good heavens! I never did such a thing in my life – how am I to begin now' (p. 345).

Despite the dating insecurity, compounded later by the re-dated volume edition of *The Woman in White*, the periodical reader might experience time passing in life and in the diary, and would also have to account in her reading processes for the other items within an issue of *All the Year Round*. The diary model impacts firstly on the focused and controlled action of an instalment on a given day and secondly on the 'open' act of reading those 'miscellaneous contributions' which make up the whole issue of the periodical. A diary was authorized to accommodate the daily or trivial incident in a similar way.

On 24 March 1860, the periodical reader can read Marian's continuing diary entry for 4 July 1850 which opens issue 48 of *All the Year Round* and concludes: 'There will be a change tomorrow'. A week later for the periodical reader that diary continues with an entry for 5 July: 'The events of yesterday warned me to be ready, sooner or later, to meet the worst. To-day is not yet at an end; and the worst has come' (p. 293). In the interim, however, the serial reader has lived her own life. She may have reread Marian's diary looking for clues about the next episode. Assuming she was reading the issue in sequence, she could learn immediately in *All the Year Round* about 'Life in Danger' from drowning in the Serpentine (*AYR*, XLVIII (24 March 1860): 506). This would further reinforce the danger for Anne Catherick, Marian and Laura who have been walking near the lake in the instalment of *The Woman in White* just concluded. A poem called 'My Maid Marian' also features in this issue and becomes a threat to Marian and her sister by association. The poetic Marian's 'sweet eyes' are 'in dusty death now dim' (*AYR*, XLVIII (24 March 1860): 511–12).

The next instalment – having begun 'the worst has come' – concludes with Marian's ordering Laura to lock her door: 'It was a relief to me, as I walked away, to hear the key turned in the lock, and to know that the door was at her own command' (p. 308). This issue of *All the Year Round* includes a poem called 'The Caged Lark' as well as an article on 'Good Water' and another on 'Bedside Experiments' which reviews Florence Nightingale's *Notes on Nursing* (*AYR*, XLIX (31 March 1860): 537; 537–42). These miscellaneous texts would also enhance the reading experience of the serial. Marian will soon to be suffering from water-borne typhus while the doctors and Fosco squabble over her course of treatment.

The diary narrative also becomes embedded in an article entitled 'Vittoria Acorrombona' telling the story of John Webster's Jacobean play *The White Devil* which is a tragedy set in Italy about a murder which facilitates a wedding (*AYR*, XL (28 January 1860): 315). This follows Marian's closing line of the instalment: 'Has the day for the marriage been fixed in our absence?' (p. 181). 'Resuscitating Animals' (*AYR*, XLIII (18 February): 387) is printed just after the introduction of Fosco's white mice, and 'The Breath of Life' (*AYR*, XLVII (17 March): 484–8) is apparently advocating euthanasia a few pages after the reappearance of the hounded and mentally disturbed Anne Catherick.

The reading experience in so far as it can be reconstructed thus operated within the competitive discourses of the periodical. It may even have offered a vital clue to the outcome of the search for the missing date in *The Woman in White*. This is finally located in a daily record more primitive than Marian's diary. A cabman's day book proves that Laura was still alive after her apparent death certificate was signed. On 25 February 1860 (*All the Year Round*, XLIV), the fourteenth instalment of *The Woman in White* ends on page 411 in the middle of an attempt to coerce Laura into signing away her fortune. An article entitled 'Cab' on page 414 invites readers to take 'a more charitable view of the business and trials of cab driving'.

In the serial progress of his own career, Collins aspired to the greater respectability of writing in a monthly periodical. The consumption of fiction was a topic under discussion by reviewers of the serialized novel and Margaret Oliphant regarded Collins as performing with 'delicate care and laborious reticence' where other authors exploited '[t]he violent stimulant of weekly publication'.[39] When Collins's success with *The Woman in White* gave him the opportunity to write a

---

[39]   [Margaret Oliphant], 'Sensation Novels', *Blackwood's Edinburgh Magazine*, XCI (May 1862): 569.

monthly serial for *The Cornhill*, he grasped it with enthusiasm. He was paid the then unimaginable sum of £5,000 by George Smith and he refers exultantly to this in a letter to his mother Harriet Collins on 31 July 1861.[40] It was owing to Collins's contract with *All the Year Round* and a prolonged period of ill-health that this novel, his only *Cornhill* work, did not appear until four years after *The Woman in White*.

Between November 1864 and June 1866, *Armadale* was serialized in twenty monthly instalments. Again, Collins used the device of a woman's diary as narrative. This diarist was very different from the resourceful mannish spinster Marian. The flame-haired deceiver and bigamist, Lydia Gwilt offered other challenges to the readership of *The Cornhill* as an analysis of their reading experience will demonstrate.

The original circulation figures for *The Cornhill* were a publishing legend although many investigations of the records have followed.[41] The readership of the magazine was known to be family-oriented. Serial fiction was prioritized with two novels running per issue each with a significant illustration. The readers of *The Cornhill* have also attracted attention from contemporary critics who identify the particular construction of the female reader.[42] *The Cornhill* thus appears to have been designed to make a particular appeal based on Thackeray's first principle, and Collins and his publishers recognized a readership to be targeted.

Circulation was not particularly improved by Collins's novel. It was pushed to 41,000 by the first episode of *Armadale* in November 1864 but had fallen back to 39,000 by September 1865 and 32,000 by December 1867.[43] He never wrote for *The Cornhill* again. Besides the ostensibly commercial reasons of profit and loss for the periodical, there were also moral objections to the criminal activities depicted and to the sensation villainess treading in the footsteps of Lady Audley and Isabel Vane.[44] The access to such a woman's diary provoked a degree of outrage during the serialization. A bishop, who was nevertheless managing to read at an appropriate rate to consume the diary episodes, wrote in March 1866: 'Is it not marvellous that anybody could have conceived it possible for Miss Gwilt

---

[40]   Letter to Harriet Collins, 31 July 1861 (*The Letters of Wilkie Collins*, vol. 1, pp. 197–8).

[41]   See for instance Alvar Ellegård, 'The Readership of the Periodical Press in Mid-Victorian Britain', *Victorian Periodicals Review*, 13 (September 1971): 3–22 and John Sutherland, '*Cornhill*'s Sales and Payments: The First Decade', *Victorian Periodicals Review*, 19/3 (Fall 1986): 64–71.

[42]   See also Mark W. Turner, 'Gendered Issues: Intertextuality and *The Small House at Allington* in the *Cornhill Magazine,*' *Victorian Periodicals Review*, 26/4 (Winter 1993): 229) and Jennifer Phegley, *Educating the Proper Woman Reader*, p. 72.

[43]   Sutherland, '*Cornhill*: Sales and Payments': 107–8. This was partly the result of competing periodicals taking some of the original 110,000 readers who were reported to have read the *Cornhill*'s first issue in January 1860.

[44]   In Mary Elizabeth Braddon, *Lady Audley's Secret* (1861–62) and Mrs Henry [Ellen] Wood, *East Lynne* (1861).

to write such a journal? It is a comfort to think that she cannot go on much longer, and that almost the only doubt remaining is whether she is to poison or drown herself.'[45]

The reading of *The Cornhill* was a different experience from that of a weekly magazine. It concentrated on fiction and could therefore anticipate an audience attuned to the techniques by which a serial would unfold. The gaps in production and longer episodes offered both the opportunity to consume more but also to consume it in a more leisurely manner. Barbara Schmidt describes *The Cornhill* as 'a magazine to assist, inform and celebrate the rising middle-class ... to make the reader feel good for having purchased the magazine that met so many social and personal goals'. [46]

Within these parameters, *Armadale* was originally designated as the lead serial and when the novel began to be serialized it occupied this position with Elizabeth Gaskell's *Wives and Daughters* in second station. The employment of Collins was perhaps always a gamble and he had been contracted before the serialization of the novel which he wrote after *The Woman in White*. That serial, *No Name*, was published in *All the Year Round* in 1862 and attracted adverse criticism about the adventures of its heroine, an eighteen-year old girl disinherited and tainted with the residue of illegitimacy when her father dies on the way to make a new will. Andrew Vanstone has only just been able to marry Magdelan's mother following the death of his first wife who is a Bertha Rochester figure. Magdelan Vanstone adopts a series of disguises in order to recover her inheritance by marrying the repulsive legal heir but is finally rescued both from herself and from a life-threatening illness by a devoted older man. The reception of *Armadale* was thus generated within the construct of another major work of fiction also in serial and the novel was itself viewed within the serial production of Collins the novelist.

After eight instalments as lead serial in *The Cornhill* between November 1864 and June 1865, *Armadale* was moved to the second station. In July 1865, *Wives and Daughters* reassumed the lead position each month until its conclusion in January 1866 when it was replaced by Trollope's *The Claverings*. Elizabeth Gaskell had died in November 1865 without finishing the final instalment which was concluded by the *Cornhill* editor Frederick Greenwood. The very title of *Wives and Daughters* would have reinforced the appeal to a female readership. Additionally Gaskell's serial was described every month as 'An Everyday Story' emphasizing its place in the lives of women and almost a diary in itself. In a commercial sense, Gaskell never achieved the earning potential of Collins but the publisher George Smith may have been stating a return to his core audience

[45]   Bishop Thirlwall, *Letters to a Friend*, 3 March 1866 in Norman Page (ed.), *Wilkie Collins: The Critical Heritage* (London: Routledge and Kegan Paul, 1974), p. 146.

[46]   Barbara Quinn Schmidt, '*The Cornhill Magazine*: Celebrating Success', *Victorian Periodicals Review*, 32/3 (Fall 1999): 208, 205.

by re-prioritizing what would be her last novel.[47] Its move into first position may have been an attempt to restore the confidence of the public because of the outrage generated by *Armadale* and particularly by its audacious villains.

The extent to which the reading experiences of the two *Cornhill* serials in parallel or in sequence can be recuperated is limited but the impact of a commercial decision appears to have been the prioritization of a particular readership. The adjustment was made after the eighth instalment of *Armadale* which concluded by introducing in person the female villain. Her name – 'Miss Gwilt' – was its closing line which was then repeated in the opening line of the ninth instalment in second station for July 1865. Conversely, it could also be argued of course that concealing the diary and the serial within the 128 pages of the magazine ensured that it would be sought by its voracious readers and that *Wives and Daughters* would act literally as 'cover' for the less acceptable piece of reading.

The diary of Lydia Gwilt occupies five of the twenty monthly instalments of *Armadale*. The December 1865 instalment is a retrospective diary portion which appears while Lydia is writing to her former collaborator Mother Oldershaw and which concludes: 'my Diary says "Don't tell her" ... PS ... You will wonder at one or two other things, Mrs Oldershaw, before many weeks more are over your head and mine'.[48] Although the diary ostensibly withholds knowledge, the periodical has exposed it.

The instalment for January 1866 returns to omniscient narrative but February 1866 is narrated entirely by Lydia's diary. She explains in the opening entry dated '*July 28th, Monday night*' that it is 'my customary record of the events of the day' (p. 474) as if it is merely a domestic household record. By the end of this instalment, she has resolved to marry Ozias Midwinter for himself and on '*Sunday August 10th*', she concludes in spiritual diary tones, 'I have trampled my wickedness underfoot' (p. 504). There is a clear juxtaposition and dissonance between the domestically authorized diary and the character of the woman writing it.

The practice of miscellany reading is also at work. The instalment for February 1866 is followed in *The Cornhill* by an article about 'Catherine de Bourbon', a good woman with a questionable marriage which puts Lydia's decision as a bad woman into questionable context. The instalment is preceded by a diatribe from Matthew Arnold called 'My Countrymen': 'The trash which circulates here by the hundred thousand among our middle class has no readers in America: our rubbish is for home-consumption.'[49] This juxtaposition may in part represent an attempt to distance the editor from his author whilst satisfying the consuming readers of the next sensational episode.

---

[47]   Collins was paid £250 per instalment for *Armadale* and Gaskell £78 for *Wives and Daughters* (Sutherland, '*Cornhill*: Sales and Payments': 107).

[48]   Wilkie Collins, *Armadale*, ed. Catherine Peters (Oxford: Oxford University Press, 1989), p. 441.

[49]   Matthew Arnold, 'My Countrymen', *The Cornhill Magazine*, XIII (February 1866): 171.

The next instalment is entitled 'The Wedding Day' (March 1866) but actually comprises Bashwood Junior reporting the story of Lydia's criminal life to his father while the wedding takes place offstage in ironic counterpoint. It is here that Lydia marries Midwinter in his real name of Armadale. Despite her resolution to turn away from 'wickedness', this means that she can still claim later in the plot to be the widow of the wealthy Armadale as she originally schemed. The story moves on to the resumption of the diary in Naples where Lydia suffers from Midwinter's coldness and turns to her 'secret friend' once more. After entries for 10 to 13 October, the instalment concludes starkly 'Who knows!' as Allan Armadale 'blunders' – in Lydia's words – by joining his friend Midwinter and re-entering Lydia's clutches. When the instalment for April 1866 opens: 'Two days missed out of my Diary!' (p. 538), serial readers have been waiting a month. A later gap of twenty days in diary time within this instalment allows it to conclude with the dramatic appearance of 'Dr Downward' who is the subject of the opening illustration for the next instalment (May 1866). These gaps contribute to the plot but also to the sense of discord between the domestic text which is no longer daily and the increasingly evil intentions of its author.

'The Diary Broken Off' begins in April and continues into the May instalment alerting the reader to the timing of her release from this contradictory narrative. Lydia runs out of paper and must bid her diary farewell: 'I have reached the last morsel of space left on the last page; and whether I like it or not, I must close the book this time for good and all, when I close it tonight' (p. 600). In order to stress that the serial is no longer in tune with its villainess, the instalment does not run out of paper itself but continues with two chapters of 'Book the Last'. Midwinter arrives in London instead of Armadale and although he collapses when Lydia denies she is his wife, the instalment ends with his vow: 'She has denied her husband to-night ... She shall know her master tomorrow' (p. 616). The readers of the serial within the periodical would more readily have appreciated Lydia's taming by text. The article following on in this May issue of *The Cornhill* is entitled 'The Old Poets and the Seven Deadly Sins' and the wages of sin are paid in the next and final instalment of the novel.

If the fictional diaries of women which narrate the nineteenth-century novel are modelled on the diaries of real Victorian women, the appearance of a fictional diary on view to the public, bought in bookshops and at railway stations for 2d a week or a shilling a month, would offer an added dimension to the original reading experience of the periodicals' female audience. The handwritten diary, produced in the snatched moments between domestic tasks and household responsibilities, becomes a mass-produced commodity.

The periodicals themselves illustrated this clash of domestic and public, of pastoral and industrial. The very titles of the periodicals associated with Collins in the 1850s and 1860s draw up the boundaries. 'Household Words' which published 'The Diary of Ann Rodway', 'The Unknown Public' and five of the *After Dark* stories might appear to be a contribution to domestic economy as a household diary would be. The title is in reality a quotation from Henry V's speech before Agincourt, a call to nationhood and unity which Sarah Ellis would have condoned. 'All the Year Round' is also borrowed from Shakespeare but even more equivocally from a speech by Othello, a man defeated in the domestic rather than the public arena.

The Cornhill Magazine was famous for the pastoral symbols on its mass-produced cover, alluding nostalgically to less commercial days.[50] Thackeray might have insisted on the domestic scene of a family dinner but the periodical was nevertheless conscious of the need to maintain a progressive place in print culture. When George Smith contracted him to produce *Armadale*, Wilkie Collins was a marketable commodity because of his success with *The Woman in White*. The relocation of *Armadale* within *The Cornhill* may have been a response to the adverse critical feedback and falling sales but Collins returned to triumph with *The Moonstone* for *All the Year Round* in 1868.

Later novels by Collins also employ the diary as a narrative device within a serial. *The Moonstone* is partially narrated by the diary of Ezra Jennings and the diaries of both Penelope Betteredge and Miss Clack are acknowledged source material for other first-person narratives. Following on from the novels of the 1860s, Hester Dethridge's 'fragmentary journal' describes her 'separate and silent life' in *Man and Wife* (1870) and Lucilla Finch composes a diary during her interval of sight in *Poor Miss Finch* (1872). The diary letter of Sara Macallan is the final piece of evidence in *The Law and the Lady* (1875) although it is the diary of Eustace Macallan which is part of a court case re-narrated in the first-person by the heroine Valeria.[51] In 1888, Collins's last completed novel, *The Legacy of Cain*, returns to a style of complementary narration in the voices of a prison governor and two young women, Helena and Eunice Gracedieu. Although presumed to be sisters, one of the two is the daughter of an executed murderess and the novel attempts to explore the impact of heredity whilst withholding the identity of the tainted sister. The sisters' narrative is presented in the form of their diaries which compose half of the novel which was widely syndicated in newspapers in the north of England between 18 February and 7 July 1888.[52]

Mr. Gracedieu has made a present of lockable diaries to his two daughters and Eunice's first entry, rerecorded by Helena, recalls what he has told them: '[E]mploy yourselves in keeping a diary of the events of the day. It will be a useful record in many ways, and a good moral discipline for young girls.'[53] He forbids

---

[50]   See Gowan Dawson, '*The Cornhill Magazine* and Shilling Monthlies in mid Victorian Britain', in Geoffrey Cantor, Gowan Dawson, Richard Noakes and Jonathan R. Topham, *Science in the Nineteenth-century Periodical: Reading the Magazine of Nature* (Cambridge University Press: Cambridge, 2004), p. 124.

[51]   See further discussion of the 1870s novels in Chapter 8, pp. 145–9.

[52]   See Graham Law, 'Wilkie in the Weeklies: The Serialization and Syndication of Collins's Late Novels', *Victorian Periodicals Review*, 30/3 (Fall 1997): 252. He finds that '*Jezebel's Daughter* [1880] and *The Legacy of Cain* have very little to recommend them' (Law: 253).

[53]   Wilkie Collins, *The Legacy of Cain* (Stroud: Sutton, 1995; reprinted 2003), p. 43.

them to read novels and newspapers[54] but the diaries give them access to a form of self expression. In an extratextual sense, however, these diaries were already being experienced by their nineteenth-century readers in a commodified form since they become part of a novel presented in newspapers by overt commercial arrangement.

Within the plot of the novel, the family also becomes involved in newspaper reporting. Eunice, who is ultimately revealed to be the murderess's daughter, records that she has read about a photograph of the Venus de Medici in the local paper. When she views the photograph displayed in a stationer's window she finds that she has 'reason to be satisfied with [her] own figure' (p. 90). Her newspaper reading makes her conscious of herself in a way disapproved by the codes for women within which she has been brought up. Helena who is beautiful and manipulative but the daughter of a domestic paragon reads wicked French novels 'sympathetic with sin' (p. 116) and uses her unauthorized reading to devise a poisoning plot. Her diary is read in court to condemn her and her literary tastes: 'The horrid hardening of her moral sense had been accomplished by herself. In her diary, there has been found the confession of a secret course of reading' (p. 183). Collins was perhaps taking the opportunity to satirize those who had condemned his works for encouraging immorality.

The use of diary narrative within the serialized novel suggests one means by which a periodical might appeal to the woman reader. Wilkie Collins's use of the device fulfils other requirements of his novelistic intent but a reconstruction of the experience of reading *The Woman in White* and *Armadale* in periodical format creates a sense of potential reader response in the context of social and commercial imperatives.

If there is a quest for the woman reader through her diary-writing equivalent in these serialized novels, the fate of the diarists offers an equivocal commentary on the domestic fate of those readers. Lydia Gwilt substitutes herself for her husband Midwinter just as Midwinter has doubled for Armadale and dies by her own hand. Eunice Gracedieu stops writing a diary and marries the weak but eligible Philip Dunboyne. Helena Gracedieu, after only brief imprisonment despite the evidence of guilt in her diary, founds a 'rational religion' in the United States which is reported extravagantly in a newspaper as evidence of 'the mightier spirit of woman' (*The Legacy of Cain*, p. 326). Though Marian Halcombe's diary occupies a large portion of text, Walter Hartright collates it as just another document alongside the evidence of a housekeeper, an illiterate cook and a woman who lays out bodies.

In a periodical, the diary is also presented in a changed physical form as a public document interacting with other forms of printed matter such as articles, poems, reviews, scientific debate and advertisements. It is an illustration in itself of different forms of reading and of the creative tension produced by the consumption

---

[54]   Collins maintains this stance by making Mr Gracedieu a Minister in a strict Congregational church.

of the miscellany. It also introduces the sensation heroine or fallen woman into the house under cover of these intersecting sources of authorized domestic narrative.

This has implications. The periodical colludes in putting a private diary into a public space. It enacts a process of writing and reading for women in the nineteenth century. *All the Year Round* might be 'the story of our lives from year to year' and *The Cornhill* might offer domestic respectability but Lydia Gwilt and Marian Halcombe are not presented in the domestic roles of woman readers of the periodical. On the other hand, though women were unlikely to be bigamous forgers or victims of evil plots by Italian counts, they did write diaries.

The fictional diary thus bridged a gap between real life and periodical life. The diary and the periodical represent fragments becoming a whole, serial narrative building into a complete novel and appealing to the woman whose life accommodated the daily. Clashing chronologies allowed the narrative and the periodical to act and react both on the page and between issues or diary entries. Women's diaries for a female readership are not, however, given any priority in the serialized format. Although their records have been borrowed to reflect women's consumption and life patterns, both Marian and Lydia are subsumed into a safe and silent fictional life. The periodical reader has been an authorized reader of a private text, authorized by her role in a community experience created by periodical publication.

The diary and the family periodical may share a feminized inferiority as literary forms. The recreation of the reading experience of women in the 1860s, however, demonstrates that there are creative and ideological tensions between the unshaped non-retrospective daily entry of the diary and the shaped formalized fragment which is an instalment of the novel. The contradictory fragmented wholeness of the result was criticized by Dickens when he described Collins's narrative method in *The Woman in White* as 'dissective.'[55] In his review of the novel in *The Times*, however, E.S. Dallas reiterated the woman's role in accommodating those fragments. In mingled complaint and admiration, he observes: 'By a miracle of art, Miss Halcombe's diary exactly fits into all the little gaps of Mr Hartright's narrative.'[56] Having done her work in the rational approach to Collins's unknown public, Marian is made safe in her role as aunt and recategorized by Hartright as 'the good angel of our lives' (*The Woman in White*, p. 643).

---

[55]   Letter to Wilkie Collins, 7 January 1860 (*The Letters of Charles Dickens*, vol. 9, p. 194).

[56]   E.S. Dallas, *The Times* (30 October 1860); Page, p. 99.

Chapter 7
The Diary and the Documentary

The discussion of the epistolary form in Chapter 5 suggested that the role of the physical text is a significant factor in the presentation of the journal as a narrative device. Narratives of inclusion and transmission develop in parallel with the unfolding drama and tell their own tale in the competitive economy and evolution of the text. The physical existence of a letter or diary is thus a vital part of the action taking place, encompassing form and plot, asking questions about compilation and provenance and emphasizing the mimetic function of the fictional diary in a hybrid narrative.

This chapter examines the documentary life of the diary contributing to the narrative of the nineteenth-century novel. The diary as a material object is given performative agency within the novel. The narrative authority of the text and its trustworthiness – derived from both print and recording immediacy – cause the diary to become a counter in a hierarchy of documents. This can be illustrated through an analysis of the role of the diary in four novels from the latter half of the century which employ the documentary as narrative: *The Woman in White* (1860), *The Moonstone* (1868) and *The Legacy of Cain* (1888) by Wilkie Collins and Bram Stoker's *Dracula* (1897). The editorial process performed on the fictional diary becomes another version of narrative within the novel. This further level of narrative can be examined through a deconstruction of the diaries in *The Woman in White* and *Dracula*. This provides a sense of the editorial impact on the diary and the contribution of such interventions to the novel as a whole.

Returning to the diary model explored in Part 1, the main features of the diary as a piece of evidence are its confidentiality, its truthfulness, its dating and its record of passing events reinforced by the sense of a narrative occasion. The diary as a document derives some of its power from its assumed veracity and its role as evidence emerges from the immediacy with which it is believed to be composed: Richardson's 'writing to the moment' which admits it to the status of truth-telling text. In the hybrid narrative, the novel in turn organizes the diary within other recognizably 'real' formats which initially seek to give all the subsumed texts equivalence. *The Woman in White* is organized as an inquest and *The Moonstone* is a family chronicle using eye witness accounts to reconstruct Franklin Blake's own guilt in the crime of stealing the moonstone.

Dickens, as seen in Chapter 6, described *The Woman in White* as 'dissective' and any investigation of the documentary role of the diary must consider the seams which are visible when the story accumulates from its components. Other critics described the novel as a 'mosaic' and dubbed Collins 'a good constructor' with 'mechanical talent'.[1] The documents must, however, display their credentials in the real world in their attempt to present the truth. *The Saturday Review* deplored Collins's use of the footnotes of a 'veracious historian'[2] and all four novels under discussion adapt the characteristics of the real-life originals to present narratives which are intrinsically unlikely but are being passed off as true.

The use of real forms is one departure point for the modern novel which deploys letters and journals purporting to be real history. Ian Watt, writing his account of the rise of the novel suggests that documentary reality was part of the development of the genre, that 'the novel's realism does not reside in the kind of life it presents but in the way it presents it ... the genre itself works by exhaustive presentation rather than by elegant concentration'.[3] The society which developed this new mode of presentation demanded both veracity and verisimilitude within the evolving culture of print, and the nineteenth century saw increased access to, and reliance on, documents. In addition, as the exploration of the epistolary novel and the periodical has demonstrated, the private letter and the position of the female writer and reader of a circulating document were central to the novel's appeal.

Among the narrative choices which emerge is that of the novel using as its sources real events from court reporting and the newspaper.[4] Chapter 6 demonstrated how the interaction of serial narrative within the periodical format offers the reader a context for re-apprehending the action unfolding within a novel, fiction existing in close proximity to related and unrelated illustrations and to non-fictional parallels. The interaction of documents within nineteenth-century novels in volume format reproduces some of that proximity reflecting other reading experiences and encounters with print which are developing in the period.

In the earliest part of her narrative, Marian Halcombe's diary in *The Woman in White* is a vulnerable document even at Limmeridge House. When Walter writes to tell Marian that he believes that he has been followed, she writes like Dora in *A Life for a Life*: 'The merest accident might place it at the mercy of strangers. I may fall ill; I may die. Better to burn it at once, and have one anxiety the less' (p. 186).[5] She is echoing the traditional concerns about the diary being misunderstood which

---

[1]   *Saturday Review*, 25 August 1860 and *Nation,* 9 November 1865; Norman Page (ed.), *Wilkie Collins: The Critical Heritage* (London: Routledge and Kegan Paul, 1974), pp. 84, 123.

[2]   Page, p. 86.

[3]   Ian Watt *The Rise of the Novel* (London: Chatto and Windus, 1957; reprinted Pimlico: Random House, 2000, p. 11; p. 30).

[4]   Collins's use of the Lord Lytton case and others of wrongful incarceration in asylums is discussed by John Sutherland in his edition of *The Woman in White* (Wilkie Collins, *The Woman in White*, ed. John Sutherland (Oxford: Oxford University Press, 1996; reissued 1998), pp. xix–xi). Sandra Kemp describes sources for *The Moonstone* in her edition (Wilkie Collins, *The Moonstone*, ed. Sandra Kemp (London: Penguin, 1998), p. ix).

[5]   Dinah Mulock Craik, *A Life for a Life* (New Edition, London: Hurst and Blackett, n.d), Chapter 21, p. 203; see Chapter 4, p. 74.

have disturbed female diarists like Dora Johnston and Emily Shore. In *The Woman in White* this apparent commonplace becomes a matter of life and death.

Marian reads her journal to rediscover her part in arranging her sister's marriage and the security of the physical text becomes an obsession. When she returns from locking Laura's door, resolved on writing to Mr Kyrle the family lawyer for a second time, she notices 'some sheets of blotting paper, which had the impression on them of the closing lines of my writing in these pages, traced during the past night' (p. 309). These words have themselves escaped from the pages of the diary. The importance of documents as evidence to be used, manipulated or destroyed is a theme of the overall reconstruction. All forms of writing, mirrored, forged and inserted into gaps are vital to the chain of evidence which is *The Woman in White* with its 'juridical model of an inquest'.[6] Even the absence of writing must have its meaning unravelled like the blank substitute letter to Kyrle smuggled by Madame Fosco via Fanny the servant. After the letter is written noisily and handed over (p. 313; p. 316), Fanny visits Limmeridge and has tea with the Countess (p. 350). Kyrle is later concerned about the blank paper (p. 354). Fosco's much later narrative reveals how the girl was drugged 'with the assistance of chemical knowledge' (p. 618). Ultimately it is the space or absence in a church register where writing should be which betrays Sir Percival's secret.[7] Mrs Catherick's letter which explains how Sir Percival 'made an honest woman of his mother' (p. 544) by distorting the entries in the register fills this textual vacuum and circumvents bureaucracy.

The role of the diary as a document in *The Woman in White* is made suspect by the ability of other texts to contradict its assertions and apparently to confirm Laura's death. Following on from Mr Fairlie's reluctant narrative and that provided by the housekeeper, the novel is briefly narrated by the direct presentation of documents on a page: a death certificate, a statement from the woman who lays out 'Lady Glyde's' body, a dictated narrative from Fosco's cook, the legal documents which disperse Laura's inheritance and the tombstone.[8] Hartright's second and longest narrative will retell the story of their inclusion in the edited text which is the novel.

The actions of Walter Hartright, collator and controller of texts in *The Woman in White* parallel the editorial acts of the social climbing Gilbert Markham. Hartright describes his task as a means of presenting the truth in the equivalent of a legal case: 'As the Judge might once have heard it, so the Reader shall hear it now. No circumstance of importance ... shall be related on hearsay evidence' (p. 5). Some parts of his later account are clearly addressing accusations of the money motive

[6]   D.A. Miller, 'Cage aux Folles: Sensation and Gender in Wilkie Collins's *The Woman in White*', in Jeremy Hawthorn (ed.), *The Nineteenth Century British Novel* (London: Arnold, 1986), p. 102.

[7]   See Walter M. Kendrick, 'The Sensationalism of *The Woman in White*', in Lyn Pykett (ed.), *Wilkie Collins* (Basingstoke: Macmillan, 1998), p. 81.

[8]   See 'THE STORY CONTINUED IN SEVERAL NARRATIVES', pp. 407–14.

which he denies and it can be demonstrated that he is using a model of male writing, the autobiographical memoir to claim provenance for both his story and his place within society.[9]

Walter introduces Marian's diary as a piece of evidence in an apparently linear motion. A footnote explains that the presence of '***' in the text denotes 'passages omitted' which are 'only those which bear no reference to Miss Fairlie or to any of the persons with whom she is associated in these pages' (p. 163). The diary, indeed, begins with an ellipsis between the announcement of the date and the statement that: 'This morning, Mr Gilmore left us' (p. 163).

Despite this innocent progression, Walter's editorial tactics demand further analysis. For instance, Mr Gilmore's narrative occurs one fifth of the way into the novel as presented but is only supplied when he is already godfather to Walter's son and returns from his rest cure two pages before the end of the novel. Walter explains: '[H]e assisted the design of these pages, at my request, by writing the Narrative which appears early in the story under his name, and which, though first in order of precedence, was thus in order of time, the last that I received' (p. 641). After a long quest for a date and proof of a death, male social identity is reinforced by Gilmore's *post hoc* account of an inheritance, reinserted into the apparently non-retrospective, unfolding text.

This positioning is significant in terms of Walter's narratorial objectives. Marian's diary is presented as the designedly unmediated account of her struggle to save Laura, written at the time. Mr Gilmore is reflecting back more than three years and with the benefit of legal documents which have since been executed to bring about Laura's initial erasure and her ultimate inheritance. Gilmore arrives at Limmeridge in early November 1849 and young Walter is a year old in February 1853 when the narrative is composed (p. 641). The narrative of the tombstone included to dramatic effect just before Walter assumes his final narrative control is only physically recorded the day before, when Laura is restored to her position and the inscription is erased (p. 633). Laura, the blank text, is also physically recorded when she is made 'plainly visible to everyone in the room' (p. 635).[10]

The 'narrative of the conspiracy' which actually restores Laura to Limmeridge is a different account collated by Walter but not presented within the text on view. It protects Sir Percival's secret and only selected letters are used to prove that the dead woman cannot be Laura (p. 634). Mr Gilmore is needed to prove Walter's claims to social advancement and not Laura's. This is highlighted by Gilmore's assertion that this is a 'family story, of which my narrative forms a part' providing 'new links to the chain of events' (p. 128). Gilmore then closely echoes Walter's overall editorial statement when he describes Marian as narrator: 'It is not my business to relate ... imperfectly on hearsay evidence. The circumstances came

---

[9]   See for instance pp. 454 and 464–5. Shirley Stave aligns Walter with Sir Percival in the 'quest for social legitimacy' (Shirley A. Stave, 'The Perfect Murder: Patterns of Repetition and Doubling in Wilkie Collins's *The Woman in White*', *Dickens Studies Annual*, 25 (1996): 293–4).

[10]   John Sutherland provides a chronology in his edition (Appendix C, pp. 662–8).

within the personal experience of Miss Halcombe; and when her narrative succeeds mine, she describes them in every particular, exactly as they happened' (p. 148). The ongoing sense of the narrative occasion also echoes Walter's narratorial concern with 'these pages' which becomes frequent in the latter half of the novel. The settlement, however, is Gilmore's concern (and Walter's at that later point in time) 'before I, in my turn, lay down my pen and withdraw from the story' (p. 149). He concludes: 'Other pens than mine will describe the strange circumstances which are now shortly to follow ... No daughter of mine should have been married to any man alive under such a settlement as I was compelled to make for Laura Fairlie' (p.163). This was in turn the end of the *All the Year Round* instalment on 21st January 1860.

In the hierarchy of texts the diary has no power partly because of its private and subjective nature, and partly, the reader must suspect, because it is that of a woman no matter how brave and masculine she is. In addition, the date of Laura's departure from Blackwater Park, the most vital contribution to the proof of Fosco's substitution, is missing from it. This questions the very function of the diary if it cannot provide an accurate date which could have been supplied by a mere memorandum. What was missing was the diarist, too ill to continue with her routine and deprived of the diary by her own weakness. Lack of routine has also disrupted both Mr Dawson the physician's books and the housekeeping records at Blackwater Park, since Mrs Michelson 'made no memorandum at the time' (p. 365). It is a mechanical record rather than a personal text which finally fixes the missing date as 26 July 1850, one day after the death of Anne Catherick reported by the death certificate (p. 413). Walter questions the driver of the brougham ordered in Count Fosco's name and there 'the date was positively established by his master's order-book' (p. 631). The date is uncovered by perseverance and 'resolution' but documentary proof is finally supplied by an impersonal record, a 'diary' at a very primitive stage of development.

The diary is further devalued by the fact of its invasion by Fosco, a violation tantamount to rape. The text retains its documentary provenance because Fosco returns it as Arthur Huntingdon returns Helen's diary in *The Tenant of Wildfell Hall*. Fosco writes his own entry, apparently the last, in Marian's insecure journal: 'My strict sense of propriety restores it (by the hands of my wife) to its place on the writer's table' (p. 344). Fosco's invasion is prefaced by the words of an editor who apparently reports the facts, as Richardson does when intervening in the transmission or non-transmission of Pamela's letters. An ellipsis and a 'NOTE' report that Marian's entry degenerates into illegible fragments and is succeeded by 'a man's handwriting, large, bold, and firmly regular' (p. 343). Tamar Heller observes: 'The colonisation of Marian's voice is particularly villainous but it is only a more obvious version of Hartright's own strategy for containing Marian's narrative energy.'[11] This act alerts us to other violations which can be tracked through the narrative of assembly which occurs in Hartright's portions of the novel.

---

[11]   Tamar Heller, *Dead Secrets: Wilkie Collins and the Female Gothic* (New Haven: Yale University Press, 1992), p. 134.

Walter acknowledges that the diary was '[t]he first source of information to which I applied' in reconstructing the evidence (p. 444), but he also admits that Marian does not allow him to see the diary for the same reasons that Helen Huntingdon 'hastily tore a few leaves from the end' of hers: 'There were passages in this diary, relating to myself, which she thought it best that I should not see' (pp. 444–5). [12] Walter does not have the diary: 'she read to me from the manuscript, and I took the notes I wanted as she went on ... three nights were devoted to the purpose, and were enough to put me in possession of all that Marian could tell' (p. 445). This dismissive tone should also alert the reader to a mismatch between the diary read within the printed text – ellipses and all – and the edited version supplied by Marian. Walter has edited it and seemed to present it with his '***' but he is now claiming that he has only taken notes. Marian has offered him an edited version transmitted verbally which is her attempt to retain control of the unfolding narrative. Walter's aims as textual controller are better served, however, by the immediate and non-retrospective content of the real diary than those 'notes' which took only a few hours to transcribe. In the published sequence of *The Woman in White*, the reader appears to be reading the diary as Marian writes it which gives it the provenance needed to uphold Walter's case.

Walter tries to redress his social and textual exclusion on his return to the story where, instead of the confused narratives of others, he refers to 'the brief, plain, studiously simple abstract which I committed to writing for my own guidance and for the guidance of my legal adviser' (p. 422). [13] It should also be noted, however, that Marian has thwarted Walter's love during his tenure as drawing master either for reasons of loyalty to Mr Fairlie's deathbed wishes or to protect her sister from an improper or socially inferior attachment. There is a suggestion that she may want Walter or Laura for herself; she writes later of Laura's marriage to Sir Percival: 'Before another month is over our heads, she will be his Laura instead of mine!' (p. 187). Walter's editorial control may be his attempt to overcome that first rejection and tracing his use of Marian's diary uncovers the textual illusion.

The diary provides a text unable to contradict the documents which Kyrle cites as 'assertions' of Laura's death (pp. 450–51) and thus *The Woman in White* demonstrates the danger of documentary proof. The application of the diary as document revisits the circulating and re-circulating letters of the epistolary form. Despite all the evidence which can be reconstructed out of the documentary it is the date in a cabman's day book that is deemed to be the authority that restores Laura and Walter. Other contesting documents allow gaps to be filled in or discovered such as that in the marriage register, and finally the blank that is Laura. Bernard

---

[12]   Anne Brontë, *The Tenant of Wildfell Hall*, ed. Stevie Davies (London: Penguin, 1996), p. 129.

[13]   Christopher Kent suggests that Collins used his legal experience to fashion novels like *The Woman in White* and *The Mooonstone*; see Christopher A. Kent, 'Victorian Periodicals and the Constructing of Victorian Reality' in J. Don Vann and Rosemary T. Van Arsdel (eds), *Victorian Periodicals: A Guide to Research Volume 2* (New York: Modern Language Association of America, 1989), p. 7.

Duyfhuizen observes that 'Hartright intends the collective narrative to validate his wife's true identity and thus erase the forged text she has become through the fraudulent death certificate'.[14]

The status of the diary is more contained than first appears when it follows on innocently from Gilmore's narrative. Marian has edited it and Walter has rewritten and then edited what appears to be the original, which actually never leaves Marian. In the closing section of the novel when Walter takes the final initiative to deal with Fosco, he identifies Madame Fosco through 'familiarity with Marian's journal' (p. 599), echoing Fosco's own 'private familiarity with the nature of Marian's correspondence' (p. 620), a familiarity gained by deceit.

Since Marian's masculine actions cast Walter in an unfavourable light, she has to be contained as her body is contained at Blackwater Park and her diary contained within the masculine explanatory narrative. Although she offers her 'share in the risk and the danger too' (p.442) she conquers her 'weakness' for detecting through housework. Her permission for Walter's marriage to Laura is a withdrawal and re-narration of her earlier confident refusal. He rewards her by making her 'the good angel of our lives' (p. 643).

The role of women's diaries in the documentary control of *The Moonstone* is outside the linear progress of the narrative. Franklin Blake tells Gabriel Betteredge, author of the first narrative, that he and the chosen narrators are 'to write the story of the Moonstone as far as your own personal experience extends, and no further' (pp. 22–3). He tells Miss Clack, the second narrator 'to limit herself to her own individual experience of persons and events, as recorded in her diary. Later discoveries she will be good enough to leave to the pens of those persons who can write in the capacity of actual witnesses' (p. 247). She proposes to add in 'affectionate warnings' but is deterred by the cheque which Blake has sent her. She concludes with unconscious irony: 'I am not permitted to improve – I am condemned to narrate' (p. 208).

The old family servant Betteredge is heavily reliant on Daniel Defoe's *Robinson Crusoe* which he adopts as a *quasi* biblical text. Crusoe's story, of course, is partly narrated through a journal which Ian Watt describes as deriving from a 'book-keeping conscience'.[15] Betteredge also uses as a guide, however, the diary of his daughter Penelope with which he collaborates in order to fix his memories. She refuses to tell the story in person because 'her journal is for her own private eye' (p. 27) but she also advises on the structure of his narrative and helps with the summary which is required when telling the story day by day becomes too exhaustive (p. 61).

---

[14] Bernard Duyfhuizen, *Narratives of Transmission* (London: Associated University Presses, 1992), p. 128. See Kathryn Carter, 'The Cultural Work of Diaries in Mid-Century Victorian Britain', *Victorian Review* 23/2 (Winter 1997): 251–67 for the equivocal use of a non-fictional diary in a court case. See also Gwendolyn Macdonagh and Jonathan Smith, '"Fill Up All the Gaps": Narrative and Illegitimacy in *The Woman in White*', *Journal of Narrative Technique*, 26/3 (Fall, 1996): 274–91.

[15] Watt, p. 63.

When Betteredge's narrative gives way to that of Drusilla Clack, another woman's diary becomes part of the documentary structure. Unlike that of Penelope with its secrets, Miss Clack's diary has a spinsterly dailiness and is part of the night-time routine of folding her clothes learned from childhood. She uses her diary both to betray herself and to supply the narrative of Rachel Verinder's time in London which Blake needs. 'With my diary', she writes, 'the poor labourer ... is worthy of her hire' (p. 202). Miss Clack is a caricature of the spiritual diary writer and she is engaged in offstage correspondence with Blake about what she now knows in real time though she is 'cruelly limited to my actual experience' (p. 260) and 'condemned to narrate'.

Within Blake's own narrative, the servant Rosanna Spearman writes a long journal letter which he retains as evidence. He reproduces it in sequence but does not finish reading it in real time. The letter can only be read because she has failed in her effort to speak to him personally about the paint-stained nightgown which proves he has stolen the Moonstone. Like other female writers of diaries and letters, she is writing equivocally in the hope of destruction because the reality will be so much better: 'Who knows but I may have filled all these weary long pages of paper for nothing?' (p. 334). Blake, however, uses the letter 'to suggest for itself all that is here purposely left unsaid' (p. 335) and puts it unread into his pocket-book. He exonerates himself from her death and exploits the text she has left behind.

Finally, Ezra Jennings the laudanum-addicted doctor's assistant has a journal 'habitually kept' (p. 396) which is also extracted for Blake's purposes. Despite his background as a disappointed lover, it may be that Jennings's illness and unusual appearance set him apart as a feminized character and diarist who records as part of his response to a confined life: 'I turned to my Journal for relief, and wrote in it what is written here' (p. 429). The recreation of the night of the theft itself recreates Blake's assembly of the narrative that builds into the novel. Blake includes a letter from Mr Candy which accounts for the availability of Jennings's diary. In a reversal of Helen and Marian's acts of control it is itself a few pages torn from one of 'many locked volumes' (p. 460). *Pamela* is supplied as a book in the standard library in Blake's bedroom and the packet of diaries and letters which joins Ezra in his coffin is a gesture reminiscent of female diary writers' threatened concealment.

The Moonstone is fuelled by a sense of personal record which is part of the diary's impulse to write. Blake as editor is trying to exonerate himself from guilt and to narrate himself into a wife and fortune. The documentary reality of the task is reiterated on several occasions. Betteredge must use dates from Penelope's unread journal. Miss Clack punctuates her account with tags such as 'my diary informs me' (p. 202). The documentary illusion is maintained by footnotes like those of Walter Hartright and of Charlotte Barrett: 'Nothing will be added, altered, or removed ... not a line will be tampered with anywhere' (p. 202). Blake insists that the narratives will be preserved as 'genuine documents ... endorsed by the attestations of witnesses who can speak to the facts' (p. 202). Later on '[i]n the pages of Ezra Jennings, nothing is corrected, and nothing is forgotten' (p. 396).

With its allusion to fictional diarists and to diaries which act as offstage reference, *The Moonstone* is pervaded by the sources of the narrative. Betteredge reiterates his trust in the diarist of *Robinson Crusoe* against the evidence of Sergeant Cuff's detective methodology. Miss Clack is unreliable precisely because she has been educated as a spiritual diarist. Jennings offers just a fragment of his immense record which despite its scientific basis uses feminized recording techniques which might parallel the professional and personal records of Max Urquhart in *A Life for a Life*.[16] Rosanna finds an addressee to whom she is forced to write like Richardson's moated heroines, a letter she does not expect to be read unless she is already dead. The well-taught but shadowy Penelope offers documentary evidence but no words of her own like a Victorian embodiment of the Pamela of old.

The narrative methods of *The Woman in White* and *The Moonstone* attracted critical remark. Henry James, associating Collins's novels with Richardson's *Clarissa*, objected to 'diaries and letters and general ponderosity'. Trollope commented in his *Autobiography* published in 1883 that he could 'never lose the taste of the construction'.[17] Both were popular novels throughout the century and never out of print. It is therefore feasible that critics reading *Dracula* in 1897 should link the novels when the construction of Bram Stoker's novel was described in *Punch* as 'a rather tantalising and somewhat wearisome form of narration, whereof Wilkie Collins was a past-master'.[18] Although the female diarist Mina comes closest to acting as editor, the narrative approach in *Dracula* re-presents a set of co-ordinating documents without an apparent collator even in the outermost frame. [19]

Like Franklin Blake and like Walter Hartright, the Preface to *Dracula* insists:

> All needless matters have been eliminated, so that a history almost at variance with the possibilities of latter-day belief may stand forth as simple fact. There is throughout no statement of past things wherein memory may err, for all the records chosen are exactly contemporary, given from the standpoint and within the range of knowledge of those who made them. (p. 6)[20]

The novel's controlling consciousness is unidentified and the preface perfunctory compared with the carefully explanatory prefaces to *The Tenant of Wildfell Hall*

---

[16] It may also allude to another non-fictional narrative, Samuel Warren's *Passages from the Diary of a Late Physician* as indicated in Chapter 5, p. 97, n.36.

[17] *Nation*, 9 November 1865; Page, p. 122; *Autobiography* quoted by Page, p. 223.

[18] Quoted by Mark M. Hennelly Jr., 'Twice-Told Tales of Two Counts: *The Woman in White* and *Dracula*', *Wilkie Collins Society Journal*, 2 (1982): 29, note 2). The *Bookman* (August 1897) was more complimentary: 'Since Wilkie Collins left us we have had no tale of mystery so liberal in manner, and so closely woven. But ... the audacity and horror of *Dracula* are Mr Stoker's own' (Nina Auerbach and David J. Skal (eds), *Dracula The Norton Critical Edition* (New York: Norton, 1997), p. 366).

[19] See David Seed, 'The Narrative Method of *Dracula*', *Nineteenth Century Literature*, 40/1 (June 1985): 61–75.

[20] Bram Stoker, *Dracula*, ed. Maurice Hindle (London: Penguin, 1993).This is comparable with Blake's instructions in *The Moonstone*, pp. 22–3, 247.

and *The Woman in White*. It is then flatly contradicted by Jonathan Harker's last 'Note': 'we could hardly ask anyone, even did we wish to, to accept these as proofs of so wild a story' (p. 486). By 1897 when *Dracula* was published the documentary process has undergone a change in textual terms. The multiple narrators finally achieve the same viewpoint through typewriting but despite her control of the resulting papers the female diarist shares the domestic fate of Marian Halcombe forty years before.

Mina Harker and Van Helsing collate their information so that the narrative process is smoothed for the benefit of their readers, and Alison Case believes that they are competing with each other in this task. [21] The texts appear in an order which retells overlapping incidents in the first half but becomes linear in the second; dates but not events overlap during the converging journeys to Transylvania. The diaries are latterly aligned to the same goals. The only incident retold in the latter half is the episode of Mina's drinking Dracula's blood which Seward first dictates from his own experience, and then revisits later in the same entry by retelling Mina's account. [22]

People invade each other's accounts just as the Count takes possession of his victims. Mina pastes cuttings into her journal and removes pain from the phonograph recordings by typewriting them. Van Helsing records messages which Jonathan relays to Mina. Dr Seward records what Jonathan cannot bear to write about the Burial Service, and Van Helsing writes memoranda during the ride into Transylvania when Mina 'make no entry into her little diary' (p. 466). Repeated consultation of the pooled evidence provides clues and reminders of locations and, in default of action, Mina revisits what she has written until her memoranda of Dracula's whereabouts solidify the evidence. The narrative is often prosaic and deductive against the backdrop of the horror which it represents. Finally, however, Mina must resume her traditional role as exemplar and mother whom 'some men so loved ... that they did dare much for her sake' (p. 486).

The preface proposes a narrative order for *Dracula*, the telling of the truth, just as Walter Hartright offers his story 'told by more than one pen ... to present the truth always in its most direct and intelligible aspect'. [23] Jonathan Harker describes his diary, however, as 'horribly like the beginning of the Arabian Nights' (pp. 43–4) where a life depends on a tale, and this is echoed by his exclamation in Varna that 'this very script may be evidence to come between some of us and a rope' (p.430). [24] When added to the dailiness of diary entries, the recovery of dates from the phonograph and the papers relating to house purchases, the collation of

---

[21]   Alison Case, 'Tasting the Original Apple: Gender and the Struggle for Narrative Authority in *Dracula*', *Narrative*, 1/3 (1993): 230.

[22]   *Dracula*, pp. 362–4; 368–71.

[23]   *The Woman in White*, p. 5.

[24]   Scheherazade is often used in narrative theory as an example of a participative but absent and therefore intradiegetic-heterodiegetic narrator; see Shlomoth Rimmon-Kenan, *Narrative Fiction: Contemporary Poetics* (2nd edition, London: Routledge, 2002; reprinted, 2003), pp. 96–7. In the uncertainty of narrative authority in *Dracula*, Jonathan occupies most of the levels of narrator in turn along with many of the participants in the novel.

evidence accumulates documents which are beyond belief but must be obsessively reread to save Mina's soul. John Paul Riquelme concludes that 'the issue of the narration's reliability is bottomless' and he describes the last pages as the 'high point of indeterminacy'.[25]

The process of the transmission and collation of the physical texts making up *Dracula* is complex at both a documentary and psychological level. The untitled preface to the novel might almost be a description of the documentary process itself and the reader is alerted to the narrative of inclusion: 'How these papers have been placed in sequence will be made manifest in the reading of them' (p. 6). The competing texts appear in an order the reader later discovers has been supplied by Mina. She preserves on record both their mode of recording – such as shorthand or phonograph – and linguistic quirks such as Van Helsing's 'puddles' of English and Mr Swales's Yorkshire dialect. At one point the text presented on the page is a supplement to a sea captain's log which was found in a glass bottle on board the *Demeter*. This has been translated for a journalist by a government official and then pasted into her journal by Mina as Mina Murray so that she can 'understand the terrible events at Whitby' (p. 288) which her diary at the time was still struggling to fit into the pattern of an ordinary life.[26]

The various diaries are collated and accumulated into the overall text in a similar way – '[I]t does make a pretty good pile', Mina observes (p. 294) – although some process of normalization has to take place before this happens. Mina's own diary as a physical text has been redesignated to take on the task of narration although it was ostensibly intended only for Jonathan's gaze. She writes to Lucy in her first transcribed letter: 'I don't mean one of those two-pages-to-the-week-with-Sunday-squeezed-in-a-corner diaries but a sort of journal which I can write in whenever I feel inclined' (p. 74). In spite of her domestic goals, she is already considering the physical nature of a text and its separateness from mere household record.

Mina also writes to Lucy that the package originally made of Jonathan's 'foreign journal' is 'wrapped up in white paper, and tied with a little bit of pale blue ribbon which was round my neck, and sealed over the knot with sealing wax, and for my seal I used my wedding ring ... an outward and visible sign for us all our lives that we trusted each other' (p. 139). In the arena of competing texts this package is reminiscent of those planned by Dora at Urquhart's request or by Pamela under pressure from Mr B.[27] Mina's is a promise not to read Jonathan's journal, of course, as well as a means of providing uncontaminated evidence. He is uneasy about his encounter with the vampire women and Mina is in a disadvantaged position compared with the reader who has had access to the whole text. In *Dracula* issues

[25] John Paul Riquelme 'Doubling and Repetition/Realism and Closure in *Dracula*', in John Paul Riquelme (ed.), *Dracula Case Studies in Contemporary Criticism* (Boston: Bedford/St Martin, 2002), p. 569, p. 71.

[26] *The Dailygraph* articles are on pp. 109–14.

[27] *A Life for a Life*, Chapter 37, pp. 357–8; Samuel Richardson, *Pamela*, ed. Thomas Keymer and Alice Wakely (Oxford: Oxford University Press, 2001, p. 237.

of trust, authorized reading and the role of the audience cohere around the sharing of documents and their relative secrecy. The reader of the novel is often invited to consider the new readers who were not the original audience of the diaries but have become authorized by the nature of the quest. Mary Fitzgerald observes that '[t]he use to which Mina puts these letters and journals is not one that was foreseen at the moment of production, and it is usage which confers power'.[28]

Mina continues to write after she has been excluded by her femininity, and Jonathan justifies his entries at this time: 'I write all these things in my diary since my darling must not hear them now; but if it may be that she can see them again; they shall be ready' (p. 422). This authorizes the reading of the final published text at the same time as dangerously undervaluing Mina's role. There is a struggle going on for textual authority as there is in the earlier novels by Shelley, Brontë and Collins, and Van Helsing insists, 'Our hope now is in knowing all' (p. 367). In the documentary world of *Dracula*, this constant re-transcribing of evidence finally lends the papers equal status and appears to unite the hunters across racial and gender divides, although Alison Case concludes that 'the thematization of copying, transcribing and translating stresses the artificiality of that effect'.[29]

Documents which do not serve their purpose prove fatal such as the delayed telegram from Van Helsing which reaches Seward too late (p. 184). Two 'unopened' letters to Lucy also maintain their textual position even though they remain unread by the designed recipient (pp. 199, 204). They are available to be reread like that of Evelina's mother long delayed in Burney's novel. There is a constant need to be up to date, '[t]hen we shall be ready for other eyes if required' (p. 232). Facsimile and replication are the keys[30] and the very method of production and equalization is a constant source of discussion. The phonograph is described as 'a wonderful machine, but it is cruelly true' (p. 285) in the performativity of its narrative; its tones have to be neutralized by the act of typewriting. Mina tells Seward that 'the cylinders ... contained more than you intended me to know' but she has 'copied out the words on my typewriter, and none other need now hear your heart beat, as I did' (p. 286). This prepares the reader for the future devaluation of evidence which is caused by copying.

Mina's entry for '*30 October evening*' when the vampire hunters reach Galatz summarizes the process of keeping up with the evidence: 'I asked them to lie down for half an hour whilst I should enter everything up to the moment. I feel so

---

[28]   Mary Fitzgerald, 'Mina's Disclosure: Bram Stoker's *Dracula*', in Toni O'Brien Johnson and David Cain (eds), *Gender in Irish Writing* (Buckingham: Open University Press, 1991): p. 45.

[29]   Case: 239. Maurice Hindle writes that the court evidence approach 'appealed to the lawyer in Stoker' (*Dracula*, p. xxv). Stoker was called to the bar but, like Wilkie Collins, never practised.

[30]   As Jennifer Wicke points out, replication by 'manifold' itself replicates *Dracula's* method of producing vampires which are copies of the original (Jennifer Wicke, 'Vampiric Typewriting: *Dracula* and Its Media', *ELH*, 59/2 (Summer 1992): 476).

grateful to the man who invented the "Traveller's" typewriter ... I should have felt quite astray doing the work if I had to write with a pen' (p. 450). She is describing the mode of production and textual equalization. She also demonstrates the use of both everyday and new-fangled recording as a means of thwarting an ancient and corrupted regime. As in *The Woman in White*, however, it is another primitive record of the daily which helps them forward when the 'hieroglyphical entries in thick, half-obliterated pencil' in carrier Smollet's notebook (p. 336) reveal the whereabouts of Dracula's boxes in London.

Writing itself is claimed to be safe, scientific, empirical and truthful, and this is reinforced through the admission of diaries to the textual hierarchy of the nineteenth-century novel. It is notable, however, that by reimposing a hierarchy through nested narrative, by limiting Mina's access to events and trying to exclude her and her diary from the action so that she merely minutes their meetings, the vampire hunters find themselves failing in their quest to protect her. She initially learns typewriting as an extension of her wifely role but it is this skill which permits the equality and free flow of information. She and her diary are the living performed embodiment of the equality of texts.

In *Dracula*, however, words circulate like blood in the documents, and it is blood which changes the nature of the recipients or readers. Dracula himself values evidence when he destroys 'every scrap of paper' belonging to Jonathan (p. 60). In London, he also burns the phonograph cylinders but misses the copy in the safe (p. 367) which has been generated by the modern technique of 'manifold'. Despite the fact that this knowledge can be regenerated by the vampire hunters, it later loses its validity as external evidence. The diary as a form in *Dracula* resists closure and is set against items which contest its space; not just the other documents but also the plots of Shakespeare plays, fantasy tales and the theories of Cesare Lombroso.

The overall narrative structure endeavours to valorize daily life and set it against inexplicable occurrences. The lack of a controlling authority other than the anonymous preface suggests the border with a modernist approach and a loose note and a quotation from Van Helsing are its final texts. The mass-produced words are denigrated by Jonathan who writes that last 'note': 'in all the mass of material of which the record is composed, there is hardly one authentic document; nothing but a mass of typewriting' (p. 486). The era of mass production is disdained as inauthentic copying along with the strange story, and Mina replicates her diary's fate. Despite her editorial extradiegetic detective role within the collated tale, she is re-confined, like Marian, to the silent role of angel in the house.

Although *Dracula* was acknowledged at the time to have similarities with the style of Wilkie Collins's 1860s novels, Collins had also returned to his documentary style in his last completed novel serialized and published in 1888, less than ten years before Stoker's. *The Legacy of Cain* demonstrates other links with *Dracula* through its subject matter of degeneration and criminal heredity but it also presents directly within the text the diaries of two women.

The documents which make up *The Legacy of Cain* are easily deconstructed. A large part of the narrative is supplied by the unnamed Prison Governor who is the collator of evidence. About two fifths of the novel is presented in diary format, largely the diary of Helena Gracedieu. Her journal returns in the Third Period of the novel by which time her sister Eunice has given up the dangerous practice of diary-keeping. In addition, a small portion is narrated at a crucial time by the spinster companion Miss Jillgall until the Governor recovers from his gout. Letters from the two Dunboynes as well as the odious Mrs Tenbruggen are edited and abridged by the Governor who adds other layers of comment in addition to that provided by Helena.

This means of narration is designed specifically to confuse the issue of parentage. The minister Mr Gracedieu has adopted Eunice on the eve of her mother's hanging and his own wife has died when their daughter Helena was very young.[31] The First Period is composed by the Governor. He has written his account of the adoption of a female toddler who is daughter to a murderess 'at the request of a person who has claims on me that I must not disown'.[32] He claims discretion in naming people and places and is thus cautious in his narrative: 'Viewing my task by the light which later experience cast on it, I think I shall act wisely by exercising some control over the freedom of my pen' (p. 1). This is later echoed in the court's opinion of the entries in Helena's diary 'guardedly as some of them were written' (p. 311). When the Governor concludes his account of the events of 1858–59, he draws attention to his distance from the story in both time and place; this was after all a letter: 'My pen is laid aside, and my many pages of writing have been sent to their destination' (p. 40).

The Second Period is composed of a hundred pages of 'The Girls and their Journals' set in 1875. The diaries of Helena and Eunice are interlocking even embedded one within the other and this section closes with Eunice's nightmare vision of her murderous mother apparently encouraging her to kill the 'sister' who has stolen her fiancé. She concludes: 'I lock up this journal of misery' (p. 149). The now retired Governor takes up the narrative when he returns from a rest cure and visits the girls' ailing Minister father. He begins to suspect that Helena the apparent 'pattern of propriety' (p. 153) is actually the murderess's daughter touched with a 'hereditary taint'. The Governor has himself been alerted to the possibilities of the angel in the house actually being a devil from his own observations of Helena's real mother. On meeting her, he observes 'The lady's temper looked at me out of

---

[31]   Catherine Peters regards the unnoticed two-year gap in age between the two as absurd (Catherine Peters, *The King of Inventors: A Life of Wilkie Collins* (London: Minerva Press, 1991), p. 425). The novel is briefly discussed by Barbara Leckie in *Culture and Adultery: the Novel, the Newspaper, and the Law, 1857–1914* (Philadelphia: University of Pennsylvania Press, 1999) pp. 17–19 and by Piya Pal Lapinski, 'Chemical Seductions: Exoticism, Toxicology and the Female Poisoner in *Armadale* and *The Legacy of Cain*' in Maria K. Bachman, and Don Richard Cox (eds), *Reality's Dark Light: The Sensational Wilkie Collins* (Tennessee Studies in Literature, 41, Knoxville: University of Tennessee Press, 2003), pp. 120–21.

[32]   Wilkie Collins, *The Legacy of Cain* (Stroud: Alan Sutton Publishing, 1993; reprinted 2003), p. 1.

the lady's shifting eyes, and hid itself again in a moment' (p. 31). Mr Gracedieu, however, writes to him 'my household is irradiated by the presence of an angel' (p. 35). Apparently under orders, the Governor asks permission not to record the Minister's letter directly but to 'give only the substance of it in this place' (p. 151) so avoiding any reference to the girls' parentage.

In his continuation of the Second Period the Governor also re-edits a portfolio of letters which Helena produces to exonerate herself from blame in Eunice's illness. This produces a mini epistolary novel (pp. 209–17) which Helena has edited and the Governor extracted as 'necessary information to the present history of events' (p. 208). He proposes to 'present them here, to speak for themselves' (p. 208). He quotes, abridges and comments, however, and allows the correspondence to return to Helena. He also makes a memorandum of the reported response of her fiancé Philip's father to a letter reporting her conduct towards Eunice, and even reads the last known entry in Eunice's journal which is again locked as evidence.

This echoes the use of documents at a trial, and he also uses newspaper accounts of Helena's actual trial to abridge letters from Miss Jillgall. Her Miss Clackian deterioration in expression authorizes his use of the summary: 'I shall avoid presenting at a disadvantage a correspondent who has claims on my gratitude, if I give the substance only of what she wrote – assisted by the newspaper which she sent to me, while legal proceedings were in progress' (p. 309). The doctor's diary and pharmacist's records are quoted in evidence along with Helena's own diary where she has recorded the story of suspicion transferred by a poisoner to an innocent servant. The Governor observes primly: 'I expressed a wish to see what revelation of a depraved nature the entries in the diary might present ... At a fitter time, I may find an opportunity of alluding to the impression produced on me by the diary' (pp. 314–15). By means of the documentary assemblage of the novel, the reader has, of course, already gained access directly to this diary, but can now officially appreciate the significance of the poisoning plot in prompting Helena's actions.

The Legacy of Cain is thus constructed from a range of the traditional materials of a Collins novel: the diary of a poisoner, the letters of a spinster, the omniscient words of a sometimes conveniently absent narrative controller, the abridged and edited letters. We never discover the identity of the Governor's sponsor whom he cites at the end of the First Period, although the need for evidence aligns his task with the actions of Collins's previous editors, Hartright and Blake. In a documentary sense, the assembly is perhaps less proficient than Collins's earlier novels – this is his last completed work – but he returns significantly to the narrative device of the diary or diaries. Eunice's remains locked but available within the narrative in linear sequence; Helena's suffers the opposite fate when it is read in court, reread in newspaper reports, and read again by the Governor.

The Legacy of Cain dramatizes the actual use of the woman's diary as evidence not just its use internal to the novel. The presentation of evidence to support Hartright and Blake's cases in *The Woman in White* and *The Moonstone* was private and now becomes public. The transmission of the diary through

Helena's prosecution replicates its appearance within the novel, suggesting that the circulation of the diary as a document is now inevitable along with the belief in its truthfulness.[33] There is a sense of unease about *The Legacy of Cain* which derives in part from Collins's waning powers but the return to the woman's diary as a narrative device suggests that the agency of the documentary is still part of the reception of the novel in the last decade of the nineteenth century.

In their different ways, the four novels under discussion in this chapter protest the validity of the court reporting process. The performativity of the woman's diary as evidence proceeds from both the document and the diarist. The evidence of assembly is also a narrative which justifies the performance of the cloistered author. She has no other reason to write unless impelled by the need to tell the truth and to give testimony by narrative occasion which must now be submitted to the public gaze.

Ultimately, however, *Dracula* denies the potency and conquest of the written word. The diaries, newspapers, letters and wills which have fuelled the novel in its second century – and have been promoted by mass production and mass literacy – are copies which cannot be trusted. Reading, writing, editing and performing are still presented as dangerous activities for women. The trustworthiness has been lost in the typewriting and replication in which Marian and particularly Mina are plainly implicated.

The diaries of nineteenth-century women have a function as documents in public which undermines their existence as a private and personal record. At the documentary level, there are a number of layers of interpretation to be derived from immediacy, veracity, assembly and the print medium. In the nineteenth century, the growth in literacy, in printing and in bureaucracy brings varieties of public and private text into competition with one another. The novel narrated by diary permits both the performance of that ostensibly private narrative and an interrogation of its transmission as a competitive text.

The diary is thus a pivotal document as a physical object and as a medium for narrative. Not only must the novel account for its access to the woman's writing, but it must recount the editorial acts performed to bring that writing into public view. The woman's diary becomes an object which can be violated and manipulated within a novel professing to use its veracity and documentary provenance to tell the truth.

The diary as a document is moated, suspected, enclosed and replicated as evidence. Its survival becomes equivocal because it testifies to female performance on the narrative occasion and self-projection outside ideologically approved environments. Attention to the physical text and the compilation of documents – the 'pile' or packet – positions the diary as an object which can be contained within the structure of the novel and at the same time have an agency of its own.

---

[33]   See Kathryn Carter's account of the diary produced in a case of adultery (Carter: 259–61).

Chapter 8
The Diary and Sensation Fiction

The public appearance of a domestic record in print is one element of the sensation created by novels which are narrated through women's diaries. The diary as women's writing and as a realistic document contributes to the phenomenon of sensation through its lack of narrative authority and its subversion of domesticity. The woman's place as narrator through her diary causes gaps in language. Often the diarist also exhibits a compulsion to write equivalent to the diseased appetite of reading which sensation fiction is accused of feeding. The means of textual transmission is also a part of sensation; the possession of the diary equates to a violation of the woman herself.

Critics of sensation fiction drew attention to the ideological conflict between domestic settings and the criminal acts portrayed in the novels. In company with female authors such as Mary Elizabeth Braddon and Mrs Henry Wood, Wilkie Collins was credited as an originator of the genre. [1] Using the domestic text of a diary to enhance sensation effects, Collins exploits reactions to the genre by creating internal female authors. In this context, the acts of diary-writing presented in *The Woman in White* and *Armadale* can be re-examined along with diary narrative in Collins's later fiction leading up to *The Legacy of Cain* and finally to Bram Stoker's *Dracula*. Jonathan Loesberg observes that by 1870 sensation fiction had 'lost its definition and ... ceased to be controversial'.[2] Although sensation had itself been defused, the elements of its impact through diary narrative can still be traced through the latter years of the nineteenth century.

Sensation fiction was much discussed by reviewers. There are, however, five areas which highlight the diary in its sensational context namely: the clash between everyday and sensation, the lack of narrative authority, the power of consumption related to serial reading and writing, the gaps in recording language and the alternative commentary on domestic womanhood. These areas can be explored through the contemporary response to the novels as well as through the novels themselves.

---

[1]   For discussions of sensation fiction see Winifred Hughes, *The Maniac in the Cellar: Sensation Novels of the 1860s* (New Jersey: Princeton University Press, 1980), Patrick Brantlinger, 'What is "Sensational" about the Sensation Novel?' in Lyn Pykett (ed.), *Wilkie Collins* (Basingstoke: Macmillan, 1998), pp. 30–57 and Lyn Pykett, *The Sensation Novel: From 'The Woman in White' to 'The Moonstone'* (Plymouth: Northcote House Press, 1994).

[2]   Jonathan Loesberg, 'The Ideology of Narrative Form in Sensation Fiction', *Representations*, 13 (Winter 1986): 115.

The clash between everyday and sensation has its origin in the novel's claims to documentary realism. George Eliot laid down the Victorian realist *credo* in Chapter 17 of *Adam Bede*, her first full length novel published in 1859. It was at this time that sensation began to make its mark on print culture not only through fiction but through the review articles which defined it. Although Eliot's own novels, with the exception of *Daniel Deronda*, were situated in a completed past whose lessons could be learned and preached, she was also influenced by the genre. An article reviewing *Felix Holt* observed that Lady Audley and Mrs Transome were 'true twin-sisters of fiction' and *Daniel Deronda* also illustrates elements of sensation.[3] *Adam Bede*, however, stresses the significance of an omniscient and trustworthy moral perspective, of life presented like 'Dutch paintings'.[4] Instead of that safe narrative distance and confiding narrative voice, sensation fiction introduced present immediacy and responded to local demands. In 1865, Henry James announced: 'To Mr Collins belongs the credit of having introduced into fiction those most mysterious of mysteries, the mysteries which are at our own door.'[5] Mystery and proximity became the issues that reviewers such as Margaret Oliphant and Henry Mansel deplored when they denounced sensation fiction as a dangerous cultural phenomenon, depicting crime in a domestic modern setting.[6] The private diary might be a real and familiar form with a domestic application like a 'Dutch painting' but the publication of the edited private document partook of sensation, what Mansel termed the 'Newspaper Novel'.[7]

It is the recognition of modern life in sensation fiction that makes the novels unfit for polite reading and discussion. Elaine Showalter points out that 'murder was made modern and suburban, with villas and railways replacing dungeons and tumbrels' and Winifred Hughes describes the sensation novel as an 'antidote to ... respectability' with its 'unsettling distortions and juxtapositions of material ... drawn from the context of modern urban experience'.[8] The place for bigamy, fraud

---

[3]   *Contemporary Review*, V (June 1867): 178–9. Eliot and sensation is discussed in Ann Cvetkovich, *Mixed Feelings Feminism, Mass Culture and Victorian Sensationalism* (New Bruswick New Jersey: Rutgers University Press, 1992), pp. 128–32 and Marlene Tromp, *The Private Rod: Marital Violence, Sensation, and the Law in Victorian Britain* (Charlottesville, VA: University of Virginia Press, 2000), pp. 200–24.

[4]   George Eliot, *Adam Bede*, ed. Stephen Gill (London: Penguin, 1980; reprinted 1985), p. 223.

[5]   *Nation*, (9 November 1865); Norman Page (ed.), *Wilkie Collins: The Critical Heritage* (London: Routledge and Kegan Paul, 1974), p. 122.

[6]   See [Margaret Oliphant], 'Sensation Novels', *Blackwood's Edinburgh Magazine*, XCI (May 1862): 564–84, 'Novels', *Blackwood's Edinburgh Magazine*, XCIV (August 1863): 168–83 and 'Novels', *Blackwood's Edinburgh Magazine*, CII (September 1867): 257–80; [Henry Mansel], 'Sensation Novels', *Quarterly Review*, CXIII (1863): 481–514.

[7]   Mansel, p. 501; see also Thomas F. Boyle, 'Fishy Extremities': Subversion of Orthodoxy in the Victorian Sensation Novel', *Literature and History*, 9/1 (Spring 1983): 93.

[8]   Elaine Showalter, 'Desperate Remedies: Sensation Novels of the 1860s', *Victorian Newsletter*, 49 (Spring 1976): 2; Hughes, pp. 36, 53.

and murder is a continental past and Mansel fears the sensation novel as 'a tale of our own times' will expose the Lady Audleys and Count Foscos in their midst for '[p]roximity is, indeed, one great element of sensation'. Lady Audley would be safe as the 'White Devil' of European history; Mansel does not want to suspect she is his next door neighbour.[9]

A second element of sensation to which the diary contributes is the lack of narrative authority. The diary ostensibly represents an everyday recording device but its use as a voice within the novel undermines the narrative authority which critics were seeking from novels in the mid nineteenth century. This departure is signalled and exploited in earlier forms of the novel such as epistolary fiction. As indicated in Chapter 5, Samuel Richardson struggled with the (mis)interpretations of his heroines arising from the reading experience of their letters in print and through the juxtaposition of those letters with other narrative voices.

Some novelists of the nineteenth century used extradiegetic interventions in an attempt to fix meaning. The implied author in Anthony Trollope's *Barchester Towers*, for instance, insists that dubious meanings will not arise from the progress of this novel. At the end of Chapter 15 a new narrative voice denies the potential for any sensational effects by assuring the reader that there are no secrets and that the experience of reading the novel will not produce any shock or violation of principle. 'Our doctrine is, that the author and the reader should move along together in full confidence with each other,' he explains. The characters may be part of a 'comedy of errors ... but let the spectator never mistake the Syracusan for the Ephesian; otherwise he is one of the dupes, and the part of the dupe is never dignified'.[10] This unnamed voice offers opinions which are meant to be trusted and morally sound. The role of the reader is to look on and to be 'dignified' unlike the duped reader of the detective story or the diseased consumer of weekly episodes.[11]

Henry Mansel's *Quarterly Review* article accuses sensation authors of misusing this narrative authority.[12] Where narrative structure and authorial intervention are considered in the sensation context, they are linked with the concept of 'non-seriousness' and lack of trust. In the novel of sensation, form, content and means of

---

[9]   Mansel, p. 488. Part of the diary narrative of *The Woman in White* was embedded in a serialization of the story of the 'White Devil' in *All the Year Round* (see Chapter 6, p. 111).

[10]   Anthony Trollope, *Barchester Towers* ed. Robin Gilmour (London: Penguin, 1982; reprinted 1994), p. 127. This is his second Barchester Chronicle, published in 1857 and roughly contemporary with both Craik's *A Life for a Life* and Collins's novels of the early 1860s.

[11]   Collins's novel *No Name* which followed after *The Woman in White* defused some element of the secret of the Vanstone sisters' illegitimacy in the early chapters and seems to allude to such a practice. Collins explained this at some length in the preface to the volume edition. (Wilkie Collins, *No Name*, ed. Mark Ford (London: Penguin, 1994), pp. xxi-xxii.) *No Name* is the Collins novel included in Mansel's discussion of sensation in *The Quarterly Review* (Mansel: p. 496).

[12]   Mansel, p. 482.

production are all means of subversion. Authorial control on Victorian realist moral principles should ensure that lessons can be taught. Ironically, however, the use of realistic devices 'writing to the moment' such as diaries and letters undermines the authority of factual material. Lyn Pykett discusses 'the dispersal of narrative authority' which occurs also in *Bleak House* and *Great Expectations*.[13] Narrative gaps open up; alternative, dangerously seductive viewpoints are presented.

Contemporary critics also decried the influence of appetite on the production and consumption of sensation fiction. In her first article on the subject, Margaret Oliphant criticized the 'violent stimulant of serial publication' and wrote in 1863 that 'variety demands the frequent production of a sensational monster to stimulate the languid life'. Mansel describes the novels as 'called into existence to supply the cravings of a diseased appetite ... to stimulate the want which they supply'.[14] Mansel too blames the reader for demanding novels in forms such as the periodical, the volume in the circulating library and the 'railway novel'.[15] Oliphant's objection to weekly publication interacts with the diary's narrative role in forwarding a plot within a serial. The forward movement and anticipation of the next day's entry is a feature of sensation reading exacerbated by the gap between consumption and anticipation.[16]

The genre of sensation also provided an alternative commentary on domestic womanhood. Novels are seen to subvert the domestic space and articulate a revolt by women against their ideologically constructed image. New and disturbing secrets emerge beyond those of the text and the interrogation of cultural norms is not made safe by the traditional ending. In *A Literature of Their Own*, Elaine Showalter describes 'golden-haired killers whose actions are a sardonic commentary on the real feelings of the Angel in the House'. Showalter parallels criminal secrets with the domestic ones which concern the subversion of home life and the roles defined by it, and Winifred Hughes points up this subversion by putting her 'maniac in the cellar'.[17]

Oliphant specifically draws attention to the duplicity of the woman reader by presenting a metafictional moral conundrum. The reader of sensation fiction will herself become its subject because she will not be able to speak freely of her reading matter and so, like the fictional Lady Audleys, will have a secret, perhaps a 'second self': 'We should no longer be able to discuss, as we do now

---

[13]   Pykett, *The Sensation Novel*, p. 38. See also Hughes, p. 24 and Brantlinger, p. 31.

[14]   Oliphant, 'Sensation Novels': 569; 'Novels' (1863): 168; Mansel, p. 483.

[15]   Mansel, pp. 484–6. See Nicholas Daly, 'Railway Novels: Sensation Fiction and the Modernization of the Senses', *ELH*, 66/2 (Summer 1999): 461–87.

[16]   Susan David Bernstein discusses sensation in the context of Victorian anthropological interest in the primitive and in appetites stimulated by increased consumerism (Susan David Bernstein, 'Dirty reading: sensation fiction, women, and primitivism', *Criticism*, 36/2 (Spring 1994): 235–6).

[17]   Elaine Showalter, *A Literature of Their Own: British Women Novelists from Brontë to Lessing* (London: Virago, revised edition 1982), p. 28, p. 158). See also Boyle, pp. 92–6.

continually, the books that we are reading and the thoughts we are thinking'.[18] Sensation is also regarded as ideologically suspect and subversive because the 'golden-haired killers' are manipulating their ideological position in order to complete their criminal tasks. The appropriation of a feminine form like a diary adds to the potential for 'maniacs in the cellar.' The use of the diary as a household recording device, travel record or family chronicle emphasizes the possibility that 'the mysteries at our own door' and the concealment of criminality are unfolding within otherwise trivial and daily writing. The act of rereading the resulting plot for oneself in a diary or as a novel reader is itself a further indication of consumer passions.

Lyn Pykett concludes that sensation is constructed through 'narrative concealment and delay or deferral'.[19] The appetite for the novel is influenced by an absence or lack of language and in this, the diary would seem to offer the perfect vehicle for deferred stimulus and constructed anticipation. Sensation is built from the diarist's choice of subject, the absence of language, the suppression of voices and the dubious authority of the text. A consequence of what Pykett terms the 'multi-voiced narrative'[20] without narrative control was a gap in expression into which the consuming reader could insert her own interpretation. Plot gaps between documents and letters, language gaps in the expression of experience in a diary and even the commentary of an editor with the ellipses which indicated his presence would allow sensational events to be imagined and in a sense narrated by the reader through her own experience of the genre. Within the context of these five elements of sensation, the diary offers distortions of narrative authority, gaps in language and expression, and a serial appetite for reading and writing. The ideological discrepancies of the woman's diary of the nineteenth century emphasize the ideological questions raised by sensation in its presentation of alternative domestic womanhood.

Contemporary critics were uncomfortable with Wilkie Collins's use of the diary as a storytelling device. *The Dublin University Magazine* complained of *The Woman in White*: 'Had the story been wrought out in the old-fashioned way it could have been told far more effectively and in less space.'[21] Of *Armadale*, *The Saturday Review* observed:

> Considering how much Miss Gwilt tells us of herself, and the length to which she prolongs her diary and her correspondence, it is singular how indistinct is the image she leaves upon the mind at the end, except that she is wicked and audacious, and that she has got very red hair.[22]

---

[18] Oliphant, 'Novels', (1867), p. 258.

[19] Pykett, *The Sensation Novel*, p. 4.

[20] Lyn Pykett describes Collins's novels as 'fragmented, multi-voiced narratives' (Pykett, *The Sensation Novel*, p. 14).

[21] *Dublin University Magazine* (February 1861); Page, p. 107.

[22] *Saturday Review*, (16 June 1866); Page, p. 152.

The use of women's diaries is a regular occurrence in Wilkie Collins's fiction including these substantial diary narratives.[23]

Collins, of course, brought with him to the work of novelist the training of a lawyer reliant on documents. His first complete work of literature was the *Memoir* of his father which used letters and journals in its construction.[24] William Collins attempted to shape the record of his life in preparation for his son's publication and indeed authorizes it in an entry for the New Year, that traditional turning point for addressing a diary anew: 'As I think it quite possible that my dear son, William Wilkie Collins, may be tempted ... to furnish the world with a memoir of my life, I purpose occasionally noting down some circumstances as leading points, which may be useful.'[25] This entry suggests a means of transforming an unfolding record into a coherent whole which Collins adapted in his fiction.

In the Victoria and Albert Museum, there are also extant diaries written by Collins's mother Harriet. Angela Richardson describes the tiny diary for 1835 with three-line entries for each day in which 'only the most dramatic, irritating or important events are recorded'. The lack of space required Harriet to be her own editor. In 1836 during the family's tour of Italy, she used an old 1834 Kirton's Royal Remembrancer and Pocket Diary which she began in September, which meant that she had to correct the dates as she went along. She also folded and stitched in extra pages for Easter in Rome and the last three months of 1837.[26] This process gives some sense of the diary as a woman's record. The possibility of writing only in another document is reminiscent both of Catherine in *Wuthering Heights* and of Mrs Armadale in *Armadale* who writes verses in a volume of Felicia Hemans's poetry about her sad life after the death of her husband while she waits for Allan to be born.[27] Diaries act as both formats for the text and contextual reference points for the documentary style which Collins developed. They also allow him to exploit the additional sensation of having a woman narrating the depraved tales demanded by the public and deplored by Oliphant and Mansel.

Both Marian Halcombe and Lydia Gwilt comment on the discipline of diary writing and the corresponding dailiness which authorizes it as a female record. Both, however, take that record out of the domestic sphere. Marian demonstrates

---

[23]   There is an overview in Chapter 6, p. 116. The sequence is 'The Diary of Anne Rodway' (*Household Words*, 19 and 26 July 1856); *After Dark* (1856); *The Woman in White* (1859–60); *Armadale* (1864–66); *Man and Wife* (1870); *Poor Miss Finch* (1872); *The Law and the Lady* (1875); *The Legacy of Cain* (1888).

[24]   It was entitled *Memoirs of the Life of William Collins, Esq., R.A. With selections from his journals and correspondence. By his son, W. Wilkie Collins* (2 vols, London: Longman, 1848).

[25]   1 January 1844; quoted by Catherine Peters, *The King of Inventors: A Life of Wilkie Collins* (London: Minerva Press, 1991), p. 61.

[26]   Angela Richardson '"Dearest Harriet": On Harriet Collins's Italian Journal, 1836–7', *Wilkie Collins Society Journal*, n.s. 7 (2004): 44; 45.

[27]   Wilkie Collins, *Armadale*, ed. Catherine Peters (Oxford: Oxford University Press, 1989), pp. 175–6.

a detective's insight into the structure of the overall text and the unravelling of the plot of *The Woman in White* when she insists on 'the regularity of the entries in my journal'.[28]

Lydia makes similar claims about writing a diary to countermand 'the fear of forgetting'. When her Diary first intrudes into the text nearly two thirds of the way through *Armadale*, she needs to keep a clear record of her shifting identity as both plotter and detective. She writes that 'it would be madness to trust to my memory' and relies on her diary to 'show me what my head is too weary to calculate without help' (p. 411). Echoing Marian's reliance on daily record she reminds herself that '[t]he smallest forgetfulness of the slightest event that has happened ... might be utter ruin to me' (p. 411). It is thus that the diary as a source of household accounting is put to unfeminine uses by both women.

The inadequacy of language as a vehicle for describing female experience has already been discussed.[29] Marian reports in the diary a conversation with Laura when her sister agrees to marry Sir Percival: 'The simple illusions of her girlhood are gone; and my hand has stripped them off' (p. 188). That 'forbidden subject' (p. 216) of confidences about the marriage indicates the topics without a written or publishable language which can be suggested by Marian's apparent reticence. The daring approach to a discussion of sex is made possible without violating the reader's sense of propriety.

Lydia struggles with the overt expression of her own plot when she comments on 'something ... which I daren't write down even in my own private diary' (p. 417). She observes that she has missed two days when she resumes the diary after her marriage: 'I must have been afraid of what I might write about him ... if I indulged in the dangerous luxury of opening these pages' (p. 538). The reader must reconstruct for herself the failed attempt to poison Allan Armadale which cannot even be confided to the diary: 'I had a few minutes thought with myself, which I don't choose to put into words, even in these secret pages' (p. 546). If sex is the unwritten subject for Marian, for Lydia it is murder.

Marian's entries on the day of Laura's marriage indicate agitation. In *Armadale* too, Lydia betrays emotion with shorter entries and elliptical clues to her past life: '*Two o'clock* ... I have made up my mind to close my Diary. ... *Seven o'clock* The letter has gone to the post ... *Three o'clock*. – I mark the hour. He has sealed his own doom. He has insulted me' (pp. 437; 439). Like Marian, Lydia seeks 'resolution' from rereading her entries and so disrupts the non-retrospective reality of the unmediated story: 'books don't interest me ... I think I shall look back through these pages, and live my life over again when I was plotting and planning, and finding a new excitement to occupy me in every new hour of the day' (p. 534). She is acknowledging her life as a novel, as a performance, and encouraging that consumption of her own writing which the critics feared. Emboldened with the idea

---

[28]   Wilkie Collins, *The Woman in White*, ed. John Sutherland (Oxford: Oxford University Press, 1996; reissued 1998), p. 290.

[29]   See, for instance, Harriet Blodgett, *Centuries of Female Days: Englishwomen's Private Diaries* (New Brunswick: Rutgers University Press, 1989), p. 62.

of substituting one Armadale for another, she exclaims: 'The whole thing has been in my Diary, for days past, without my knowing it!' (p. 434). She also demonstrates some of her own vulnerability in an entry about authorship: 'Why do I keep a diary at all? ...Why am I not always on my guard and never inconsistent with myself like a wicked character in a novel?' (p. 547). Lydia is a suspect character partly because of her paraded knowledge of the staged performance which is a woman's life. Her knowledge of the ideological models which she must fulfill to achieve her goals and her resourcefulness in seeking advice and forwarding her own interests make her the dangerous 'White Devil' in the house.

These examples demonstrate how both novels use elements of the diary-writing trope. The records of both Marian and Lydia are ostensibly unmediated by retrospect and undiluted by any planned communication with an audience external to the diary itself. In their dailiness and reticence, they should remain a cross between a spiritual monitor and a contribution to the household accounts. The transmission of the two texts, however, is controlled in different ways which reframe the roles of the diarists and partly explain the variant receptions of the diaries within the novels overall. A nineteenth-century interpretation of womanhood would ultimately valorize Marian's role as silent spinster aunt but an exploration of the diary as narrative identifies points of both dissonance and convergence between the diarists and their chosen texts. The ideological conflict within these two hybrid diary novels of the 1860s and an element of their impact on the fiction of sensation can be observed through the positions occupied by the female diarists in the context of narrative and textual transmission.

The narrative control and collation of *The Woman in White* are almost as complex as the detective story itself. Initially, Marian's diary remains among those documents which fail to restore Laura Fairlie's identity. Marian's narrative comes to an end with Count Fosco's shockingly invasive entry into the diary, tantamount to textual rape as Marian lies close to death. It is prefaced, however, by the words of an editor who reports the facts but also preserves Fosco's monstrous act as he manipulates a woman's diary for his own purposes. The pace of events and Marian's recording of them ultimately authorizes her account of the removal of her own petticoats as part of the violent stimulus of consumption and production.

The assembly of the text and its transmission as a document discussed in Chapter 7 are important elements of the sensational effect and of the role of the alternative angel in the house. Access to Marian's diary appears to be controlled by Walter's taking notes and defusing it, but the narrative assembly itself betrays the effect of a Lady Audley-esque suppression. Marian visits the asylum only to rescue Laura. but is ultimately confined in society outside the asylum by her gender role as angelic aunt.

The transmission of Lydia's diary is more simply traced. She never relinquishes narratorial control although she originally chooses to give up writing the diary on her marriage as some diary-writing models would recommend.[30] The narrative

---

[30]   See Cynthia Huff, *British Women's Diaries: A Descriptive Bibliography of Selected Nineteenth Century Women's Manuscript Diaries* (New York: AMS Press, 1985), p. xxix.

demands, however, that this is a resolution which lasts only two months. 'Why have I gone back to this secret friend of my wretchedest and wickedest hours?' Lydia asks in Naples. She might expect to need no 'secret friend' after her marriage. She continues: 'My misery is a woman's misery and it *will* speak – here rather than nowhere; to my second self, in this book' (p. 532). Midwinter, however, already has his 'second self' in Allan Armadale, Allan the Fair. Midwinter struggles with his own interpretation of this relationship whether in the sense of a forbidden homosexual attraction or of his role as a psychological Other, Allan's murderous 'dark side.'[31] Despite her monstrous plans for control of Armadale, Lydia continues to insist that her diary partakes of the feminized, domestic and personal privacy of the diary model; she shows no other inclination to share it or to offer it as a public document.

Lydia has commented like Marian on the composition of the diary and even reports buying writing materials for its production but there is no sense of the physical transmission of the text within the completed story. When she returns to plotting, she records her thoughts with this proviso: 'I can easily tear the leaf out, and destroy it, if the prospect looks too encouraging' (p. 535). Soon, however, she prioritizes the aesthetics of the text in order to authorize her actions and the continuing existence of the plot: 'My Diary is so nicely bound – it would be a positive barbarity to tear out a leaf' (p. 537).

For Lydia, it is the element of its physical existence which ironically brings the diary to an end. Marian continues to act within the narratives of others and reports that she has suppressed her talent for detection by applying herself to the housework. Her diary has returned to its place in the home. Lydia's record is stopped not by illness or domesticity but ostensibly by the diary itself, by a problem of production or, in sensation terms, by the loss of food for an appetite:

> I might be in a humour to sit here for some time longer, thinking thoughts like these, and letting them find their way into words at their own will and pleasure – if my Diary would only let me. But my idle pen has been busy enough to make its way to the end of the volume. I have reached the last morsel of space left on the last page; ... Good-by, my old friend and companion ... I half suspect myself of having been unreasonably fond of *you*. (p. 600)

She has promoted a book to the status of a friend and consumed every 'morsel' of paper so that a physical text no longer exists except in the imagination of the reader who has also consumed it in monthly serial form. Despite her death, Lydia still looks boldly out from the pages of *Armadale*. The surviving characters are made safe by Allan's marriage, and through Midwinter's devotion to his writing, they are released from Lydia and from the threat of the prophetic dream.

---

31 See Maria K. Bachman and Don Richard Cox, 'Wilkie Collins's Villainous Miss Gwilt, Criminality and the Unspeakable Truth', *Dickens Studies Annual*, 32 (2002): 319–37: 'the text assiduously uncovers the homoerotic bond between Allan Armadale and Ozias Midwinter' (322).

Sensation is also created by the woman's being given a voice which causes other voices to be suppressed. This raises ideological concerns about the circumstances of saying 'I' and of the woman as narrator of her own story. Marian can argue that her diary-writing plays a role in combating the actions of Glyde and Fosco but their plan to acquire Laura's money is only a logical consequence of the laws governing matrimony at the time. That juxtaposition of the prosaic and daily facts of life with the development of a plot to incarcerate Laura in an asylum is itself a reflection of the potential married life of women and is, of course, the ultimate fate of Lady Audley two years later. Marian states both her household and detective credentials through the diary but she is also using it to record rebellion against the wishes of a father, an uncle and society in general. The lack of an extradiegetic overview in the novel at this point causes the plot to be more shadowy and sinister although the reader should always remember that Walter ultimately controls what is being presented. The suppression of other voices during diary narrative[32] is a sensational effect partly because those voices may later present alternative viewpoints in the hybrid narrative or explain the incidents initially observed and classified for record by the diarist. This additional layer of mediation differentiates the texts here from those of single viewpoint diary fiction. The negotiation for the attention of the reader is then made more complex by the editing and framing process.

The roles of Marian and Lydia are heightened by their unique positions as narrators internal to the plot of Collins's novels. They are women who write diaries authorized by domestic practice but their positions are changed by acts of reading which constitute the final phase of transmission. When Walter concludes, 'let Marian end our Story' (p. 643), he seems effectively to have reinstated gender boundaries and left Marian with asterisks, silence and a questionably private diary. Tamar Heller points out that 'the silence after this line emphasizes the irony of his expecting to speak through a woman who has been silenced'.[33] Marian may still be writing a diary but its text is apparently restored with her to the socially acceptable ideological position.

Lydia is silenced by the loss of her means of production. She simply stops writing and the reader is then offered the safer context of an extradiegetic narrator who provides a distancing framework for the closing episodes of *Armadale*. Lydia herself has two fragmentary textual interventions to make. She uses a housekeeper's pencil to write a last message to the unconscious Midwinter and, in the absence of the necessary paper, she writes on the blank sheets of a deathbed letter from the Reverend Decimus Brock, mentor to the two men: 'Even my wickedness has one merit – it has not prospered. I have never been a happy woman' (p. 653). Her textual intrusion into an already written letter echoes the diary's first intrusion

---

[32]   See H. Porter Abbott, *Diary Fiction: Writing as Action* (Ithaca: Cornell University Press, 1984), p. 11.

[33]   Tamar Heller, *Dead Secrets: Wilkie Collins and the Female Gothic* (New Haven: Yale University Press, 1992), p. 141.

into the text and might signify the plot of the novel as a whole.[34] The other piece of text is her tombstone which bears nothing 'but the initial letter of her Christian name, and the date of her death' (p. 656). Even in death she resists reinscription into respectable society.

Both the ideologically sound Marian and the vilified Lydia write diaries within the terms of the diary model. The absence of overt framing by another fictional character is a shocking factor in *Armadale*. Part of the critical reception of *Armadale* is attributable to the reader's wariness in having a relationship directly with the diary. Instead of the masculine frame of Walter's narrative, the reader is asked to accept direct access to the thoughts of a bigamous and dangerously attractive poisoner who dabbles in forgery and disguises her age. Reading the reaction of Bishop Thirlwall, it would appear that the act of writing the diary and allowing it to be read is more sinful than the performed acts of criminality.[35] It is as if the bishop feels that he has been lured into the position of a Fosco, an unauthorized reader violating a private text.

Collins's two novels of the 1860s which use the diary-writing trope thus differentiate between the diary writers in the ultimate presentation of their diaries to the reader. The role of the diary in serving up sensation is controlled through access. The framing and transmission of Marian's diary in *The Woman in White* is part of the process of making her safe in all her detective resourcefulness and mannish courage. Its place within the narrative makes the diary appear to be unfolding in real time which adds to the sensational impact. The later revelation of Walter Hartright's role in presenting Marian's text as evidence makes it more secure in representing the dominant ideology of womanhood and Marian remains admirable within contemporary mores. Lydia Gwilt in *Armadale* is more shocking because she faces directly into the narrative and offers to present her diary and then to withhold it. And yet it has already been read along with the letter in which she debates having it read. The audience is thus implicated in the unauthorized reading of a private text and Lydia has led her reader on to play a role like Fosco's in entering the diary of a woman uninvited.

Transmission is a significant element of sensation genre in that it both draws attention to the multi-voiced narrative and also permits the withholding of vital information. Conversely, the threat of the female diarist's control over the text is another element of the sensation generated by these novels. Marian Halcombe finally accepts the control of domesticity for herself and for the text she has used for surveillance and resolution. Lydia Gwilt retains control and is reduced to the final initial on her tombstone.

In the interim between the substantial diary narratives of *Armadale* and *The Legacy of Cain*, Wilkie Colllins employed women's diaries in three novels of the 1870s. The interaction of the diary with sensation can be further explored in the post-sensation narratives *Man and Wife, Poor Miss Finch* and *The Law and the Lady*.

---

[34] It echoes too the writing within other texts performed by Catherine in *Wuthering Heights* and Mrs Armadale (see note 27 above).

[35] See Chapter 6, pp. 112–13.

In *Man and Wife* published in 1870, the female diarist is also the murderer of her abusive husband. Hester Dethridge's story must be told by her own hand because she is mute either as an involuntary psychological response to her crime or possibly as a self-inflicted punishment. In this she has literally suppressed even her own voice and can communicate only in writing. She first appears as an efficient housekeeper writing messages on a slate. In the context of the novel where women and particularly wives are abused in the name of the law, this is perhaps the desirable state for a woman or at least for a servant who will satisfy Lady Lundie, the overbearing woman who employs the novel's heroine Anne Sylvester as a governess. A diary along with letters, a visiting list, memorandum book, desk, envelope case, bills and ledgers are among the 'domestic business' of Lady Lundie, 'the British matron on her throne ... formidably full of virtue'.[36]

Despite her role as housekeeper to this respectable establishment, Hester Dethridge's journal is of a very different kind; she keeps it in a 'secret pocket hidden in the inner side of her stays' (p. 549). Like Pamela's, this journal becomes part of her and it is an act of violation when Geoffrey Delamyn reads it. This occurs at the point in the novel when he wishes to murder Anne who is, inconveniently and for reasons of Victorian propriety, his wife. He guesses that Hester, with whom they now lodge, has used a device to murder someone in the past. This echoes the situation in Collins's early short story 'A Terribly Strange Bed.' The story featured in the *After Dark* collection of 1856 framed by 'Leah's Diary' and was first published in *Household Words* on 24 April 1852. [37]

Hester entitles her journal 'My Confession. To be put into my coffin, and to be buried with me when I die' (p. 549). This transforms her into an uneasy cross between Rosanna Spearman whose letter is read because she is dead, and Ezra Jennings who allows part of his journal to be spared burial to support Blake's case in *The Moonstone*. Hester writes her life in retrospect: 'This is the history of what I did, in the time of my married life' (p. 559). She has been repeatedly forced to return to her drunken husband Joel who uses up any resources she has gathered because it is his right and divorce is impossible.

Despite the fact that this confession will never be read, Collins must give Hester a reason to decide on murder as her only solution. He has already had to avoid mentioning Anne's pregnancy, and her miscarriage is daringly presented although still veiled. Like Helen Huntingdon in *The Tenant of Wildfell* Hall, Anne takes the name 'Mrs Graham' when she runs away to Glasgow. When visiting a lawyer, Anne is 'seized with giddiness, and with some sudden pang of pain' (p. 305). In the following chapter her landlady finds her trying to write a letter 'her handkerchief twisted between her set teeth, and her tortured face terrible to look at' (p. 306). The landlady reports later 'A child born dead' and the blotted fragments of the letter (p. 307) in the manner of Marian's last diary entry.

---

[36]   Wilkie Collins, *Man and Wife* (Stroud: Alan Sutton Publishing, 1990; reprinted 1993), p. 283.

[37]   See Wilkie Collins, *Mad Monkton and Other Stories*, ed. Norman Page (Oxford: Oxford University Press, 1994), pp. 1–20.

When Hester narrates her husband's return in her journal, she appears to be describing rape as the final trigger:

> I leave the rest untold, and pass on purposely to the next morning. No mortal eyes but mine will ever see these lines. Still, there are things a woman can't write of even to herself. I shall only say this. I suffered the last and worst of many indignities at my husband's hands – at the very time when I first saw, set plainly before me, the way to take his life. (p. 577)

After the murder, Hester chooses like Rosanna Spearman her 'separate and silent life' (p. 580) but Geoffrey violates her again when he finds and reads her 'fragmentary journal' (p. 584). He can then both implicate and include her in his own crime, although he does not succeed because Hester strangles him. On the evidence of the diary, she is removed to an asylum to end her days in the manner of sensation heroines. Through Hester's intervention, Anne survives to marry the elderly but reliable uncle and becomes the next Lady Lundie. The diary has allowed Hester to tell and perform the truth, but her text and the reading of that text confines her just as her marriage did. She echoes, albeit in miniature, the situation of Helen Huntingdon in *The Tenant of Wildfell Hall*.

Collins uses a larger journal portion in his next novel, *Poor Miss Finch* published in 1872. The journal element constitutes about one eighth of the novel[38] which is otherwise narrated throughout by Madame Pratolungo, companion to the eponymous Miss Lucilla Finch. Madame Pratolungo alludes throughout the diary section to her overall control of the text and has previously indicated that, because she is blind, Lucilla can only write her own thoughts though dictation. During Madame Pratolungo's absence, the temporary cure of this blindness allows Lucilla to become independent and she is persuaded to leave the protection of her home with the twin brother of her fiancé. Oscar Dubourg has allowed his brother Nugent to present himself as her lover because he, Oscar is suffering from epilepsy and his medication turns him a shade of blue. When blind, Lucilla has expressed total aversion towards the colour and Oscar fears that she will reject him.

Although his brother exploits this position because he is in love with Lucilla, Lucilla herself suspects that she is not with the correct twin. She allows her blindness to recur by straining her sight to write the diary and is finally at peace with the man she loves whilst Nugent is lost in an expedition to the North Pole. The diary has a practical application or narrativity in that it allows the novel to continue without Madame Pratolungo's being present. There is also a sense that diary writing is dangerous particularly when it allows a woman clear sight of her true position, and Lucilla must therefore return to dependency and domestic containment. Sensation is created by the reader's knowing that Lucilla has put herself in the power of the other brother but at the same time recognizing that her morbid hatred of blue will undermine the original relationship anyway.

---

[38] Wilkie Collins, *Poor Miss Finch* (Stroud: Alan Sutton Publishing, 1994), pp. 256–96.

In a short space of time – some forty pages composed during her one week of sight – Lucilla's writing demonstrates many of the features of diary-writing. She begins by closely echoing Burney's reason for writing, 'My one confidential friend is my Journal. I can only talk about myself *to* myself in these pages' (p. 261). She picks up the need for confidentiality which is once again undermined by the reader's access to her 'private record': 'My book locks up, and my book can be trusted with the truth' (p. 271; 261). There is a Burneyesque compulsion to write, feeding the reader's depraved need to read, when she writes that she 'can't do without' the Journal (p. 288). She is conscious too of the narrative occasion and use of the retrospective entry when she offers to write 'the long story of yesterday' (p. 291). By now, however, the entries are in fading ink to represent her returning blindness and she concludes with the secret which will be maintained and sensationalized by her suppression as a narrator: 'Something has happened which I must positively set down in this history of my life' (p. 296). She expects to continue, but her writing now tapers off like Marian's. She can never keep a personal diary again because she will always have to use an intermediary. She will also be married with no need for a confidential friend although this event is still to be narrated.

Madame Pratolungo regains narrative control and makes some editorial claims to information which should be secret. She observes that 'the Journal will show you I calculated right' (p. 301). She keeps a letter which proves that Lucilla really believed that Nugent was Oscar observing that 'After events make it necessary to preserve this note also' (p. 298). Madame Pratolungo is not, however, a wholly trustworthy narrator. She is protecting her own position as much as her male counterparts Walter Hartright and Franklin Blake. She clearly misunderstands the situation she is narrating but has the privilege of final retrospection. The lack of narrative authority is therefore maintained even when she is in control but the diary section reiterates the absence of omniscience and heightens the tension of Lucilla's plight.

The Law and the Lady, Collins's novel of 1875, uses a first person female narrator who is writing in instalments but insists towards the end of her narrative 'I write from memory, unassisted by notes or diaries'.[39] This is partly because the diary narrative is being saved for a very different purpose as court evidence and as the final piece in the sensational puzzle. Valeria Macallan who is a resourceful woman in the mould of Marian Halcombe, nevertheless draws attention to the unfolding story on a regular basis. Immediately after discovering that she has been married under an assumed name, she writes: '[l]et me dry my eyes and shut up my paper for the day' (p. 12). Her narrative act, '[w]riting as I do long after the events' (p. 156), is to rewrite the record of her husband's trial for the murder of his first wife which has received the verdict 'not proven' under Scottish law. This has left Eustace Macallan forever under suspicion of Sarah's murder. In the novel, it

---

[39]   Wilkie Collins, *The Law and the Lady*, ed. Jenny Bourne Taylor (Oxford: Oxford University Press, 1992; reissued 1999), p. 399.

is Eustace's diary which is unlocked and read out at his trial.[40] Valeria records the court reporter's opinion of 'the silent evidence of the letters and the Diary ... the prisoner's daily record of domestic events, and of the thoughts and feelings which they aroused in him at the time' (p. 156).

Eustace's friend Miserrimus Dexter regards a diary as an expression of weakness, a feminizing record; 'the more or less contemptible outpouring of vanity and conceit which the writer dare not exhibit to any mortal but himself' (p. 175). It is Dexter, however, who has destroyed a journal letter written by Sarah Macallan in the last hours of her life, another 'Wife's Confession' through which he is partially implicated in her death. Dexter has shown Eustace's diary to Sarah who is bedridden trying to cure her bad complexion in an attempt to regain her husband's affection. Eustace has married her because of a misunderstanding which compromised her honour; he is really in love with another woman staying with them in Scotland. Dexter loves Sarah himself although he is a deranged and disabled man, but he hopes to separate the couple. Instead, Sarah writes of her slow poisoning by her own hand. She indicates clearly that there were moments when Eustace could have pulled her back but that he acted coldly towards her. He has in effect killed her, but it is Valeria who chooses that he should never know this fact. The journal letter is rediscovered as a result of some wild clues thrown out by Dexter and is recovered from the rubbish pile at the family house. It is a diary dismembered and reread from its reconstructed fragments. Valeria reviews the case with Benjamin the lawyer and decides that a personal record denotes 'the existence of dangerous domestic secrets in the locked-up pages' (p. 401). The diary cannot be the source of her narrative because the diary has become a suspect device whilst she is on a quest for the truth. Her decision to keep another woman's diary a secret spares Eustace the knowledge of his complicity in Sarah's death, but it also transfers power to Valeria. Their final domestic bliss may not be undermined by a diary but Valeria demonstrates that the ideological role of angel must include duplicity as well as courage.

Helena Gracedieu in *The Legacy of Cain* manipulates more obviously the role of domestic paragon because her diary is made available. It demonstrates significant elements of full-blown sensation fiction – the lack of narrative authority, the power of consumption, the lack of language and the alternative commentary on domestic womanhood – as late as 1888. The documentary presentation, serialization and role of the diarists have been discussed in previous chapters. This chapter notes that in the sequence of women's diary narratives this novel is important despite its poor critical reception since *The Legacy of Cain* acts as a bridge to the latest woman's fictional diary of the nineteenth century, that of Mina Harker in *Dracula*.

The Preface to *Dracula* offers a disembodied extradiegetic viewpoint which is not identified with either the author or a character. It insists that, like Walter Hartright and Franklin Blake who have a homodiegetic existence within their own narratives, the story has been presented as evidence by those who were present.

---

[40]   Ibid., p. 146; pp. 161–5.

At some moments there are signs of the practice of an editor, but one who shows no respect for the actual boundaries between diary entries. A higher controlling force – like that of Gilbert's ordering Helen's diary in *The Tenant of Wildfell Hall* – appears to be allocating the chapter divisions of the novel which are often inserted at moments of high tension; for instance when Jonathan awakes after his encounter with the vampire women and when Seward's diary continues after Van Helsing has claimed Lucy to be the 'bloofer lady'.[41] As demonstrated in Chapter 7, however, this fragile narrative authority is summarily withdrawn by Jonathan's final 'Note' which denigrates the 'proofs' provided.[42]

Within the novel as a whole, the collation of information by Mina and Van Helsing gives an illusion of narrative authority. Mina must, however, be dismissed from the process to avoid any direct communication with Dracula. This suggests the danger of engaging directly with a force which offers women the power of vampirism. Multiple layers of translation present accounts from a ship's log in another language which becomes part of the diary via a translator and the pages of the newspaper. This opens questions of narrative authority in the early part of the novel. At the end of *Dracula*, however, multiple transcription and removal from the original authority of the text means that it can no longer represent the truth, a danger which the real diary itself encounters.

The use of everyday narrative vehicles such as the letter, diary or newspaper is designed like sensation fiction to adapt the actions of everyday to the Gothic horror of Dracula's quest for blood. The novel also employs means of recording appropriate to the era with a facsimile, typewriter and phonograph as devices which reproduce text, but these media cannot finally give credence to the original information. Mina initially imitates her fiancé Jonathan's approach to the descriptive travel diary and this helps to align Transylvania with Whitby, an exotic wilderness with the daily domesticity of the holiday resort. Although Mina has not read Jonathan's diary at this stage, the combination of a personal travel narrative with Gothic touches such as her reference to the Abbey 'where the girl was built up in the wall' in *Marmion* (p. 85) is reminiscent of her fiancé's style. Jonathan uses everyday memos to remind him to find recipes for Mina in almost the same paragraphs as he observes the peasants crossing themselves. Mina herself observes an injury on Lucy's neck: 'I trust her feeling ill may not be from the unlucky prick of the safety pin ... the tiny wounds seem not to have healed' (p. 127), and it has been suggested that the diarists in *Dracula* are always trying to cling to everyday details in the face of the horrifying events they witness.[43] The elision between their innocent observations and the incidents they have to observe often verges on the comic.

---

[41]   Bram Stoker, *Dracula*, ed. Maurice Hindle (London: Penguin, 1993), p. 57; p. 250.

[42]   *Dracula*, p. 486; p. 6. Alison Case identifies an atmosphere of suspicion created by the absence of a master narrator (Alison Case, 'Tasting the Original Apple: Gender and the Struggle for Narrative Authority in *Dracula*', *Narrative*, 1/3 (1993): 236).

[43]   See David Seed, 'The Narrative Method of *Dracula*', *Nineteenth Century Literature*, 40/1 (June 1985): 64–5.

The need to consume and retell is an obsessive one because writing itself is claimed to be safe and scientific. The domestic incident is recorded in the hope that it can 'counter strangeness'[44] but it is Mina's typewriting skills as a performance of narrativity which permit this free flow of information. When she has provided a verbal overview of Dracula as a criminal type, Van Helsing tells Mina: 'You must be scribe and write him all down, so that when the others return from their work you can give it to them; then they shall know as we do' (p. 441). Mina knows more partly because of her telepathic contact with Dracula and partly because of the blood shared through transfusions. Her diary represents the new and illusory equality of texts. Words and blood circulate. The reproduced diaries of Mina, Jonathan and Dr Seward also contribute to the obsession with writing and reading, the narrative of inclusion which is the text for their quest. Since this parallels Dracula's own appetite for circulating and prolonging life, the power of the female collator must also be destroyed along with the vampire.

Despite the number of accounts and recording devices in *Dracula* there are still difficulties in expression even within the scientific records of Van Helsing and Seward. On his return from Transylvania, Jonathan does not wish Mina to read his diary and his use of shorthand symbolizes the language gaps in the first half of the novel. In addition, the rereading and sharing of texts does not always bring the truth to light. Some points of crisis are left un-narrated such as Mina's pallor when the men return from that first trip to Carfax. The narrated silence between husband and wife causes Mina some tears and an ellipsis which is followed by an aside: 'lest it should ever be that he should think for a moment that I kept anything from him, I shall keep my journal as usual' (p. 330). Recollecting Lucy's fate brings on more tears and another ellipsis as if concealment 'is one of the lessons that we poor women have to learn ...' (p. 331). Mina also narrates at this point the clues that remind the reader of the novel that Dracula has been present although she herself does not make that connection (pp. 332-4). In a text which is no longer being shared Jonathan writes ominously of his belief that 'the ceasing of telling things had made no difference' (p. 344).

When Mina is allowed to narrate Dracula's second attack it is only as a replica of Seward's diary entry. The attack is thus told and retold in the performed language of the phonograph but doubly removed and qualified so that the vampire hunters can record it safely. When Mina retypes it on her restoration to her former position in their confidence, her energetic note-taking and research is suspect because of her new telepathic communication with Dracula.[45] It is Seward who comments on a continuing language gap: 'I fear that in some mysterious way poor Mrs Harker's tongue is tied. I know that she forms conclusions of her own ... but she will not, or cannot give them utterance' (p. 414). Van Helsing likens her also to Lucy who

---

[44] Ibid.

[45] Jennifer Wicke points out that she is a medium and 'telepathic double' and not just a secretary (Jennifer Wicke, 'Vampiric Typewriting: *Dracula* and Its Media', *ELH*, 59/2 (Summer 1992): 485).

'did not speak, even when she wrote that which she wished to be known later' (p. 415) but Mina's diary at least manages to narrate its silences to help in the eventual circulation of information when records are pooled once more.

The lack of a language creates the gaps into which Dracula can insert himself in opposition to everyday, open communication and to the technological safeguards which the vampire hunters believe will defeat him. The equivocal role of Mina as transcriber and object exposes society to the dangers which Dracula represents in elevating women to the status of undead and consuming vampires. By the end of the novel, Mina is contesting domestic womanhood by driving a carriage and toting a gun – and perhaps contesting the control of blood and words with Dracula himself. The scientific and socially dominant men have also found themselves considering alternative roles for women, tempted by the appearance of Lucy and the other vampire women. Although she claims opposition to the feminist ideas of the New Woman, it is Mina who discusses this in her early journal. She comments after a 'severe tea' at Robin Hood's Bay: 'We should have shocked the "New Woman" with our appetites' but adds that New Woman would not make a good 'job' of proposing (pp. 118–19). Her final restoration, however, is for the purposes of motherhood and *Dracula* finally downgrades the text and the diarist. Blood flows into her son and the hard-won words in the 'mass of typewriting' (p. 486) are discounted as evidence even though both the assembly and inclusion of the materials remain as narrative on the page.

The fear of or fascination with the New Woman informs the gender clash within *Dracula* just as the alternative commentary on domestic womanhood fuelled sensation fiction earlier in the century. The vampire hunters have shared blood with Mina, and her son now shares their names. Marian Halcombe shares the upbringing of Walter's son in *The Woman in White*. The diarist Lydia Gwilt takes the poison she had designed for Armadale in order to save Midwinter and declines her share in another form of domesticity within the triangle of name exchange and male bonding which have enveloped her.[46] The redemption which a domestic environment offers the other fictional diarists is not available having been subverted in *Armadale* by the relationship between the two men.

In *The Woman in White*, Walter Hartright controls the means of narration which Lydia Gwilt denies to everyone. The lack of a controlling authority other than the anonymous preface to *Dracula* borders on a more modern approach to narrative despite similarities with novels of the 1860s and 1870s. The diary as narrative played a role in the contemporary response to sensation fiction and those elements

---

[46] Bachman and Cox point out that the homosexual secret is unspoken because Lydia frees Midwinter by dying herself (Bachman and Cox: 332). Marian could be seen to be part of her own domestic triangle with Walter and Laura at the end of *The Woman in White* although Richard Collins prefers to describe her as 'safely unsexed [in] angelic androgyny' (Richard Collins, 'Marian's Moustache: Bearded Ladies, Hermaphrodites and Intersexual Collage in The Woman in White', in Maria K. Bachman and Don Richard Cox (eds), *Reality's Dark Light: The Sensational Wilkie Collins, Tennessee Studies in Literature* 41 (Knoxville: University of Tennessee Press, 2003), pp. 158–9).

it helped to create are consistently present at the end of the century when the male diarists in *Dracula* are denied veracity along with the female. Critics in the 1890s may still have described diary fiction as a 'wearisome form of narration'[47] but the lack of narrative authority and the debate over alternatives to domestic womanhood remain overt issues for Stoker's *fin de siècle* society.

The use of female diary writers as narrators presents the possibility that characters like Lydia Gwilt and Helena Gracedieu are even closer to home. Women are thus implicated in the production of sensation as either authors in their own right, or as writers of diaries and letters within the novel. Ann Cvetkovich observes that the popularity of the genre was constructed out of 'nineteenth-century discourses suspicious of working class readers, female audiences and affectively powerful or nonrealist literature'.[48] The moral confusion was seen significantly to be generated through women writers. Oliphant deplored the fact that '[t]his new and disgusting picture of what professes to be the human heart comes from the hands of women, and is tacitly accepted as real'.[49] Sensation fiction was defined particularly as being the result of the act of reading, and the means by which the novels gained access to the home was through female authors and upright domestic publications aimed at women.

Women are further implicated as readers of these novels in serial form and as potential authors of their own personal diaries. This raises the question of what they are writing themselves as diarists and as family chroniclers. They may be writing in their diaries the truth of their 'secret course of reading' which they cannot discuss within the family circle.[50] The sensation novel shares with the diary a sense of literature as a commodity in public circulation. It shares the sense too of a protest against domestic restrictions by presenting an alternative narrative of life written by a 'second self'.

---

[47] In *Punch*; quoted by Mark M. Hennelly Jr., 'Twice-Told Tales of Two Counts: *The Woman in White* and *Dracula*', *Wilkie Collins Society Journal*, 2 (1982): 29, note 2.

[48] Cvetkovich, p. 15. See also the ideological juxtaposition of home and marketplace discussed in Bernstein, pp. 235–6. The documentary facts of death certificates and tombstones were also 'affectively' imported into sensation fiction.

[49] Oliphant, 'Novels', (1867), p. 260.

[50] Wilkie Collins, *The Legacy of Cain* (Stroud: Alan Sutton Publishing, 1993; reprinted 2003), p. 183). See Chapter 6 for a discussion of serial reading and role of woman as reader.

PART 3
The Diary as Narrative

Chapter 9
The Diary Narrating the Novel

This study has investigated the significance of women's diary narrative in the nineteenth-century novel using both the ideological model of women's diary writing and a critics' model of diary fiction. The readings in Part 2 are grounded in literary analysis contextualized by nineteenth-century printing and reading practices. The diary's structure, its language and narrative occasion, are the means of interrogating the novels and their contemporary reception. Women as writers, readers and subjects become performers through the medium of the diary record.

This concluding chapter provides a review of diary narrative and reaches a number of conclusions about its impact on the reading and reception of the novels. It theorizes the use of women's diaries as narrative – their narrativity – and considers the diary as a physical text, as a nineteenth-century feminine form and as a structure for narrative. In assessing the heritage and chronology of the diary in fiction, areas for further development are identifiable in women's biographies of women, in the serialization of novels and in the diary narrative of the twentieth century.

Despite the fifty-year time span across the core novels, there is an identifiable continuity in the treatment of the fictional woman and her text. The non-fictional diary might be regarded as non-narrative because it does not set out to tell a story and is, in narrative terms, the raw materials for the autobiography or narrative of a life. The plotlessness of the diary described by D'Israeli[1] is, however, undermined by the presence of a controlling intelligence which selects the issues worthy of record using a technique which includes that of narrative. The retrospective imposition and re-reading techniques of the non-fictional female diarists of Chapter 2 reiterate this process. In conjunction with its non-fictional counterpart the diary as a narrative device raises questions about dailiness and authenticity, about the role of non-retrospection and the sense of the audience or addressee. In considering how a narrative operates when a diary is invoked as a source, the authority and transmission of the text is a significant factor. Its survival and preparation or collation will authorize it as a factual or reliable document and re-enact narratives of composition, inclusion and transmission exterior to the narration of events.

In codifying the system of narrative discourse, classic structuralist theory would describe the diary as a sign system or medium with shared ordering principles.[2]

---

[1]   See Chapter 1, pp. 10–11, 19.

[2]   See Mieke Bal, *Narratology: Introduction to the Theory of Narrative* (first published 1980; translation Toronto: University of Toronto Press, 1985), pp. 5–7. See also Wayne Booth, *The Rhetoric of Fiction* (first published 1961; 2nd edition, Harmondsworth: Penguin: 1991), Gerald Prince, *Narratology: The Form and Functioning of Narrative* (New York: Mouton, 1982), and Shlomoth Rimmon-Kenan, *Narrative Fiction: Contemporary Poetics*

For Roland Barthes the diary would form one of the 'elementary combination schemes' of narrative and Barthes comments on the role of domestic forms such as letters within an epistolary novel as signs that 'don't look like signs'.[3]

Basing her discussion on the work of Gerard Genette, Shlomoth Rimmon-Kenan discusses types of narration in terms of their temporal relationship with events, and in these terms, the diary is intercalated narration. Within the hybrid form of the novel, the diary fits the term 'intercalated' more closely than the level of simultaneity or minimal distance within which Rimmon-Kenan classifies the single viewpoint text. [4] As a device for telling a story, the diary is a hypodiegetic narrative which presents events told by characters who are themselves internal to the novel.

In novels which use the diaries of women as intercalated narration, the diary positions its female narrator at an intradiegetic or second level, below that of the extradiegetic narrator. The authors of the novels explore narrative levels by using internal narrative collators or editors who have an extradiegetic function. In the hybrid diary novel, the woman's narrative thus always operates at a level beneath the extradiegetic collator, at the level of story. Rimmon-Kenan observes, 'Narration is always at a higher level than the story it narrates'[5] and in the typology of narrators the diarist is always lower in the hierarchy even during the time when the diary is be used as a narrative device. This is made clear by the additional narrative of inclusion replayed in framing documents but, as the chapters in Part 2 have demonstrated, the overall authors of the novels also use this level to expose the collators and to provide an extra-extradiegetic commentary. Narrative theory

---

(first published 1983; 2nd edition, London: Routledge, 2002; reprinted, 2003). The development is outlined by Gerard Prince, 'Narratology', in Raman Selden (ed.), *The Cambridge History of Literary Criticism: Volume 8 From Formalism to Poststructuralism* (Cambridge: Cambridge University Press, 1995), 110–30. In the later 1980s, critics developed applications of the theoretical models. See Wallace Martin, *Recent Theories of Narrative* (Ithaca: Cornell University Press, 1986; reprinted, 1994); Steven Cohan, and Linda M. Shires, *Telling Stories: A Theoretical Analysis of Narrative Fiction* (London: Routledge, 1988; reprinted, 1997); Seymour Chatman, *Coming to Terms: The Rhetoric of Narrative in Fiction and Film* (Ithaca: Cornell University Press, 1990) which itself updates his *Story and Discourse* (Ithaca: Cornell University Press, 1978). These are the summarized or cumulative techniques used for discussions of novels by Bernard Duyfhuizen and to an extent Lorna Martens and H. Porter Abbott although as indicated in Chapter 1of this book the latter critics are theorizing diary narrative for the modern novel. At the level of theory the diary as fiction has stimulated areas of analysis both narrower and broader in definition. Prince, for instance, moves from 'The Diary Novel as Sub Genre' (1975) to closely-reasoned narratological theory in *Narratology* (1982) and Abbott moves from *Diary Fiction* (1984) to his guide to narrative: H. Porter Abbott, *The Cambridge Introduction to Narrative* (Cambridge: Cambridge University Press, 2002).

   [3]   Roland Barthes, *Image Music Text: Essays Selected and Translated by Stephen Heath* (London: Fontana, 1977), p. 81; p. 116. The process is termed in translation 'disinaugurating' (p. 116).

   [4]   Rimmon-Kenan, pp. 90–92. The term 'nested' which might also apply has come to be interpreted within linguistics as having hierarchical associations.

   [5]   Rimmon-Kenan, p. 93.

thus demonstrates that nineteenth-century women could narrate at the level of story where they remained contained, but the manipulation of narrative levels questions both the cultural significance of their role and the performative potential of their private text.

Classic theory reiterates Plato's distinction between 'mimesis' and 'diagesis'.[6] In terms of this book's engagement with self-representation for the nineteenth-century diarist, the diary as a narrative device is one element of performance, balanced between 'showing' and 'telling'. The diary as a physical text within a hybrid or intercalated narrative draws attention to the existence of a text which can be shown as well as told. Leaving the sign system of domestic record in place, the transmission or framing of the written diary makes that text into a performative or 'shown' text. The authority of the collator is undermined when the woman's diary ceases to narrate. This is partly because the collator must offer a documentary record of his access to the still private diary. The 'recuperable record' in Seymour Chatman's terms[7] is disrupted by the female diarist and by the circulation of her text through the overall unifying agency supplied by the real author – Brontë, Craik, Collins or Stoker. There are different degrees or kinds of telling exemplified within the core texts where the authors of the novels exploit the mimetic qualities of the diary as narrative.

Analysis of both fictional and non-fictional diaries demonstrates the exploitation of the gaps which become apparent in this showing and telling, between recording, writing and reading. This is because a publicized personal record has many facets including the rationale for publication, the role of editorial choice and the means of telling a story which is imposed on the unmediated record. At the time of composition of the core texts analysed in this study when the novel was valued for its realism, the use of realistic documents perversely undermined all veracity. In fact the dailiness and immediacy of the record generate anxiety about the absence of narrative control and this is exacerbated by the use of female intradiegetic narrators from Pamela in 1740 to Mina in 1897. The distribution of authority amongst competing narratives raises questions not only about the instructional value of the text but about unauthorized readers and other unread diaries. The diary narrative also contains both the oppressive voices which colonize the female diarists and the suggestion of those suppressed voices which are not heard because the diaries speak in their stead.

The diary's alleged privacy during the nineteenth century contributes to its status as a feminine form. The impulse to write and to perform should be regarded as suspect for nineteenth-century women whose exemplary selflessness cannot be sustained by the egoism of a diary. Linda Anderson describes the diary as a 'provisional voice' because the woman's lack of public access results in the 'denial of narrative' and Rebecca Hogan concludes that the diary became an unread, silent

---

[6]   This was developed originally by Gerard Genette in *Narrative Discourse* (1972; translated 1979). See also Lorna Martens, *The Diary Novel* (Cambridge: Cambridge University Press, 1985), p. 6 and Bernard Duyfhuizen's reading of Mikhail Bakhtin in *Narratives of Transmission* (London: Associated University Presses, 1992), p. 40.

[7]   Chatman, *Coming to Terms*, p. 83.

text.[8] Sidonie Smith regards the diary as a form in which the woman is 'culturally silenced' and 'doubly estranged' because she is both marginalized and denied the possibility of self-writing.[9]

The codes of privacy and performance in the nineteenth century, however, can be reread through the diary to demonstrate that domestic space did in fact offer women a voice and a narrative opportunity. The private diary becomes a vehicle for narratives which might otherwise be unwritten and the fictional diarists in the core texts are writing journals because they are forced to rebel or to take action like men. Helen in *The Tenant of Wildfell Hall* is secretly fallen because she acknowledges a sexual attraction first to Arthur and then to Gilbert. She is doubly fallen because she enacts her fallenness first by escaping and then by allowing Gilbert to read her private diary. Her return to nurse Arthur is narrated by other competing documents from a distanced place. Marian in *The Woman in White* is emphatically described as masculine with her moustache and man's umbrella, and the removal of her petticoats dramatizes her masculine resolve. Mina has 'man's brains' according to Van Helsing but she must finally accept motherhood as an alternative to the power which Dracula offers her. Helena in *The Legacy of Cain* is rebelling first against domesticity and then against her unrequited physical attraction to Philip. She enacts in her housekeeping her own monstrous form of ideological conformance inherited from her mother.

These women can say 'I' because they are employing a record which is authorized within their cloistered and moated lives. They are in this sense 'cloistered' by their womanhood like nuns echoing the plight of Eloisa, and 'moated' by circumstances relating to an interaction with the world controlled by men. The transmission of the diaries of Helen and Marian onto the page is part of a male negotiation for social acceptance which is also conducted by Franklin Blake in *The Moonstone*. The direct picture of Lydia in *Armadale* is sustained without male control and she has finally only an initial on a tombstone to be her record. All, however, are keeping household records, adapting the diary as a reflection on their own conduct and spiritual experiences, and using the diary as a substitute for a confidential friend in terms which echo Burney's published *credo* to 'Nobody.'

The fictional diary, like Burney's renarration of the events of her life, is offering a woman's story in public. The diary is a confirmation of what is being written in secret which has been published both to make it safe and to make an informal legal case – or at least to reconstruct an exemplar in the tradition of the spiritual diary. A women's diary can be put to ideological use partly because controlling the diary appears to control the woman especially if the text is literally sewn into her clothes as the journals of Richardson's Pamela and Hester in *Man and Wife* are. The diaries allow impropriety – domestic abuse, alcoholism, poisoning plots and

---

    [8]   Linda Anderson, 'At the Threshold of Self: Women and Autobiography' in Moira Monteith (ed.), *Women's Writing A Challenge to Theory* (Brighton: Harvester Press, 1986), p. 61; Rebecca Hogan, 'Engendered Autobiographies: The Diary as a Feminine Form', in Shirley Neuman (ed.), *Autobiography and Questions of Gender* (London: Cass, 1991), p. 99.

    [9]   Sidonie Smith, *A Poetics of Women's Autobiography: Marginality and the Fictions of Self-Representation* (Bloomington: Indiana University Press, 1987), pp. 43–4; p. 49.

even murder – to be renarrated. The change of addressee into the public sphere neutralizes the fear of what is being written in private and the majority of the texts under consideration reabsorb the female diarist and her diary into (authorized) male texts. As a result, diaries can still be written and indeed there is a sense in which the diarists' return from the public into the private sphere allows them to have the luxury of befriending 'these pages' once more.

It may also be that the diary as a 'second self' encodes a space for the truth. Elaine Showalter has observed, 'for the Victorian woman, secrecy was simply a way of life'.[10] The diary as a text uses the discourse of showing and performance within an authorized domestic framework and this allows a woman to act with immediacy within that space and its traditions, to perform a life which ought to remain private. Jane Austen's original allusion suggests that it is practice which makes it possible to 'perform to strangers';[11] by the nineteenth century it is print which enacts that possibility. The availability of documents, the appetite for reading and the technological achievement of the publishing industry influence both readership and the market, bridging a gap between the public and the private, the home and the world, the woman and her audience.

The idea of performance is not, however, without precedent as a part of women's ideological determination. Sarah Ellis herself defines 'the true Englishwoman whose peculiar charm is that of diffusing happiness without appearing conspicuously as the agent in its diffusion'.[12] There is a performance at the heart of every nineteenth-century home which Elizabeth Langland describes as 'a theatre for the staging of a family's social position'.[13] This performance is at the very core of female responsibility which Ellis promotes: 'it is her peculiar duty as a wife ... to make all her domestic concerns appear before her husband to the very best advantage'.[14] As late as 1894, Inez in Henry Arthur Jones's play *The Case of the Rebellious Susan* describes a woman's 'treasures of deceit – loving, honourable deceit, and secrecy and treachery'.[15] Despite Sarah Ellis's insistence that any focus on self-presentation is 'evil', domestic life is a staging of the self: 'while affording

---

[10]   Elaine Showalter, *A Literature of Their Own: British Women Novelists from Brontë to Lessing* (London: Virago, revised edition 1982), p. 158.

[11]   See Introduction, p. 2.

[12]   Sarah Stickney Ellis, *The Women of England* (London: Fisher and Son, 1839), p. 273.

[13]   Elizabeth Langland, *Nobody's Angels Middle Class Women and Domestic Ideology in Victorian Culture* (New York: Cornell University Press, 1995), p. 9.

[14]   Sarah Stickney Ellis, *The Wives of England* (London: Fisher and Son, 1843), p. 181.

[15]   Henry Arthur Jones, *The Case of the Rebellious Susan*, in Russell Jackson (ed.), *Plays by Henry Arthur Jones* (Cambridge: Cambridge University Press, 1982), Act II, p. 125. Catherine Wiley observes that, 'social acceptance was only guaranteed by the sincere performance of conventional femininity' (Catherine Wiley, 'The Matter with Manners: the New Woman and the Problem Play', in James Redmond (ed.), *Women in Theatre* (Cambridge: Cambridge University Press, 1989), p. 109).

pleasure to all who live within the sphere of their influence, [women] shall be conscious of the charm by which they please'.[16]

Unpublished diaries of the time offer a model for the diary discourse which could develop within the space permitted for women's narrative of themselves. The acts of writing with immediacy and identifying the narrative occasion suggest that the diary's entries are live and unmediated. The non-fictional unpublished diaries of Emily Shore and Elizabeth Gaskell illustrate this sense of the areas of domestic space in which to write, the fear of publication and the sense of self-defined roles which will develop into the performance characteristics of the published fictional diary. The influence of the performative aspect of a diary is peculiarly apparent in the multiple techniques of Burney's *Diary and Letters* negotiating their appearance and attempting to act out the roles allocated by society. As Julia Epstein observes, 'Burney used her correspondence to dramatize personal experience and thereby to take retrospective control over it.'[17] In her introduction to the first volume in 1842, Charlotte Barrett as editor even reframes the defining event of the edited version by describing how Burney told her father of her hitherto concealed authorship of *Evelina* despite 'confusion at acknowledging her authorship and dread of his desiring to see her performance'.[18] This interest in viewing the self is demonstrated by Anne Lister too. On 26 January 1826, she records the death of her uncle and the inheritance of the Shibden estate jointly with her father: 'I read aloud the will [and] felt frightened to think I could think, at such a moment, of temporal gain ... He was the best of uncles to me ... I shed a tear or two when my father and Marian came and stopt once in reading the will ... Lord have mercy on me.'[19] God is invoked on this momentous occasion but the will also becomes a performed text within the mimetic action of producing a diary. Lister records not only what she must do in memorial terms ('the best of uncles') but in a performed act of reading which lays claim to her new role. She balances her female sorrow with her thoughts of 'temporal gain'. She then renarrates the experience in a text she will use as a conduct guide for the next fourteen years.

Performativity is a product both of immediacy and of the narratives of inclusion which the diary presents. The non-fictional diaries demonstrate a sense of self

---

[16]   Sarah Stickney Ellis, *The Daughters of England* (London: Fisher and Son, 1842), pp. 97–100. Rebecca Stern discusses this subversive content in Ellis's manuals: 'repetitions of the gestures and signs of cheerfulness, wit, and so on, become scandalous because they strip those qualities of their essentialist claims and reduce them to manufactured products' (Rebecca F. Stern, 'Moving Parts and Speaking Parts: Situating Victorian Antitheatricality', *ELH*, 65/2 (1998): 423).

[17]   Julia Epstein, *The Iron Pen: Fanny Burney and the Politics of Women's Writing* (Bristol: Bristol Classical Press 1989), p. 50.

[18]   *Diary and Letters of Madame D'Arblay* (7 vols, London: Colburn, 1842–46), 'Editor's Introduction', vol. 1, p. xix. See also the discussion of Burney's experience at the theatre when her heroine Cecilia is mentioned on stage (Chapter 3, p. 42).

[19]   Quoted in Jill Liddington, *Female Fortune: Land, Gender and Authority: The Anne Lister Diaries and Other Writings 1833–6* (London: Rivers Oram, 1998), p. 21.

which puts the diarist into a story which is unfolding and which she evaluates. Emily Shore and Elizabeth Gaskell provide contained examples of this; Frances Burney's is a complex performance linked with her own public persona as an author and Court attendant; Lister is always negotiating her public and private selves. In the context of fiction, Helen's diary in *The Tenant of Wildfell Hall* provides a model of the possibility of performing by allowing a text to be read. Marian's record is manipulated into immediacy by the assembly of the text which is *The Woman in White* making use of non-retrospection, gaps in language and editorial practice. Hers is a conditional performance partially withheld whereas Lydia Gwilt's is part of the deceitful act which is her whole life. The diary is the most transparent element of her representation within *Armadale*. Between the dramatizations of Marian and of Lydia, Collins's intervening novel *No Name*, serialized in 1862, includes a heroine who impersonates other characters both in a play and more extensively in her own plot to regain her inheritance. The novel includes some documents in a style similar to *The Woman in White* and *Armadale*, but Magdelan Vanstone actually does perform to strangers and therefore needs no diary.[20]

Sidonie Smith points out that there is a need to 'assign narrative coherence' to something termed a 'life' through which 'the autobiographical speaker becomes a performative subject [with] certain narrative itineraries'.[21] It is the dramatization of the writing and reading experience of diaries which makes them equivocal recording devices for nineteenth-century women. Writing is performed by the interpretation of the narrative occasion and by the preservation of the text, and reperformed by the acts of reading which make it a public text or narrative device.

This performance for the nineteenth-century diarist is authorized within the context of other performative narratives such as the conduct book, spiritual guide or court case. It allows a story to be told closer to actual experience as Anne Brontë observed in her foreword to *The Tenant of Wildfell Hall*. It is also performed as a social duty to fulfil Ellis's stipulation for domestic happiness and to keep in place society's 'friendly hedge'.[22] This should be a warning to women that their textual performance is nonetheless restricted. Magdelan Vanstone is restored to society by the death of her husband/cousin Noel, by the passive non-conspiratorial actions of her sister Norah and by an older man who rescues her from both death

---

[20]   Magdelan is frequently discussed and narrated within the novel. The lack of personal perspective on her actions is critical the night before her wedding when she is described performing the act of counting ships as a way of making the decision about her choice between suicide or going ahead with her plot (Wilkie Collins, *No Name*, ed. Mark Ford (London: Penguin, 1994), pp. 408–9). The diary in *Armadale* provides a more direct way of accessing Lydia's indecision.

[21]   Sidonie Smith, 'Performativity, Autobiographical Practice, Resistance', in Sidonie Smith and Julia Watson (eds), *Women Autobiography Theory: A Reader* (Madison: University of Wisconsin Press, 1998), p. 108; p. 110. The article originally appeared in 1995 which also postdates Smith, *A Poetics of Women's Autobiography* (1987).

[22]   Ellis, *Daughters of England*, p. 220.

and fallenness. Lydia Gwilt is a diarist who manages her extreme version of the domestic performance; she is her own collator and cannot be redeemed.

In a documentary sense, the fictional diaries are organized, concealed, printed, loaned, stolen, read, returned and even burned. Their provenance and survival as evidence is designed to fulfil their narrative purpose just as Pamela records how Reverend Williams, beset by thieves, 'by good Chance has sav'd my Papers'.[23]

The importance of, and appetite for, writing is reflected by the design and physical appearance of the diary which may be locked, pre-printed, customized, and even inscribed on another document. Catherine Earnshaw writes to put her mark in texts used to oppress her. Emily Shore describes her new volumes in detail using their first entries as subsidiary anniversaries in her life and Dora Johnston is particularly pleased to begin her diary bought with the money saved by not buying a new bonnet. Lydia reflects Richardson's Pamela in her absorption in the means of production and her inability to tear out a page even though it may incriminate her. Ezra Jennings, female in his sickness and Hester Dethridge, manly in her resolution both consider their physical texts essential to their second selves and the all-consuming secrets of their lives; their diaries are destined to be put into their coffins unread. In the latest novel of the sequence, however, Mina Harker's active collation and rereading come to nothing through the loss of all textual agency and authenticity. In *Dracula*, the second death of Lucy who wished to marry all three of her suitors defeats the threat of appetite and Mina as wife embodies her own original denial of New Womanhood.

The diary format enables the diarist to sift and evaluate her experiences. This is particularly evident in the construction and revision of Mina's diary and the other texts in *Dracula*, but all the fictional diarists use a sifting process to which their diaries contribute. Like Frances Burney, Helen writes entries which allow reflection and sifting by revisiting events after a long interval. She writes prospective as well as retrospective entries: 'I must have recourse to my diary again; I will commit it to paper tonight, and see what I think of it tomorrow.' She counteracts Hargrave's offensive but possibly tempting approaches by rereading her diary entry about his 'indescribable looks' which she has 'done well to record ... so minutely'.[24] Marian Halcombe's diary is part of Walter's chain of evidence but she also rereads later entries made with immediacy at the time. She uses these to review 'the fatal error of [Laura's] marriage' and to record Kyrle's letter when the original is destroyed for reasons of safety. [25] Walter as editor preserves the entries which make his case and afterwards make Marian safe for life in his own household. Helen's entries remain written so that Gilbert can read and edit them later.

---

    [23]   Samuel Richardson, *Pamela*, ed. Thomas Keymer and Alice Wakely (Oxford: Oxford University Press, 2001), p. 150.

    [24]   Anne Brontë, *The Tenant of Wildfell Hall*, ed. Stevie Davies (London: Penguin, 1996), pp. 164, 309.

    [25]   Wilkie Collins, *The Woman in White*, ed. John Sutherland (Oxford: Oxford University Press, 1996; reissued 1998), pp. 271, 373.

The core texts at the level of their overall narrative structure incorporate the nineteenth-century woman, the nineteenth-century diary and the hybrid narration of the novel. The intervention of the narrating editor promotes both clarity and conciseness and testifies to the proper sources of the evidence. The editor justifies through narration the overall assembly of the narrative which is the novel.

The acts of editing in the novels are based on non-fictional arguments for exposing otherwise private material. Max Urquhart, although not a collator, regularly discusses texts and their production or preservation. Likewise the Governor in *The Legacy of Cain* controls access to some of the information. Editors like Gilbert, Walter and Franklin Blake seek protection, propriety and posterity, the narrative of their own social inclusion. The exploitation of non-retrospective immediacy can accommodate the confirmatory acts of narration which give the text provenance. Confirmation is also sought through the already existing traditions of the woman's diary in sifting for meaning, compiling a memory bank, exploring advice and recording family history. Even what is not written makes its contribution through ellipses, which indicate a reticence or the lack of writing opportunity. In turn, these elisions are exploited in the editing situation and create the irony that there is always space to read further meaning in. Having hijacked its veracity, the editor creates gaps to improve readability and this generates the textual narrative of inclusion such as the one which arises between the originally written diaries and letters of Frances Burney and the originally printed text of Madame D'Arblay's *Diary and Letters*.

The resulting text bears the imprint of editing practice and editorial choice. Each document of a hybrid or intercalated narrative in the novels thus exists through its own narrative of inclusion. As Valerie Raoul has observed, the fictional diary is fiction 'flaunted' in that it 'reveals something about narration, rather than something about a particular self'.[26] The editors and other exterior compilers such as the outer voice of *Dracula* and the neutral controller of *Armadale* arrange the intersection of competing narratives such as letters, memoranda and newspaper cuttings. The impact of these realistic sources ranges from the fight for proof which occurs in *The Woman in White* to the final lack of proof in *Dracula*. What is clear is that documents can distort the truth and the diary is implicated in this distortion along with the products of nineteenth-century bureaucracy such as letters and death certificates. Even technological advances such as facsimile and phonograph recordings are made suspect and at one further remove, diary narrative acquires additional paratextual associations when interacting with the miscellany reading of the serial.

The overall editor also structures the narrative by choosing its vehicles and voices. In the hybrid novel, the diary functions as narrative through the suppression of other voices and this suppression, resulting in the prioritization of 'I', represents another equivocal area of performance by nineteenth-century women. The women

---

[26] Valerie Raoul, *The French Fictional Journal: Fictional Narcissism/Narcissistic Fiction* (Toronto: University of Toronto Press, 1980), p. 11.

who do not have a voice within the novels act as implicit commentary on the women who do. These other voices exist either within the private record of the chosen diarist or within colonized accounts provided by the editors but the resulting act of suppression by the diarist makes her into a fallen woman or would-be man.

The diary of Helen Huntingdon's aunt compiled as a conduct book, might offer an insight into the life of an unhappily married woman which could have altered the course of *The Tenant of Wildfell Hall*. The model of Penelope in *The Moonstone* is a reminder that women's diaries can stay hidden and still prompt a narrative as hers does for the recollections of her father Gabriel Betteredge. The diary of Rachel Verinder in that novel must be suppressed for a different reason – just as the diaries of Laura Glyde and Anne Catherick in *The Woman in White* cannot be revealed without undoing the plot. In a sense, the latter two women have 'second selves' in each other and need no textual confessor. In *Armadale*, access is briefly provided to the narrative of Mother Oldershaw through her letters whose role is to facilitate plotting and also to give Lydia a different voice. Lydia's diary in turn contains Oldershaw as if she were herself a textual controller and suppressor of other voices. There may be some contrast in elegance and ambition between Gwilt and her former mentor but there is a sense in which Oldershaw provides further warnings of what enterprising women will achieve by manipulating nineteenth-century codes of accomplishments, good dress sense and cosmetics.[27] Lucy in *Dracula* is a putative New Woman with her Dracula-induced appetite for men, and access to her thoughts is both unwise and unplottable. She is allowed several coy communications with Mina about her marriage prospects but a one-page diary and a failed letter are her only other contributions to the 'narrative patchwork.' She, like her own letter, must be read too late in order to give the men grounds for action and for their own Fosco/Walter-like violation with a stake.

The combined lack of language and lack of access have an impact both on the plot and on the other interpretations of domestic womanhood from Penelope Johnston to Mother Oldershaw and Lucy Westenra. The role of the diarist in suppressing these other voices contributes to her nature as a fallen or mannish woman who is the protagonist in her own story and must be renarrated within the confines of a male text. In the cases of Dora, Lydia and Helena, the suppression is managed by the diarist herself; in the cases of Helen and Marian by a male editor. In *Dracula*, the supreme equivalence of voices finally undermines the very case under investigation. In these core novels, the diaries disappear from the narrative as a result of negotiations within the overall text and the diarists are themselves suppressed by the social obligation of (re)marriage, death or being an aunt.

---

[27]   Her role in Lydia's life has some echoes in the situation of Edith Dombey and her mother. The positions of the women groomed for a life which will make them fallen women is pointed up by the existence of Edith's illegitimate cousin Alice Marwood and her mother in *Dombey and Son*. The example of Estella and Miss Havisham in *Great Expectations* comes from the same decade as *Armadale*.

Gilbert Markham, Walter Hartright and Franklin Blake and to a lesser extent Madame Pratolungo and Valeria Macallan are engaged in projects which construct narrative for their own purposes. The facsimile of reality which they control – Gilbert in a letter, Walter and Franklin as supervising editors and the two women as first-person narrators who enclose other documents – is itself a reflection of print culture as they seek verification through evidence. Anne Brontë and Wilkie Collins present their diarists so that their evidence can appear in print and then be refracted within printed and reread versions of edited material. In *Dracula*, the final act of framing and obsessive reworking of evidence is literally a facsimile as no original documents remain and indeed no record is deemed to be authentic.

It is at this level of extratextuality that the 'convoluted plot'[28] generates narratives of assembly, transmission and inclusion which bring the authority of the collator into question as part of the reading process. Diary-writing creates a narrative occasion and the ability to record events. The preservation, equivocal privacy and transmission of the diary are translated into a fictional context. The novel in turn takes on the fiction of editing which complicates any reading of a hybrid narrative and questions the role of both reader and collator in their access to the text.

The value of print brought into question in hybrid diary narratives from 1848 to 1888 is finally defused in *Dracula* where documents cannot be a version of the truth because they are (re)printed. In terms of its heritage and incorporation of other forms of print, the fictional diary in the later nineteenth century engages with a complex set of references when it forms a narrative voice in the hybrid form of the novel. The non-fictional diary of a woman exemplified by that of Frances Burney had to negotiate with its household and spiritual traditions in order to appear in print at all. Just like her non-fictional counterpart, the female fictional diarist explores her own narrativity in conjunction with the contemporary texts she absorbs; from the epistolary novel to the conduct book and childcare manual; from the published diary to the court case.

The analysis in Part 2 characterizes the narrative application of the diary in the writing and reading of women as subjects, fictional diarists and consumers. Women writers could use the diary as narrative as a result of their own engagement with the diary-writing traditions of the early nineteenth century. The published diary of Frances Burney illustrates the potential for a woman's diary as narrative in a public form. At the same time the inclusion of the diary in narrative is a development leading from the epistolary form of the first novels of the early and mid eighteenth century. This is reiterated by the writing advice offered by manuals of the period which themselves fictionalize situations in which appropriate letters may be written in series. Serial narrative appeals to women as both letter writers and readers of fiction, and the serial like the diary during its process of composition offers delayed gratification but conversely operates under strict authorial control and with knowledge of the outcome. A reading and writing miscellany which puts

---

28   Martens, p. 37.

the diary into context can be recovered from the periodical in order to reinterpret the reading experience of the first consumers. The document as a potential fictional device emerges through the reported appearance of documents in court in parallel with the private miscellany of diary compilation which might include cuttings and copied material. The mid nineteenth-century phenomenon of sensation fiction acts as a miscellany genre by utilizing the traditions of writing already visited – the role of women, court reporting, the document and the serial consumption of fiction. In this way, the fictional diary becomes a tool for promoting sensation through both deferral within the plot and the use of a feminine form of writing to narrate monstrous actions.

Against this background an assessment of the chronology or evolution of the diary as a narrative device becomes possible using the evidence of the core texts. For contemporary critics, the double diary of *A Life for a Life* became linked with *The Woman in White* which was in turn identified with *Dracula* when it was published in 1897. *The Woman in White* sold well throughout the century and may have been the main influence on Stoker, but some of the documentary approach of *Dracula* shows traits identifiable in *The Legacy of Cain* which itself partakes of the heredity debate and the degeneration which *Dracula* fears.

As a modern day editor, John Sutherland regards *A Life for a Life* as a source for the narrative method of *The Woman in White*.[29] Unlike Collins's novel, however, *A Life for a Life* does not contain ostensible authorial intervention and may even anticipate in itself the intertwined complexity of *Dracula*. There is a sense in which all the fictional diaries within hybrid narratives offer just such an interwoven set of references. *Wuthering Heights*, for instance, frames an oral story retold in a man's diary which contains a woman's diary. In the third volume of the novel as it was originally published, the final pages of *Agnes Grey* claim the authority of a diary.[30] The fertilization of ideas between the Brontë sisters then appears to develop into the framing and framed diaries of *The Tenant of Wildfell Hall*. *The Woman in White* connects with *The Tenant of Wildfell Hall* through the textual collators and class movers Gilbert and Walter who take on editorial roles over strong women.

The time frame of influence of Dinah Craik on Wilkie Collins which Sutherland proposes is not easy to establish despite the link made by at least one critic in the 1860s.[31] The model of Burney's *Diary and Letters* from 1842–46 was re-emphasized by Macaulay's *Edinburgh Review* article in January 1843 which was then reprinted in his *Critical and Historical Essays* throughout the 1840s

---

[29]   Sutherland refers to *A Life for a Life* in his Introduction to the Oxford edition (*The Woman in White*, p. xv). Wilkie Collins had himself acted in a one-act farce about a diary in 1851. See Kathryn Carter, 'The Cultural Work of Diaries in Mid-Century Victorian Britain', *Victorian Review*, 23/2 (Winter 1997): 256 for his part in Charles Dickens and Mark Lemon's *Mr Nightingale's Diary* (1851). Collins had also written 'The Diary of Ann Rodway' for *Household Words* as well as 'Leah's Diary' in *After Dark* in 1856.

[30]   See Chapter 4, p. 59.

[31]   *Dublin University Magazine* (February 1861) in Norman Page (ed.), *Wilkie Collins: The Critical Heritage* (London: Routledge and Kegan Paul, 1974), p. 106.

and 1850s. Collins had used letters and journals in his *Memoir* of his father published in 1848. Craik had published *Bread Upon the Waters* for the Governess's Benevolent Association in 1852, but this was before the success of *John Halifax Gentleman* and it is unlikely that its circulation was very wide. A cheap edition of *The Tenant of Wildfell Hall* was issued in 1854 and its authorship was much discussed with the publication of Gaskell's *Life of Charlotte Bronte* in 1857. *A Life for a Life* was originally published in August 1859 and the first instalment of *The Woman in White* appeared in *All the Year Round* on 26 November 1859 with Marian's first diary entry on 28 January 1860.

The refraction of literary and documentary forms in Part 2 has, however, generated an identifiable coincidence of approaches between Craik and Wilkie Collins. Their shared interest in the use of the diary represents one of several possible associations between their novels from 1852 to 1875 and there are further continuities or thematic parallels between Craik and Collins beyond the use of diary narrative which are worthy of exploration. The investigation of the mature and later periods of their writing highlights further potential intersections of subject matter in the area of gender roles.[32] The role of Phineas Fletcher who narrates *John Halifax Gentleman* using his background diary suggests that disabled men are women. Collins's plots may rely on strong women from Marian to Helena but his weak men are womanly and must take control. For Craik, marginalized men like Halifax or Max Urquhart are women in disguise and their actions indicate how women would behave if the world were theirs to run.[33]

There is a sense also in which Craik's is a separate tradition despite links with the conduct book and the diary-writing intentions of Burney. Without offering a direct rebellion, she allows Dora's resurrected diary to be the last entry in the novel. It is a record that could carry on even if it were re-embraced by the four traditions and no longer a public document. It is, however, Dora who chooses to stop writing or at least to stop the reader from reading in a way which surprisingly allies her with Lydia Gwilt. Although the two women finally appear in plainly different domestic contexts, Lydia expects to stop writing on her marriage as Dora

---

[32] *John Halifax Gentleman* (1856) provides the portrait of a blind and angelic daughter which may have influenced the portrayal of Lucilla in *Poor Miss Finch* (1872). Collins's disabled character Miserrimus Dexter in *The Law and the Lady* (1875) is a madman who taunts Valeria both with his appearance and the threat of sexuality by contrast with her weakly conventional husband Eustace. Craik has already presented the Earl of Carnforth in *A Noble Life* (1866) as a disabled man doing good and providing himself with an heir through a totally asexual process. In *A Brave Lady* (1869), Craik returns to the idea of a background journal which is utilized by the first person narrator Winifred. The composition of the journal in French for one hour a week is presented in the context of Craik's own horror of the idea of being 'cursed with a biographer' (*A Brave Lady* (London: Harper, 1870), p. 43). The 'brave' Josephine is a mouthpiece for Craik's concerns with the Married Women's Property Act which Collins exposes at around the same time through the character of diarist Hester Dethridge in *Man and Wife* (1870).

[33] This is discussed by Sally Mitchell, *Dinah Mulock Craik* (Boston: Twayne, 1983).

does. Midwinter's belief in the dream in *Armadale* which predicts that he will repeat his father's act of murder by murdering Allan Armadale, is the complex context for the behaviour which drives Lydia back to her plot. Dora's situation might in other lights also be seen as sensational since she inadvertently falls in love with and eventually marries the murderer of her own half brother. The use of immediacy in Max Urquhart's answering diary letter defuses this situation. He writes to the very 'moment' his discovery that his hitherto unknown victim was Harry Johnston.[34] Diary sharing causes Dora to be redeemed and to retain her means of personal expression where Lydia is absorbed into omniscient narrative.

Within this overview of fifty years of diary narrative, the influence of Frances Burney's diaries may also extend to the end of the century. Reprints and rediscoveries of Burney were taking place between 1889 and 1892 when new editions and new material emerged. W.C. Ward's standard edition of the *Diary* was published in 1890–91 in a series entitled 'The Cream of the Diarists and Memoir Writers.'[35] An abridged Swan Sonneschein edition from 1892 retains Charlotte Barrett's frame.[36] Ward, however, announces that his is the unaltered popular edition. He removes Barrett's introduction, uses Macaulay's review in its stead and ignores 'Nobody.'

The 1890s appear to have stimulated a revival of interest in the diary as a literary and biographical device. Annie Raine Ellis's edition of Burney's early diaries was published in 1889[37] and in 1891 Emily Shore's sisters decided to publish her diary which was reprinted in 1898. In another parallel development, John Lister of Shibden Hall produced a two hundred thousand-word transcript of Anne Lister's diary for the *Halifax Guardian* which was published between 1887 and 1892. Elsewhere and even before the publication of *Dracula* in 1897, Gwendolen Fairfax in Act II of *The Importance of Being Earnest* pronounced the diary in 1895 'something sensational to read on the train'. In Wilde's play the appearance on stage of the fictional lover conjured by Cecily Cardew's diary suggests that all diary writing is fiction. In the wake of such developments at the end of the nineteenth century, the ongoing fictional device of the woman's diary

---

[34]   See Dinah Mulock Craik, *A Life for a Life* (New Edition, London: Hurst and Blackett, n.d), Chapter 25, p. 244.

[35]   *The Diary and Letters of Madame d'Arblay* (3 vols, London: Virtue/Vizetelly & Co, 1890–1). The Preface acknowledges that the entries have been reselected from 'Mrs. Barrett's' edition. Barrett died in 1870 and Ward describes her as the 'former editor' (p. x).

[36]   *Diary and Letters of Madame D'Arblay as edited by her niece Charlotte Barrett* (3 vols, London: Swan Sonneschein, 1892). There had been an intervening reprint of the 7–volume edition by Hurst and Blackett in 1854. Bell's (1891) and Frederick's (1892) editions also retained Barrett's introduction.

[37]   *The Early Diary of Frances Burney, 1768–1778*, ed. Annie Raine Ellis, (2 vols, London: G. Bell & Sons, 1889). Bell would produce the 10–volume Wheatley edition of Pepys's diaries (1893–99) in a reverse of Colburn who had turned to Burney after Pepys in the 1840s. Joyce Hemlow observes that Ellis printed all she could read of Burney and Barrett's selections 'making no discriminatory deletions of her own' (*The Journals and Letters of Fanny Burney* (12 vols, Oxford: Clarendon Press, 1972–1984), vol. 1, p. vi).

in the twentieth century could in turn be refracted against the categories of literary production considered in Part 2.[38]

The writing and publication of Emily Shore's diary represents one arc within which the core texts for this study of the nineteenth century sit. In 1891 her editor sisters take control to explain 'her heart was a shrine whose veil was never, or but a corner of it, lifted'.[39] In her preface to the 1991 reprint of this text, Barbara Gates speculates on the 'sisterly selectivity' of Louisa and Arabella Shore and she makes the significant distinction that 'the sisters were orchestrating a memoir; Emily was unfolding a life'.[40] Shore's diary is thus not only a model for nineteenth-century diary-writing but also a case study for the presentation of women in print, of the diary becoming biography.

In this context, the actions of Louisa and Arabella Shore and those of Charlotte Barrett in positioning Emily Shore and Frances Burney for the market present the possibility of a specific role for the female biographer of a female family member.[41] Charlotte Brontë's reconstruction of Emily and Anne Brontë has been briefly considered in this study in Chapter 4; Cassandra Austen was part of the Austen family project in the choice of her sister's surviving letters and Lucy Aikin wrote an introductory memoir to the 1825 edition of her aunt Anna Laetitia Barbauld's *Works*. Although she began a diary, Elizabeth Gaskell resisted biography for herself but used the documents of a sister author to create *The Life of Charlotte Brontë* in 1857.[42] This 'selectivity' and the editing of other documents such as diaries, letters and testaments can be seen by acts of omission or inclusion to narrate other

---

[38] Such a study of the first part of the twentieth century might include Charlotte Perkins Gilman's *The Yellow Wallpaper* (1892), Austin Dobson's 'English Men (*sic*) of Letters' account of Burney (1903) and his edition of her *Diary* (1905–6), Virginia Woolf's 'Journal of Mistress Joan Martyn' (1906), the publication of Anne Clifford's Diary (1922–3), Magdelan King-Hall's *Diary of a Young Lady of Fashion* (1924), Vera Brittain's *Testament of Youth* (1933) and the serial *The Diary of a Provincial Lady* (*Time and Tide* 1929–40). Elizabeth Gaskell's diary was published in 1923 and in 1938 the librarian Muriel Green produced a transcript of 395 of Anne Lister's letters entitled *A Spirited Yorkshirewoman*. Green also wrote articles for the *Halifax Courier* (which had amalgamated with the *Halifax Guardian*) although the topic of Lister's sexuality was not discussed.

[39] Emily Shore, *The Journal of Emily Shore*, ed. Barbara Timm Gates (Charlottesville: University Press of Virginia, 1991), p. 178. Shore's diary was originally written between 1831 and 1839. It was published in 1891 and reprinted in 1898.

[40] Ibid., pp. vii, xviii.

[41] The manuscript of two volumes of Shore's diary has become available for study. See Barbara Timm Gates, 'Self-Writing as Legacy: *The Journal of Emily Shore*', http://rotunda.upress.virginia.edu:8080/EmilyShore/make-page.xqy?id=jes-intro (accessed 15 March 2007).

[42] Dinah Craik described biography as the act of 'literary ghouls' in an article which dramatizes a protest from the spirit world against Gaskell's *Life*; see 'Literary Ghouls: A Protest from the Other World', *Chamber's Journal* (21 August 1858) reprinted in Dinah Mulock Craik, *Studies from Life* (London: Hurst and Blackett, [1861]), pp. 225–48.

women for posterity. Enough evidence exists to justify further consideration of these 'sisterly' acts, the creation of print portraits of women by women.

By 1846, the diary of a woman was familiar in print, part of the commodification of the personal. The emergence of the diary into print culture was linked clearly with the availability of material and the existence of an audience for its appearance as a publication. At the level of contemporary serial consumption, the initial exploration of reading in *All the Year Round* and *The Cornhill* in Chapter 6 demonstrates ways in which the serialized novel also interacted with the other material of the periodical miscellany as part of the reception of the fictional diary in print.[43] Critics responded with little enthusiasm to the fictional device, finding the narratives of inclusion undramatic. A reviewer of *The Tenant of Wildfell Hall* wrote in 1848 of the transitions between Gilbert's narrative and Helen's diary: 'After so long and minute a history, we cannot go back and recover the enthusiasm which we have been obliged to dismiss a volume and a half before'.[44] Dickens found the method of *The Woman in White* 'dissective', and critics at the end of the century continued to bemoan the 'wearisome narrative' bequeathed by Collins to Stoker.

Fictional diaries including six within the core texts have been studied here using a nineteenth-century model. In each case, a woman's diary written for the private 'audience of one'[45] is asked to reinscribe itself with a new addressee, to 'perform to strangers'. Women's diaries were permitted in private because a fragmented form of writing was possible in the context of household responsibility and the tasks imposed by routine. In their dailiness, diaries too represent that routine. They become authorized records because they fit into daily duty and feed the other authorized texts – letters, household accounts, family history – which act as moral reference points. As records within the traditions and practices of diary-writing, women's non-fictional diaries are in themselves multi-voiced. Diaries can also narrate experiences outside language because they have been moved to the private sphere where narrative gaps are a factor of women's lived experience. Whether they are valuing a domestic record or revaluing an experience by recording it, women's diaries act out tensions between private and public domains.

The fictional diary takes from its non-fictional counterpart the role of editor and the need for provenance as well as the equivocal role of the diarist herself.

---

[43]   Other Collins novels in *All the Year Round* such as *No Name* and *The Moonstone* could be studied in the same way in addition to *A Tale of Two Cities* and *Great Expectations* from a similar period. The serialization of Gaskell's novels and stories in different types of periodicals from *Household Words* ('Lizzie Leigh', the *Cranford* group, *North and South*) to *The Cornhill* (*Cousin Phillis*, *Wives and Daughters*) could also be re-examined in this light along with Collins's novels of the 1870s serialized in *Cassell's Magazine* and *The Graphic*. This would build on the work in Linda K. Hughes and Michael Lund, *The Victorian Serial* (Charlottesville: University Press of Virginia, 1991), specifically pp. 17–108.

[44]   *The Examiner* (29 July 1848); Miriam Allott (ed.), *The Brontës: The Critical Heritage* (London: Routledge and Kegan Paul, 1974), p. 255.

[45]   Cheryl Cline, *Women's Diaries, Journals and Letters: An Annotated Bibliography* (New York: Garland Press, 1989), p. xiii.

Three of these fictional diarists occupy a distant intradiegetic place in the 'narrative recess' of the novel. Helen is a tenant within a male journal, and Mina is replicated like her diary, not as a vampire but as an ideologically sound woman. Marian is renarrated into her place as another woman in white, reduced to blank or at least private pages. As collator, Walter makes this recess even more distant when he announces casually more than four fifths of the way into *The Woman in White* that for Laura's sake he tells this 'story under feigned names' and has renamed himself 'right-hearted'.[46] At some points within the narrative these diarists may own the ellipsis as editors themselves but control of the diary finally controls the women. Dora, Lydia and Helena appear to maintain some form of agency as a result of being diarists. Despite her accounts of her own passivity, Dora marries Max as she set out to do in defiance of her father and of society. Lydia and Helena use the diary to articulate the performance of staged domesticity as part of their plots; one must die, and the other emigrates.

These diaries are part of the hierarchy of documents building into a text which narrates its own assembly. The narrative of their inclusion is a significant part of the creation of meaning just as the narrative occasion is a part of the evolution of the diary. *The Tenant of Wildfell Hall* presents the act of reading a diary already written and *A Life for a Life* is in the form of a 'double diary' shading into sympathetic letters which discuss the nature of being an addressee. *The Woman in White* unfolds a diary as written immediacy which is reconstructed as evidence whilst the diary in *Armadale* reinforces Lydia's villainy by being outside any male or other narrative control. *The Legacy of Cain* revisits the double diary and also looks forward to the textual indeterminacy of the last decade of the nineteenth century when the diaries and co-operating texts in *Dracula* are finally discounted.

Diary replication and re-enactment shift the focus from the private back to the public sphere so that Gilbert and Walter are regenerated as gentlemen, and the vampire hunters defy *fin de siècle* gender anxiety. The provenance and physical survival of the diaries as texts secures their place in the chain of evidence. All the diaries are acts of renarrated impropriety but the propriety of telling is maintained by their being first of all devalued as private documents and then revalued as contemporaneous accounts. In this way it is possible to tell a woman's story as closely as possible to actual experience without the mediation of her retrospective narrative control. The diaries can only be made public because they are unrevised but the reader must always suspect that the role of addressee has been hijacked and that she is implicated in that duplicity. In effect, publication neutralizes the fear of what is being written in private and the nineteenth-century dilemma over women's private texts is thus resolved. Diaries might be written in private, but they can be used in public for ends which exploit their method and subject matter.

---

[46] *The Woman in White*, p. 556. The name 'Fairlie' is close to 'Fairly' which is the name chosen by Burney to disguise the identity of Stephen Digby in Volume IV of her *Diary*.

In *Dracula*, at the end of the century, the diary performance is safely marginalized at the expense of all textual authenticity.

This conclusion posits a continuity of response as well as a chronology of women's diaries narrating the novel. The diary has a competing role with the other documents in the hybrid form of the novel. While the diary acts as narrative, other voices are suppressed as in the model of the non-fictional diary made public. There are both silenced narrators and non-narrators within this narrative matrix, and the diary made public has readers both authorized and unauthorized through the act of editing and the transmission of the text.

As a physical artefact the diary is both a written and a transmitted document. In its fictional role, the diary novel narrates its own assembly and generates narratives of inclusion at the time of recording and at the time of collation. This reflects the commodified status of the private diary in print.

The diary of a nineteenth-century woman acting as a narrative device exploits the ideological clash between the feminine form and a public document. The diary is the woman. It offers her the possibility of saying 'I' in the guise of a 'second self' who can compose an alternative conduct book to challenge the narrow definition of her privacy. The ideology of domestic womanhood is reinterpreted by the use and inflection of the authorized interwoven traditions of accounting, spiritual reflection, family chronicle and travel journal; and by the act of showing this diary as a performance of the self.

Thus *The Woman in White* as a novel offers the reader access to a homely female record within a purportedly judicial format. It appears on the page in reported immediacy as an ongoing diary by an ordinary Victorian woman and yet that diary conceals scenarios of spying and illegal detective work, forgery and social climbing. Despite the use of a realistic document, Marian's diary records the characters of a manly woman, a womanly man, a controlled feminist, unfaithful husband and unnatural mother. The inheritance of the aristocracy is found to be illegitimate on the grounds of bigamy, and the older generation of male guardians is useless. The diary contains these 'mysteries at our own door' and demonstrates that there is criminal activity at the heart of the nineteenth century even in its domestic recording practices.

This study of the diary as narrative assesses the treatment of women's diaries as commodities in fiction. Critics argue that the diary is a feminine form of writing. The nineteenth-century novel puts a private document into the marketplace where the fictional diaries of women both preserve and question a contested domestic space. 'Marian Halcombe,' a woman made doubly fictional and fallen by an unauthorized act of renaming, narrates her second self in a diary which is forced to perform for a male textual collator. At one crucial moment, she records in the diary her escape through a low window into the grounds of Blackwater Park: 'I ran out to hide from them in the darkness; to hide even from myself.'[47]

---

[47]   *The Woman in White*, p. 293.

Bibliography

Primary Sources

All the Year Round, XXXI–LII (26 November 1859–21 April 1860).

Austen, Jane, *Catharine and Other Writings*, ed. Margaret Anne Doody and Douglas Murray (Oxford: Oxford University Press, 1993; reissued 1998).

Braddon, Mary Elizabeth, *Lady Audley's Secret*, ed. David Skilton (Oxford: Oxford University Press, 1987).

The British Letter-Writer: or Letter-writer's Complete Instructor (London: J. Cooke, 1760).

Brontë, Anne, *Agnes* Grey, ed. Angeline Goreau (London: Penguin, 1988).

———, *The Tenant of Wildfell Hall*, ed. Stevie Davies (London: Penguin, 1996).

Brontë, Emily, *Wuthering Heights*, ed. Pauline Nestor (London: Penguin, 1995; reissued 2003).

Burney, Frances, *The Journals and Letters of Fanny Burney*, ed. Joyce Hemlow (12 vols, Oxford: Clarendon Press, 1972–1984).

———, *The Early Journals and Letters of Fanny Burney*, ed. Lars E. Troide (6 vols, Oxford: Clarendon Press, 1988–).

———, *Evelina*, ed. Margaret Anne Doody (London: Penguin 1994; reprinted 2004).

Collins, Wilkie, *Mad Monkton and Other Stories*, ed. Norman Page (Oxford: Oxford University Press, 1994).

———, *After Dark*, ed. W.A. Brockington (London: Gresham, n.d).

———, 'The Unknown Public', *Household Words*, XVIII (21 August 1858): 217–22.

———, *The Woman in White*, ed. John Sutherland (Oxford: Oxford University Press, 1996; reissued 1998).

———, *No Name*, ed. Mark Ford (London: Penguin, 1994).

———, *Armadale*, ed. Catherine Peters (Oxford: Oxford University Press, 1989).

———, *The Moonstone*, ed. Sandra Kemp (London: Penguin, 1998).

———, *Man and Wife* (Stroud: Alan Sutton Publishing, 1990; reprinted 1993).

———, *Poor Miss Finch* (Stroud: Alan Sutton Publishing, 1994).

———, *The Law and the Lady*, ed. Jenny Bourne Taylor (Oxford: Oxford University Press, 1992; reissued 1999).

———, *The Legacy of Cain* (Stroud: Alan Sutton Publishing, 1993; reprinted 2003).

———, *The Letters of Wilkie Collins*, ed. William Baker and William M. Clarke (2 vols, Basingstoke: Macmillan, 1999).

The Complete Letter-Writer containing Familiar Letters on The most common Occasions in Life (Edinburgh: Paterson, 1776).

The Cornhill Magazine, X–XIII (November 1864–June 1866).

Craik, Dinah Mulock, *Bread Upon the Waters: A Governess's Life* (Leipzig: Tauschnitz, 1865) Collection of British Authors Vol. 807, pp. 7–86.

———, *John Halifax Gentleman* (29th edition, London: Hurst and Blackett, n.d.).

———, *A Life for a Life* (New Edition, London: Hurst and Blackett, n.d).

———, *Studies from Life* (London: Hurst and Blackett, [1861]).

———, *A Brave Lady* (London: Harper, 1870).

Diary and Letters of Madame D'Arblay: author of 'Evelina', 'Cecilia', &c. (7 vols, London: Colburn, 1842–46).

Dickens, Charles, *The Letters of Charles Dickens*, ed. Graham Storey (12 vols, Oxford: Clarendon Press, 1965–2002), vols 9 and 11.

D'Israeli, Isaac, 'Diaries Moral, Historical and Critical', *Curiosities of Literature*, vol. 2 (New edition, London: Warne, 1881), 206–15.

Ellis, Sarah Stickney, *The Women of England* (London: Fisher and Son, 1839).

———, *The Daughters of England Their Position in Society, Character and Responsibilities* (London: Fisher and Son, 1842).

———, *The Wives of England* (London: Fisher and Son, 1843).

Eliot, George, *Adam Bede*, ed. Stephen Gill (London: Penguin, 1980; reprinted 1985).

Gaskell, Elizabeth, 'The Diary' in *The Works of Elizabeth Gaskell*, ed. Joanne Shattock (10 vols, London: Pickering and Chatto, 2005), vol. 1, ed. Joanne Shattock, pp. 5–25.

———, *Cranford* in *The Works of Elizabeth Gaskell*, ed. Joanne Shattock (10 vols, London: Pickering and Chatto, 2005), vol. 3, ed. Alan Shelston.

Gisborne, Thomas, *An Enquiry into the Duties of the Female Sex* (London: Cadell, 1797).

Household Words, CCCXXX–XXXI (19 and 26 July 1856).

[Jewsbury, Geraldine], *'A Life for a Life'*, *The Athenaeum* (6 August 1859):173–4.

Johnson, Charles, *The Complete Art of Writing Letters* (London: T. Evans, 1779).

Jones, Henry Arthur, *The Case of the Rebellious Susan*, in Russell Jackson (ed.), *Plays by Henry Arthur Jones* (Cambridge: Cambridge University Press, 1982), pp. 103–61.

Lister, Anne, *I Know My Own Heart: The Diaries of Anne Lister (1791–1840)*, ed. Helena Whitbread (London: Virago, 1988).

[Mansel, Henry], 'Sensation Novels', *Quarterly Review*, CXIII (April 1863): 481–514.

[Oliphant, Margaret], 'Sensation Novels', *Blackwood's Edinburgh Magazine*, XCI (May 1862): 564–84.

———, 'Novels', *Blackwood's Edinburgh Magazine*, XCIV (August 1863): 168–83.

———, 'Novels', *Blackwood's Edinburgh Magazine*, CII (September 1867): 257–80.

'Our Female Novelists', *The Christian Remembrancer*, CV/ii (1859): 305–21.

[Parr, Harriet], 'The Author of *John Halifax*', *British Quarterly Review*, XCVII (July 2 1866): 32–58.

Richardson, Samuel, *Pamela; or, Virtue Rewarded*, ed. Thomas Keymer and Alice Wakely (Oxford: Oxford University Press, 2001).

Shelley, Mary, *Frankenstein*, ed. Maurice Hindle (London: Penguin, 2003).

Shore, Emily, *The Journal of Emily Shore*, ed. Barbara Timm Gates (Charlottesville: University Press of Virginia, 1991).

The Spectator, CCCXVII–XXIII (4–11 March 1712): 394–423.

Stoker, Bram, *Dracula*, ed. Maurice Hindle (London: Penguin, 1993).

Trollope, Anthony, *Barchester Towers*, ed. Robin Gilmour (London: Penguin, 1982; reprinted 1994).

Wood, Mrs Henry [Ellen], *East Lynne*, ed. Norman Page (London: Everyman, 1994).

Secondary Sources

Abbott, H. Porter, 'Letters to the Self: The Cloistered Writer in Nonretrospective Fiction', *PMLA*, 95 (1980): 23–41.

———, 'Diary Fiction', *Orbis Litterarum*, 37 (1982): 12–31.

———, *Diary Fiction: Writing as Action* (Ithaca: Cornell University Press, 1984).

Allott, Miriam (ed.), *The Brontës: The Critical Heritage* (London: Routledge and Kegan Paul, 1974).

Altick, Richard D., *The English Common Reader: A Social History of the Mass Reading Public, 1800–1900* (Chicago: University of Chicago Press, 1957; revised 1983).

Altman, Janet Gurkin, *Epistolarity: Approaches to a Form* (Columbus: Ohio State University Press, 1982).

Anderson, Linda, 'At the Threshold of Self: Women and Autobiography', in Moira Monteith (ed.), *Women's Writing: A Challenge to Theory* (Brighton: Harvester Press, 1986), pp. 54–71.

———, *Autobiography* (London: Routledge, 2001).

Armstrong, Nancy, *Desire and Domestic Fiction: A Political History of the Novel* (Oxford: Oxford University Press, 1987).

Auerbach, Nina and David J. Skal (eds), *Dracula The Norton Critical Edition* (New York: Norton, 1997).

Bachman, Maria K. and Don Richard Cox, 'Wilkie Collins's Villainous Miss Gwilt, Criminality and the Unspeakable Truth', *Dickens Studies Annual*, 32 (2002): 319–37.

Bachman, Maria K. and Don Richard Cox (eds), *Reality's Dark Light: The Sensational Wilkie Collins* (*Tennessee Studies in Literature*, 41, Knoxville: University of Tennessee Press, 2003).

Bal, Mieke, *Narratology: Introduction to the Theory of Narrative* (Toronto: University of Toronto Press, 1985).

Barker, Juliet, *The Brontës* (London: Weidenfield and Nicholson, 1994).

Barthes, Roland, *Image Music Text: Essays Selected and Translated by Stephen Heath* (London: Fontana, 1977).

Beetham, Margaret, 'Open and Closed: the Periodical as a Published Genre', *Victorian Periodicals Review*, 22/3 (Fall 1989): 96–100.

Bell, Bill 'Fiction and the Marketplace: towards a study of the Victorian Serial', in Robin Myers and Michael Harris (eds), *Serials and their Readers 1620–1914* (Winchester: St Paul's Bibliographies, 1993).

Bernstein, Susan David, 'Dirty reading: sensation fiction, women, and primitivism', *Criticism*, 36/2 (Spring 1994): 213–41.

Blair, David, 'Wilkie Collins and the Crisis of Suspense', in Ian Gregor (ed.), *Reading the Victorian Novel: Detail into Form* (London: Vision Press, 1980), 32–50.

Blodgett, Harriet, *Centuries of Female Days: Englishwomen's Private Diaries* (New Brunswick: Rutgers University Press, 1989).

Blodgett, Harriet (ed.), *The Englishwoman's Diary* (London: Fourth Estate, 1992).

Booth, Wayne, *The Rhetoric of Fiction* (2nd edition, Harmondsworth: Penguin: 1991).

Botonaki, Effie, 'Seventeenth-Century Englishwomen's Spiritual Diaries: Self-Examination, Covenanting and Account-Keeping', *Sixteenth Century Journal*, 30/1 (Spring 1999): 3–21.

Bottoms, Janet, 'Sisterhood and Self-Censorship in the Nineteenth Century: Writing Herself: the Diary of Alice James', in Julia Swindells (ed.), *The Uses of Autobiography* (London: Taylor and Francis, 1995), 110–19.

Boyle, Thomas F., 'Fishy Extremities': Subversion of Orthodoxy in the Victorian Sensation Novel', *Literature and History*, 9/1 (Spring 1983): 92–6.

Brake, Laurel, *Print in Transition, 1850–1910: Studies in Media and Book History* (Basingstoke: Palgrave, 2001).

Bray, Joe, *The Epistolary Novel* (London: Routledge, 2003).

Bullock, Meghan, 'Abuse, Silence and Solitude in Anne Brontë's *The Tenant of Wildfell Hall*', *Brontë Studies*, 29 (July 2004): 135–41.

Bunkers, Suzanne and Cynthia Huff (eds), *Inscribing the Daily: Critical Essays in Women's Diaries* (Amherst: University of Massachusetts Press, 1996).

Bunkers, Suzanne L., 'Whose Diary Is It, Anyway? Issues of Agency, Authority, Ownership', *A/B: Auto/Biography Studies*, 17/1 (Summer 2002): 11–27.

Butler, Judith, *Gender Trouble: Feminism and the Subversion of Identity* (London: Routledge, 1990).

Campbell, Gina, 'How to Read Like a Gentleman: Burney's Instructions to her Critics in *Evelina*', *ELH*, 57/3 (Autumn 1990): 557–83.

Cardinal, Roger, 'Unlocking the Diary', *Comparative Criticism*, 12 (1990): 71–87.

Carnell, Rachel K., 'Feminism and the Public Sphere in Anne Brontë's *The Tenant of Wildfell Hall*', *Nineteenth Century Literature*, 53/1 (June 1998), 1–24.

Carter, Kathryn, 'The Cultural Work of Diaries in Mid-Century Victorian Britain', *Victorian Review*, 23/2 (Winter 1997): 251–67.

Case, Alison, 'Tasting the Original Apple: Gender and the Struggle for Narrative Authority in *Dracula*', *Narrative*, 1/3 (1993): 223–43.

Castle, Terry, *Clarissa's Ciphers: Meaning and Disruption in Richardson's 'Clarissa'* (Ithaca, New York: Cornell University Press, 1982).

Chatman, Seymour, *Coming to Terms: The Rhetoric of Narrative in Fiction and Film* (Ithaca: Cornell University Press, 1990).

Cline, Cheryl, *Women's Diaries, Journals and Letters: An Annotated Bibliography* (New York: Garland Press, 1989).

Cohan, Steven and Linda M. Shires, *Telling Stories: A Theoretical Analysis of Narrative Fiction* (London: Routledge, 1988; reprinted, 1997).

Cook, Elizabeth Heckendorn, *Epistolary Bodies: Genre and Gender in the Eighteenth-Century Republic of Letters* (Stanford: Stanford University Press, 1996).

Corbett, Mary Jean, *Representing Femininity: Middle Class Subjectivity in Victorian and Edwardian Women's Autobiographies* (Oxford: Oxford University Press, 1992).

Cribb, Susan M., "'If I Had to Write with a Pen": Readership and Bram Stoker's Diary Narrative', *Journal of the Fantastic in the Arts*, 10/2 (1999): 133–41.

Daly, Nicholas, 'Railway Novels: Sensation Fiction and the Modernization of the Senses', *ELH*, 66/2 (Summer 1999): 461–87.

Daugherty, Tracy Edgar, *Narrative Techniques in the Novels of Fanny Burney* (New York: Peter Lang, 1989).

Davidoff, Leonore and Catherine Hall, *Family Fortunes: Men and Women of the English Middle Class 1780–1859* (London: Hutchinson, 1987).

Davis, Tracy C., *Actresses as Working Women: Their Social Identity in Victorian Culture* (London: Routledge, 1991).

Dawson, Gowan, 'The *Cornhill Magazine* and Shilling Monthlies in mid Victorian Britain', in Geoffrey Cantor, Gowan Dawson, Graeme Gooday, Sally Shuttleworth, Richard Noakes and John R. Topham, *Science in the Nineteenth Century Periodical: Reading the Magazine of Nature* (Cambridge University Press: Cambridge, 2004), 123–50.

Donovan, Josephine, 'The Silence is Broken', in Sally McConnell-Ginet, Ruth Borker and Nelly Furman (eds), *Women and Language in Literature and Society* (New York: Praeger, 1980), 206–17.

Doody, Margaret Anne, *Frances Burney: A Life in the Works* (New Brunswick: Rutgers University Press, 1988).

Duyfhuizen, Bernard, 'Diary Narratives in Fact and Fiction', *Novel: A Forum on Fiction*, 19/2 (Winter 1986): 171–8.

———, *Narratives of Transmission* (London: Associated University Presses, 1992).

Ellegård, Alvar, 'The Readership of the Periodical Press in Mid-Victorian Britain', *Victorian Periodicals Review*, 13 (September 1971): 3–22.

Epstein, Julia L., 'Fanny Burney's Epistolary Voices', *The Eighteenth Century: Theory and Interpretation*, 27/2 (Spring 1986):162–79.

———, 'Evelina's Deceptions: The Letter and the Spirit' in Harold Bloom (ed.), *Fanny Burney's 'Evelina'* (New York: Chelsea House, 1988), 111–29.

———, *The Iron Pen: Fanny Burney and the Politics of Women's Writing* (Bristol: Bristol Classical Press 1989).

Favret, Mary A., *Romantic Correspondence: Women, Politics and the Fiction of Letters* (Cambridge: Cambridge University Press, 1993).

Fitzgerald, Mary, 'Mina's Disclosure: Bram Stoker's *Dracula*', in Toni O'Brien Johnson and David Cain (eds), *Gender in Irish Writing* (Buckingham: Open University Press, 1991).

Flint, Kate, *The Woman Reader 1837–1914* (Oxford: Clarendon Press, 1993; reprinted 2002).

Fothergill, Robert A., *Private Chronicles: A Study of English Diaries* (London: Oxford University Press, 1974).

Fraser, Hilary, Stephanie Green and Judith Johnston, *Gender and the Victorian Periodical* (Cambridge: Cambridge University Press 2003).

Fryckstedt, Monica Correa, *Geraldine Jewsbury's 'Athenaeum' Reviews: A Mirror of Mid-Victorian Attitudes to Fiction, Studia Anglistica Upsliensia*, 61 (Uppsala: [Uppsala University], 1986).

Gagnier, Regenia, *Subjectivities: A History of Self-Representation in Britain, 1832–1920* (Oxford: Oxford University Press, 1991).

Gates, Barbara Timm, 'Self-Writing as Legacy: *The Journal of Emily Shore*', http://rotunda.upress.virginia.edu:8080/EmilyShore/make-page.xqy?id=jes-intro (accessed 15 March 2007).

Gaylin, Ann, 'The Madwoman Outside the Attic: Eavesdropping and Narrative Agency in *The Woman in White*', *Texas Studies in Literature and Language*, 43/3 (Fall 2001): 303–33.

Gilmore, Leigh, *Autobiographics: A Feminist Theory of Women's Self-Representation* (New York: Cornell University Press, 1994; reprinted, 1995).

Gleadle, Kathryn, '"Our Separate Spheres": Middle-class Women and the Feminisms of Early Victorian Radical Politics', in Kathryn Gleadle and Sarah Richardson (eds), *Women in British Politics, 1760–1860: The Power of the Petticoat* (Basingstoke: Macmillan, 2000), pp. 134–52.

Goldsmith, Elizabeth C., *Writing the Female Voice: Essays in Epistolary Literature* (Boston: North Eastern University Press, 1989).

Gordon, Jan B., 'Gossip, Diary, Letter, Text: Anne Brontë's Narrative Tenant and the Problematic of the Gothic Sequel', *ELH*, 51/4 (Winter 1984): 719–45.

Greenfield, Susan C., '"Oh Dear Resemblance of Thy Murdered Mother": Female Authorship in *Evelina*', *Eighteenth Century Fiction*, 3/4 (July 1991): 301–20.

Hassam, Andrew, 'Reading Other People's Diaries', *University of Toronto Quarterly*, 56/3 (Spring 1987): 435–42.

———, '"As I Write": Narrative Occasions and the Quest for Self-Presence in the Travel Diary', *Ariel*, 21/4 (October 1990): 33–47.

———, *Writing and Reality: A Study of Modern British Diary Fiction* (Westport: Greenwood, 1993).

Heller, Tamar, *Dead Secrets: Wilkie Collins and the Female Gothic* (New Haven: Yale University Press, 1992).

Hemlow, Joyce, *The History of Fanny Burney* (Oxford: Oxford University Press, 1958).

————, 'Letters and Journals of Fanny Burney: Establishing the Text', in D.I.B. Smith (ed.), *Editing Eighteenth-Century Texts* (Toronto: University of Toronto Press, 1968), 25–43.

Hennelly, Mark M., 'Twice-Told Tales of Two Counts: *The Woman in White* and *Dracula*', *Wilkie Collins Society Journal*, 2 (1982): 15–31.

Hewitt, Martin, 'Diary, Autobiography and the Practice of Life History', in David Amigoni (ed.), *Life Writing and Victorian Culture* (Aldershot: Ashgate, 2006), 21–39.

Hogan, Rebecca, 'Engendered Autobiographies: The Diary as a Feminine Form', in Shirley Neuman (ed.), *Autobiography and Questions of Gender* (London: Cass, 1991), 95–107.

Huett, Lorna, 'Among the Unknown Public: *Household Words*, *All the Year Round* and the Mass-Market Weekly Periodical in the mid Nineteenth Century', *Victorian Periodicals Review*, 38/1 (Spring 2005): 61–82.

Huff, Cynthia, *British Women's Diaries: A Descriptive Bibliography of Selected Nineteenth Century Women's Manuscript Diaries* (New York: AMS Press, 1985).

Hughes, Linda K. and Michael Lund, *The Victorian Serial* (Charlottesville: University Press of Virginia, 1991).

Hughes, Winifred, *The Maniac in the Cellar: Sensation Novels of the 1860s* (New Jersey: Princeton University Press, 1980).

Jackson, Arlene M., 'The Question of Credibility in Anne Brontë's *The Tenant of Wildfell Hall*', *English Studies*, 63/3 (June 1982): 198–206.

Jacobs, Naomi M., 'Gender and Layered Narrative in *Wuthering Heights* and *The Tenant of Wildfell Hall*', *Journal of Narrative Technique*, 16/3 (Fall 1986): 204–19.

James, Louis, 'The Trouble with Betsey: Periodicals and the Common Reader in mid Nineteenth-Century England' in E.J. Shattock and Michael Wolff (eds), *The Victorian Periodical Press: Samplings and Soundings* (Leicester: Leicester University Press, 1982), 349–66.

Jansson, Siv, '*The Tenant of Wildfell Hall*: Rejecting the Angel's Influence', in Anne Hogan and Andrew Bradstock (eds), *Women of Faith in Victorian Culture Reassessing the Angel in the House* (Basingstoke: Macmillan 1998), 31–47.

Jelinek, Estelle C., 'Women's Autobiography and the Male Tradition', in Estelle C. Jelinek (ed.), *Women's Autobiography: Essays in Criticism* (Bloomington: Indiana University Press, 1980), pp. 1–20.

Jordon, John O. and Robert L. Patten (eds), *Literature in the Marketplace: Nineteenth-Century British Publishing and Reading Practices* (Cambridge: Cambridge University Press, 1995; reprinted 2003).

Kale, K.A., 'Could Lydia Gwilt Have Been Happy? A New Reading of *Armadale* as Marital Tragedy', *Wilkie Collins Society Journal*, 2 (1999): 32–9.

Kapetanios, Natalie, 'Hunger for Closure in *Lady Audley's Secret* and *Armadale*', *Wilkie Collins Society Journal*, 4 (2001): 18–34.

Keymer, Tom, *Richardson's 'Clarissa' and the Eighteenth-Century Reader* (Cambridge: Cambridge University Press, 1992).

Kilgow, Maggie, 'Vampiric Arts: Bram Stoker's Defence of Poetry', in William Hughes and Andrew Smith (eds), *Bram Stoker History, Psychoanalysis and the Gothic* (Basingstoke: Palgrave 1998).

Kunin, Aaron, 'From the Desk of Anne Clifford', *ELH*, 71 (2004): 587–608.

Langland, Elizabeth, *Anne Brontë: The Other One* (Basingstoke: Macmillan, 1989).

———, 'The Voicing of Feminine Desire in Anne Brontë's *The Tenant of Wildfell Hall*', in Anthony H. Harrison and Beverly Taylor (eds), *Gender and Discourse in Victorian Literature and Art* (De Kalb: Northern Illinois University Press, 1992), 111–23.

———, *Nobody's Angels Middle Class Women and Domestic Ideology in Victorian Culture* (New York: Cornell University Press, 1995).

———, *Telling Tales: Gender and Narrative Form in Victorian Literature and Culture* (Columbus: Ohio State University Press, 2002).

Lang-Peralta, Linda, '"Clandestine Delight": Frances Burney's Life-Writing', in Linda S. Coleman (ed.), *Women's Life-Writing: Finding Voice/Building Community* (Bowling Green, Ohio: Popular, 1997), pp. 23–41.

Law, Graham, 'Wilkie in the Weeklies: The Serialization and Syndication of Collins's Late Novels', *Victorian Periodicals Review*, 30/3 (Fall 1997): 244–69.

Liddington, Jill, *Presenting the Past: Anne Lister of Halifax 1791–1840* (Hebden Bridge: Pennine Press, 1994).

———, *Female Fortune: Land, Gender and Authority: The Anne Lister Diaries and Other Writings 1833–6* (London: Rivers Oram, 1998).

Liggins, Emma, 'Her Resolution to Die: "Wayward Women" and Constructions of Suicide in Wilkie Collins's Crime Fiction', *Wilkie Collins Society Journal*, 4 (2001): 5–17.

Lin, Lidan, 'Voices of Subversion and Narrative Closure in Anne Brontë's *The Tenant of Wildfell Hall*', *Brontë Studies*, 27 (July 2002): 131–7.

Loesberg, Jonathan, 'The Ideology of Narrative Form in Sensation Fiction', *Representations*, 13 (Winter 1986): 115–38.

Lonoff, Sue, *Wilkie Collins and His Victorian Readers: A Study in the Rhetoric of Authorship* (New York: AMS Press, 1982).

———, 'Multiple Narratives and Relative Truths: A Study of *The Ring and the Book*, *The Woman in White* and *The Moonstone*', *Browning Institute Studies*, 10 (1982): 143–61.

MacArthur, Elizabeth J., *Extravagant Narratives: Closure and Dynamics in the Epistolary Form* (Princeton, New Jersey: Princeton University Press, 1990).

Macdonagh, Gwendolyn and Jonathan Smith, '"Fill Up All the Gaps": Narrative and Illegitimacy in *The Woman in White*', *Journal of Narrative Technique*, 26/3 (Fall 1996): 274–91.

McMaster, Juliet, '"Imbecile Laughter" and "Desperate Earnest" in *The Tenant of Wildfell Hall*', *MLQ*, 43/4 (December 1982): 352–68.

Martens, Lorna, *The Diary Novel* (Cambridge: Cambridge University Press, 1985).

Martin, Wallace, *Recent Theories of Narrative* (Ithaca: Cornell University Press, 1986; reprinted, 1994).

Martinson, Deborah, *In the Presence of Audience: The Self in Diaries and Fiction* (Columbus: Ohio State University Press, 2003).

Matthews, William, 'Diary: A Neglected Genre', *Sewanee Review*, 85 (1977): 286–300.

Maunder, Andrew, '"Monitoring the Middle-Classes": Intertextuality and Ideology in Trollope's *Framley Parsonage* and the *Cornhill Magazine* 1859–60', *Victorian Periodicals Review*, 33/1 (Spring 1999): 44–64.

Miller, D.A., '*Cage aux Folles*: Sensation and Gender in Wilkie Collins's *The Woman in White*', in Jeremy Hawthorn (ed.), *The Nineteenth Century British Novel* (London: Arnold, 1986), 95–124.

Miller, Elizabeth, '*Dracula*, The Narrative Patchwork', *Udolpho*, 18 (September 1994): 27–30.

Mitchell, Sally, *Dinah Mulock Craik* (Boston: Twayne, 1983).

Morgan, Simon, *A Victorian Woman's Place: Public Culture in the Nineteenth Century* (London: Tauris, 2007).

Nash, Julie and Barbara A. Suess (eds), *New Approaches to the Literary Art of Anne Brontë* (Aldershot: Ashgate, 2001).

Nixon, Cheryl L. and Louise Penner, 'Writing by the Book: Jane Austen's Heroines and the Art and Form of the Letter', *Persuasions*, 26/1 (Winter 2005), http://www.jasna.org/persuasions/on-line/vol26no1/penner_nixon.htm (accessed 17 December 2007).

Nussbaum, Felicity A., 'Towards Conceptualizing Diary' in James Olney (ed.), *Studies in Autobiography* (Oxford: Oxford University Press, 1988), 128–40.

———, *The Autobiographical Self: Gender and Ideology in Eighteenth Century England* (Baltimore: The Johns Hopkins University Press, 1989).

O'Neill, Philip, 'Illusion and Reality in Wilkie Collins's *Armadale*', *Essays in Poetics*, 7/1 (April 1982): 42–61.

Orr, Dannielle, '"I Tell Myself to Myself": Homosexual Agency in the Journals of Anne Lister (1791–1840)', *Women's Writing*, 11/2 (2004): 201–22.

O'Toole, Tess, 'Siblings and Suitors in the Narrative Architecture of *The Tenant of Wildfell Hall*', *SEL*, 39/4 (Autumn 1999): 715–31.

Oulton, Carolyn, '"The Good Angel of Our Lives": Subversive Religion and *The Woman in White*', *Dickens Studies Annual*, 30 (2001): 309–20.

———, '"Never Be Divided Again": *Armadale* and the Threat to Romantic Friendship', *Wilkie Collins Society Journal*, 7 (2004): 31–40.

Page, Norman (ed.), *Wilkie Collins: The Critical Heritage* (London: Routledge and Kegan Paul, 1974).

Paige, Lori, A., 'Helen's Diary Freshly Considered', *Brontë Society Transactions*, 20/4 (1991): 225–7.

Parker, Andrew, 'Praxis and Performativity', *Women & Performance: A Journal of Feminist Theory*, 8/2 (1996): 265–73.

Parker, Andrew and Eve Kosofsky Sedgwick (eds), *Performativity and Performance* (New York: Routledge, 1995).

Patten, Robert L., 'Dickens as Serial Author: A Case of Multiple Identities', in Laurel Brake, Bill Bell and David Finkelstein (eds), *Nineteenth-Century Media and the Construction of Identities* (Basingstoke: Palgrave, 2000), 137–53.

Perkin, J. Russell, 'Narrative Voice and the "Feminine" Novelist: Dinah Mulock and George Eliot', *Victorian Review*, 18/1 (Summer 1992): 24–42.

Perkins, Pamela and Mary Donaghy, 'A Man's Resolution: Narrative Strategies in Wilkie Collins's *The Woman in White*', *Studies in the Novel*, 39 (December 1990): 392–402.

Peters, Catherine, *The King of Inventors: A Life of Wilkie Collins* (London: Minerva Press, 1991).

Peterson, Eric E., and Kristin M Langellier, 'The Performance Turn in Narrative Studies', in Michael Bamberg (ed.), *Narrative: State of the Art* (Amsterdam: John Benjamins, 2007).

Peterson, Linda H., *Traditions of Women's Autobiography: The Poetics and Politics of Life Writing* (Charlottesville: University Press of Virginia, 1999).

Phegley, Jennifer, *Educating the Proper Woman Reader: Victorian Family Literary Magazines and the Cultural Health of the Nation* (Columbus: Ohio State University Press, 2004).

Podnieks, Elizabeth, 'Private Lives/Public Texts: Women's Diary Literature', *A/B: Autobiography Studies*, 17/1 (2002): 1–10.

Price, J.M., 'A Note on the Circulation of the London Press 1704–1714', *Historical Research*, 31 (November 1958): 215–24.

Prince, Gerald, 'The Diary Novel: Notes for the Definition of a Sub-Genre', *Neophilogus*, 59 (1975): 477–81.

———, *Narratology: The Form and Functioning of Narrative* (New York: Mouton, 1982).

———, 'Narratology', in Raman Selden (ed.), *The Cambridge History of Literary Criticism: Volume 8 From Formalism to Poststructuralism* (Cambridge: Cambridge University Press, 1995), 110–30.

Pykett, Lyn, *The Sensation Novel from 'The Woman in White' to 'The Moonstone'* (Plymouth: Northcote House Publications, 1994).

Pykett, Lyn (ed.), *Wilkie Collins* (Basingstoke: Macmillan, 1998).

Raoul, Valerie, *The French Fictional Journal: Fictional Narcissism/Narcissistic Fiction* (Toronto: University of Toronto Press, 1980).

———, 'Women and Diaries: Gender and Genre', *Mosaic*, 22/3 (Summer 1989): 57–65.

Raven, James, Helen Small and Naomi Tadmor (eds), *The Practice and Representation of Reading in England* (Cambridge: Cambridge University Press, 1996).

Reitz, Caroline, 'Colonial "Gwilt": In and Around Wilkie Collins's *Armadale*', *Victorian Periodicals Review*, 32 (2000): 92–103.

Richardson, Angela, '"Dearest Harriet": On Harriet Collins's Italian Journal, 1836–7', *Wilkie Collins Society Journal*, n.s. 7 (2004): 41–58.

Richetti, John (ed.), *The Cambridge Companion to the Eighteenth Century Novel*, Cambridge: Cambridge University Press, 1996).

Rimmon-Kenan, Shlomoth, *Narrative Fiction: Contemporary Poetics* (2ⁿᵈ edition, London: Routledge, 2002; reprinted, 2003).

Riquelme, John Paul (ed.), *Dracula: Case Studies in Contemporary Criticism* (Boston: Bedford/St Martin, 2002), 559–72.

Roberts, Lewis, 'The "Shivering Sands" of Reality: Narration and Knowledge in Wilkie Collins's *The Moonstone*', *Victorian Review*, 23/2 (Winter 1997): 168–83.

Rogers, Katharine M., *Frances Burney: The World of 'Female Difficulties'* (Hemel Hempstead: Harvester Wheatsheaf, 1990).

Rowanchild, Anira, '"My Mind on Paper": Anne Lister and the Construction of Lesbian Identity' in Alison Donnell and Pauline Polkey (eds), *Representing Lives: Women and Auto/Biography* (Basingstoke: Macmillan, 2000), 199–207.

Sabor, Peter (ed.), *The Cambridge Companion to Frances Burney* (Cambridge: Cambridge University Press, 2007).

Sanders, Valerie, *The Private Lives of Victorian Women* (Hemel Hempstead: Harvester Press, 1989).

Schmidt, Barbara Q., '*The Cornhill Magazine*: Celebrating Success', *Victorian Periodicals Review*, 32/3 (Fall 1999): 202–8.

Seed, David, 'The Narrative Method of *Dracula*', *Nineteenth Century Literature*, 40/1 (June 1985): 61–75.

Senf, Carol A., '*Dracula*: Stoker's Response to the New Woman', *Victorian Studies*, 26 (1982): 37–49.

Shattock, Joanne (ed.), *Women and Literature in Britain 1800–1900* (Cambridge: Cambridge University Press, 2001).

Sherman, Stuart, *Telling Time: Clocks, Diaries and English Diurnal Form 1660–1785* (Chicago: University of Chicago Press, 1996).

Showalter, Elaine, 'Dinah Mulock Craik and the Tactics of Sentiment: A Case Study in Victorian Female Authorship', *Feminist Studies*, 2 (1975): 5–23.

———, 'Desperate Remedies: Sensation Novels of the 1860s', *Victorian Newsletter*, 49 (Spring 1976): 1–5.

———, *A Literature of Their Own: British Women Novelists from Brontë to Lessing* (revised edition, London: Virago, 1982).

Signoretti, Elizabeth, '"A Frame Perfect and Glorious": Narrative Structure in Anne Brontë's *The Tenant of Wildfell Hall*', *Victorian Newsletter*, 87 (Spring 1995): 20–25.

Simons, Judy, *Diaries and Journals of Literary Women from Fanny Burney to Virginia Woolf* (Iowa City: University of Iowa Press, 1990).

Sjöblad, Christina, 'From Family Notes to Diary: the Development of a Genre', *Eighteenth Century Studies*, 31/4 (1998): 517–21.

Smith, Sidonie, *A Poetics of Women's Autobiography: Marginality and the Fictions of Self-Representation* (Bloomington: Indiana University Press, 1987).

———, 'Performativity, Autobiographical Practice, Resistance', in Sidonie Smith and Julia Watson (eds), *Women Autobiography Theory: A Reader* (Madison: University of Wisconsin Press, 1998).

Spacks, Patricia Meyer, *Imagining a Self: Autobiography and Novel in Eighteenth-Century England* (Cambridge, Massachusetts: Harvard University Press, 1976).

———, *Novel Beginnings: Experiments in Eighteenth Century English Fiction* (Haven: Yale University Press, 2006).

Stave, Shirley A., 'The Perfect Murder: Patterns of Repetition and Doubling in Wilkie Collins's *The Woman in White*', *Dickens Studies Annual*, 25 (1996): 287–303.

Steinitz, Rebecca, 'Diaries and Displacement in *Wuthering Heights*', *Studies in the Novel*, 32/4 (Winter 2000): 407–19.

Stern, Rebecca F., 'Moving Parts and Speaking Parts: Situating Victorian Antitheatricality', *ELH*, 65/2 (1998): 423–49.

———, '"Personation" and "Good Marking-Ink": Sanity, Performativity and Biology in Victorian Sensation Fiction', *Nineteenth Century Studies*, 14 (2000): 35–62.

Straub, Kristina, *Divided Fictions: Fanny Burney and Feminine Strategy* (Lexington: University Press of Kentucky, 1987).

Suleiman, Susan Rubin, 'Diary as Narrative: Theory and Practice', in Harald Hendrix, Joost Kloek, Sophie Levie and Will van Peer (eds), *The Search for a New Alphabet: Literary Studies in a Changing World* (Amsterdam: Benjamins, 1996), 234–8.

Sutherland, John, 'Two Emergencies in the Writing of *The Woman in White*', *Yearbook of English Studies*, 7 (1977): 148–56.

———, '*Cornhill*'s Sales and Payments: The First Decade', *Victorian Periodicals Review*, 19/3 (Fall 1986): 64–71.

Taylor, Jenny Bourne, *In the Secret Theatre of Home: Wilkie Collins, Sensation Narrative and Nineteenth Century Psychology* (London: Routledge, 1988).

———, 'Psychology and Sensation: the Narrative of Moral Management in *The Woman in White*', *Critical Survey*, 2 (1990): 49–56.

Thompson, Nicola Diane, *Reviewing Sex: Gender and the Reception of Victorian Novels* (Basingstoke: Macmillan, 1996).

Tromp, Marlene, *The Private Rod: Marital Violence, Sensation and the Law in Victorian Britain* (Charlottesville: University of Virginia Press, 2000).

Tucker Irene, 'Writing Home: *Evelina*, the Epistolary Novel and the Paradox of Property', *ELH*, 60/2 (Summer 1993): 419–39.

Turner, Mark W., 'Gendered Issues: Intertextuality and *The Small House at Allington* in the *Cornhill Magazine*', *Victorian Periodicals Review*, 26/4 (Winter 1993): 228–34.

Vann, J. Don, *Victorian Novels in Serial* (New York: Modern Language Association of America, 1985).

Vickery, Amanda, 'Golden Age to Separate Spheres? A Review of the Categories and Chronology of English Women's History', *The Historical Journal*, 36/2 (June 1993): 383–414.

Wain, John (ed.), *Fanny Burney's Diary: A Selection from the Diary and Letters* (London: The Folio Society, 1961).

Watson, Nicola J., *Revolution and the Form of the English Novel, 1790–1825: Intercepted Letters, Interrupted Seductions* (Oxford: Clarendon Press, 1994).

Watt, Ian, *The Rise of the Novel* (London: Chatto and Windus, 1957; reprinted Pimlico: Random House, 2000).

Wicke, Jennifer, 'Vampiric Typewriting: *Dracula* and Its Media', *ELH*, 59/2 (Summer 1992): 467–93.

Wiley, Catherine, 'The Matter with Manners: the New Woman and the Problem Play', in James Redmond (ed.), *Women in Theatre* (Cambridge: Cambridge University Press, 1989), 109–27.

Wilson, Anita, 'Critical Introduction' to *Private Voices: The Diaries of Elizabeth Gaskell and Sophia Holland*, ed. J.A.V. Chapple and Anita Wilson (Keele: Keele University Press, 1996), pp. 11–49.

Wynne, Deborah, *The Sensation Novel and the Victorian Family Magazine* (Basingstoke: Palgrave, 2001).

Index